W9-CMB-997

14,137

DATE DUE

William the Silent

C. V. WEDGWOOD

William the Silent

William of Nassau, Prince of Orange
1533–1584

JONATHAN CAPE
THIRTY BEDFORD SQUARE LONDON

FIRST PUBLISHED 1944
REPRINTED 1944, 1945 (twice), 1948
RE-ISSUED IN *The Bedford Historical Series* 1956
RE-ISSUED IN THIS FORMAT 1967
REPRINTED 1971

JONATHAN CAPE LTD, 30 BEDFORD SQUARE
LONDON WCI

ISBN 0 224 60761 8

PRINTED IN GREAT BRITAIN BY
FLETCHER AND SON LTD, NORWICH
AND BOUND BY
RICHARD CLAY (THE CHAUCER PRESS) LTD, BUNGAY, SUFFOLK

CONTENTS

To

JAQUELINE HOPE-WALLACE

NOTE ON SOURCES

Absolute consistency in the spelling of names, where more than one language is involved, is often absurd if not actually obscure. I have as far as possible used the form of a name most familiar to English readers, whether it be French or Flemish or — like *Flushing* — a time-honoured invention of our own.

Footnotes have been reduced to a minimum and authorities only cited for direct quotation or where proof of authenticity seemed especially called for. The following list gives the full names of authorities cited in the body of the work in an abbreviated form. It is in no sense a bibliography of the subject. Bibliographies are to be found in the Cambridge Modern History, in Dahlmann-Waitz, and in Gosses and Japikse: *Handboek tot de Staatkundige Geschiedenis van Nederland*.

Alva, *Correspondence sur l'invasion du Comte Louis de Nassau*. Brussels, 1850.
Analectes Historiques, ed.: Gachard. Brussels, 1856.
Archives de la Maison d'Orange-Nassau, ed.: Groen van Prinsterer. Leyden, 1841.
Aubéry du Maurier, *Mémoires pour servir à l'histoire de Hollande*. Paris, 1711.
Bezold, *Briefen des Pfalzgrafen Johann Casimir*. Munich, 1882.
Bijdragen voor Vaderlandsche Geschiedenis en Oudheidkunde. The Hague.
Blaes, *Memoires Anonymes*. Utrecht. 1859.
Bor, *Nederlandsche Oorloghen*. Amsterdam, 1621.
Burgon, *Life and Times of Sir Thomas Gresham*. London, 1839.
Busbecq, *Lettres*. Paris, 1748.
Calendar of State Papers. Domestic and *Foreign*.
Delaborde, *Charlotte de Bourbon*. Paris, 1888.
Dorp, Arend van, *Brieven en onuitgegeven stukken*. Utrecht, 1887-8.
Duplessis-Mornay, *Mémoires*, ed.: Société de l'Histoire de France.
Gachard, *Correspondence de Guillaume le Taciturne*, Brussels, 1851.
Granvelle, *Correspondence*, ed.: Poullet. Brussels, 1879.
Haecht, *Kroniek*, ed.: Roesbroek. Antwerp, 1929-30.
Halewyn, *Memoires*, ed.: Kervyn de Volkaersbeke. Brussels, 1859.
Hoynck van Papendrecht, *Analecta Belgica.* The Hague, 1743.
Jacobs, E., *Juliane von Stolberg*. Wernigerode, 1889.
Japikse, *Correspondentie van Willem I*. The Hague, 1934.
Kervyn de Lettenhove, *Relations Politiques des Pays Bas et de l'Angleterre*. Brussels, 1882.

La Huguerye, *Memoires*. Paris, 1877.

La Noue, *Correspondence*, ed.: Kervyn de Volkaersbeke. Paris, 1854.

Philip II, *Correspondence sur les Affaires des Pays Bas*, ed.: Gachard. Brussels, 1848.

Pirenne, *Les Villes et les Institutions Urbaines*. Brussels, 1939.

Reiffenberg, *Interrogatoires de Comte d'Egmont*. Brussels, 1843.

Strada, *De Bello Belgico*.

Wesembeeck, *Memoires*, ed.: Rahlenbeck. Brussels, 1858.

THE NETHERLANDS

AT THE TIME
OF WILLIAM THE SILENT

Boundary shown thus..................

DELFZIJL   EMDEN
JEMMINGEN
LEEUWARDEN   UMMELANDEN   HEILIGERLEE
GRONINGEN
FRIESLAND   GRONINGEN

LINGEN

ALKMAAR   ENCKHUYSEN
ZUYDER
EDAM   *ZEE*   OVERYSSEL
BREDERODE   AMSTERDAM
HAARLEM   DEVENTER   OLDENZAAL
NAARDEN

N O R T H   LEYDEN   ZUTPHEN
HAGUE   UTRECHT   GELDERLAND
DELFT   UTRECHT   ZUTPHEN
S E A   SCHIEDAM   OUDEWATER
VIANEN
BRILL   ROTTERDAM
DORDRECHT   NYMEGEN
GORCUM   MOOK HEIDE
SCHOUWEN   DUIVELAND   GERTRUIDENBERG   CLEVES
ZEVENBERGEN   R. Lippe
TIOLEN   BREDA
ZEELAND
MIDDELBURG   BERGEN OP ZOOM   GELDERLAND   DUISBURG
FLUSHING   VENLOO   R. Ruhr
HOOGSTRAETEN
THOULOUSE   ANTWERP   ROERMONDE
BRUGES   LIERRE
GHENT   WILLBROEK   MALINES   COLOGNE
DENDEMONDE   SIEGEN
DUNKIRK   VILVOORDE   LOUVAIN
GRAVELINES   GAVRE   ALOST   MAESTRICHT   DILLENBURG
F L A N D E R S   OUDENARDE   BRUSSELS
YPRES   ST STROND   TONGRES
LUMBRES   COURTRAI   STIRLEMONT   LIÈGE
ST OMER   TOURNAI   RAMILLIES   SPA
TEROUANNE   GEMBLOUX   HUY
LOOS   JEMAPPES   MONS   NAMUR
HARMIGNIES
A R T O I S   HAINAULT
VALENCIENNES   R. Sambre
ARRAS   CAMBRAI
P I C A R D Y   CATEAU CAMBRESIS   L U X E M B U R G
50°

LUXEMBURG

R. Aisne   C H A M P A G N E   R. Mosel
RHEIMS

R. Marne
JOUARRE

ENGLISH MILES
20   10   0   20   40   60

CHAPTER I

GLORIOUS MORNING

1533 – 1559

I

WILLIAM, COUNT OF NASSAU-DILLENBURG, was forty-six years old when his eldest son was born. Having nothing to show for his first marriage but two daughters, he had taken as his second wife his cousin and one-time ward, Juliana von Stolberg, a handsome widow of twenty-six, the mother of four fine children. On Thursday, April 24th, 1533, as he recorded with his own hand, 'the highborn Juliana von Stolberg, Countess and lady of Nassau, between two and three in the morning – but nearer to three – in the castle of Dillenburg, gave birth to an infant of the male sex: he shall be called William'.[1] As his father had decided, so it was done, and the child was christened shortly after with considerable pomp and a great number of guests, according to the rites of that Catholic Church from which both his parents were to secede within a few months.

The exaggerated attention which the middle-aged father might have devoted to this long-awaited heir was soon healthily moderated, for Juliana, a princess, as contemporaries approvingly noted, 'of an admirable fecundity', produced in dutiful succession eleven other children, among them four more boys.

The Count of Nassau-Dillenburg was not rich. His lands, in pleasant wooded country along a tributary of the Lahn, had for centre the prosperous village of Dillenburg grouped about his old-fashioned castle, its conical turrets topping the surrounding trees. Vines grew on the sunny banks of the little river Dill, plum blossom and cherry fluttered in the spring breezes along the orchards in the valley, there was excellent hunting in the neighbouring woods. Thunder of cannon and clank of marching men were rarely heard: the Count took good care that they should not be, for his resources were small and the defences of his castle antiquated. An unambitious man, William of Nassau-Dillenburg had the joint qualities of tenacity and caution which enabled him to keep out of the religious wars then raging in Germany, without forfeiting his independence or even his integrity. His chief interest was the improvement of agriculture, and the foundation of schools, and he ruled his small estates with paternal care even in the matter of religion;

[1] Jacobs, 82.

when in 1534 he at length officially changed his faith and 'reformed' the
churches of Nassau-Dillenburg he did it with moderation and provoked no
serious protest. Also, it would seem, he did not abandon the Catholic
Church for gain, for the Catholic Church owned little of value in Nassau-
Dillenburg. His Lutheranism was genuine and personal, if not exactly
passionate.

The fourth decade of the sixteenth century was a stormy moment at which
to be born into the European world. The unsolved Protestant problem was
tearing the political framework to shreds, and the Peasants' Revolt had left
Germany raw and bitter. The voice of religious mania mingled with that of
the wretched and oppressed. In the year of young William's birth the
religious communism of the Anabaptists spread chaos in the Netherlands.
But while princes fought for the spoils of the Church and the recurrent outcry of the people was recurrently stifled, while the Anabaptist republic at
Munster was crushed by the Imperial troops and the theocracy of Calvin at
Geneva was founded and flourished, the Count and Countess of Nassau-
Dillenburg were occupied in bringing up their family.

The surviving children of both their marriages amounted to seventeen in
all: a healthy, noisy, handsome brood. In order to provide them with suitable companions their parents converted their castle into a select school
for the children of the nobility. It was a happy, peaceful place in which to
grow up in that stormy time, a backwater remote from the hubbub of
international politics, where principles of right and truth and justice could be
taught to these young members of the ruling class, without the embarrassment of daily practical contradiction outside the schoolroom. Life at
Dillenburg was pious, regulated and simple. Ponies, dogs and children
thronged the courtyards across which from time to time the head master of
the school, the learned and easy-tempered Justus Hoen of Gelnhausen,
padded on slippered feet; music tinkled from inner rooms where solemn
little girls sat at the virginals, or learnt with their brothers and cousins how to
go through the steps of the necessary dances. Juliana presided over all,
upright and handsome, innocent alike of vanity and coquetry, carrying her
pregnancies with pride under the folds of her homespun gown, her greying
hair hidden under the spotless linen coif of a housewife. She taught the girls
to sew and spin and embroider, to cook and distil and make up the homely
remedies — from herbs plucked in the castle garden — which the dietetic
habits of the time rendered essential. She cannot have been so directly concerned in the instruction of her sons, but since her husband was much harassed
with the management of his lands and she was a woman of character, her
influence on all her children was predominant. A devout Lutheran, believing in

and practising a rigid moral code, sincere, generous and simple, her energetic example and spoken precepts moulded the characters of all her children.

According to a tradition not wholly improbable, William of Nassau, in the first excitement of having an heir, had persuaded the well-known theologian, Melancthon, to cast his eldest son's horoscope. The result seemed at the time rather absurd: young William was to achieve great wealth and power, to suffer in middle life some extraordinary reverses of fortune, and to die a violent death. Since the worldly prospects of a future Count of Nassau-Dillenburg could hardly be described as great wealth and power, the rest of the horoscope was dismissed as equally ridiculous. Meanwhile, young William had ceased to be his father's only son and was learning, in the rough and tumble of family and school, the art of getting on with his fellows, an art for which he had, from the beginning, an astonishing aptitude.

The Nassau family were ancient and distinguished, though — possibly because they were more honest and less grasping than their fellow German nobles — their status had diminished rather than increased since the days when one of them had been Emperor. The Count of Nassau-Dillenburg was in any case a younger son, and the major part of the family inheritance, which was in the Netherlands, had passed to his elder brother Henry. A boyhood friend of the Emperor Charles V, Henry had married a lady of the noble French family of Chalons, heiress to the sovereign principality of Orange, a minute but technically independent state in the heart of France. Their son, René, had in course of time succeeded to the joint inheritance, becoming both Count of Nassau and Prince of Orange. René was fifteen years older than his cousin, young William of Nassau, healthy, married and the father of at least one illegitimate child. When, before setting out to the wars, he made a will in his young cousin's favour, nobody set much store by it, least of all René himself. He had drawn up the document merely to satisfy his patron the Emperor Charles V, who did not want this great inheritance to pass, by any untoward accident, into the hands of René's uncle, the elder William of Nassau, a Lutheran. Should disaster befall René, the religion of a child heir could easily be altered. Disaster did befall René, who, in July 1544, stopped a bullet in the lines before St. Dizier.

II

With mixed feelings the frugal family at Dillenburg realized that their eldest son had inherited the sovereign principality of Orange, about a quarter of Brabant, large stretches of Luxembourg, Flanders, Franche-Comté and Dauphiné, and the county of Charolais, lands valued at 170,000 *livres* a year;

not to mention more or less legal claims to the obsolete kingdom of Arles, the dukedom of Gravina, three Italian principalities, sixteen countships, two margravates, two viscountcies, fifty baronies, and about three hundred smaller estates.

Thus, at eleven years old, the heir to the unimportant county of Nassau-Dillenburg became Prince of Orange and one of the wealthiest noblemen in Europe. It was for him the end of the simple and cheerful life in the family castle. There was no help for it; he must take possession of his lands in the Netherlands, join the Imperial Court in that country, learn to be soldier, courtier, diplomat and *grand seigneur*. He must say good-bye to the strait precepts and frank good humour, the informal manners and the honest affection he had known at Dillenburg, and go out to the complicated lone-liness and intrigue of a great international Court. At eleven years old, there-fore, he renounced at his father's wish the small paternal inheritance in favour of his next brother John, and left the flagged corridors and rush-strewn sitting-rooms of home for the marble and porphyry pavements, the coffered gilt ceilings and tapestried walls of the Flemish palaces. At Dillen-burg, the spring water splashed into a round basin ornamented with crude human supporters, doubtless an object of marvel to the whole neighbour-hood, but what was this to the elegant fountain of Helicon with its nine amply sculpted muses at the royal lodge of Binche in the Netherlands? At Dillenburg they sang loud German glees or psalms in unison, but at Court in Brussels they listened to the delicate intricacies of Italian lutenists, or attended masses chanted by the well-rehearsed choir among winking pyramids of wax candles in the lofty Gothic aisles. The books at Dillenburg included histories and religious tracts and Luther's Bible, but in the royal libraries in the Netherlands there were illuminated Books of Hours, with miniatures in sharp blue, glowing red and burnished gold; there were Ovid and Petrarch and the *Miroir des Dames*, the romances of Olivier de la Marche (the Emperor's favourite reading) all the recent fashionable novels, Spanish, French or Italian, pastoral, picaresque, lightly erotic, *Amadis de Gaule*, the *Heptameron* of Margaret of Navarre, the *Diana* of Montemayor, but not of course Luther's Bible. Rather was Castiglione's *Courtier*, that brilliant and worldly hand-book of behaviour, the recommended reading for young nobles. At Dillenburg clothes were expected to last, and the girls and women had their own faces; at Court in the Netherlands the shimmering brocades, the velvets slashed with satin and laid with gold, the satin doublets sewn with pearls and the fine lawn shirts inset with Malines lace were new for every occasion. So were the ladies' faces.

The new Prince of Orange took nothing, hardly even a familiar companion, out of the old life and into the new. His father accompanied him to the Netherlands and there left him. His education and welfare in future rested with a committee of three Flemish noblemen, while the Emperor stood in lieu of father to him. So little control indeed did the Count of Nassau retain over his young son that a few years later he seems to have heard only indirectly and at second hand when the boy received a new tutor. This was Jerome Perrenot, younger brother of one of the Emperor's chief ministers, the Bishop of Arras. The Count of Nassau made the occasion an excuse for writing to the Bishop expressing his pleasure at the appointment and hinting that the Bishop might use his influence with the Emperor to forward some private affairs of his own then waiting for judgment at the Imperial Court. The Count by this time had so many children that – once the parting was irrevocable – he seems to have felt nothing but relief that his eldest son was thus settled and off his hands at eleven years old. Not so Juliana, whose maternal anxiety followed the little boy into the Netherlands, and who for many years worried impotently about the temptations and false doctrines to which he would be exposed.

Amazed, fascinated, curious, not a little bewildered, not a little home-sick, William of Nassau entered upon his life as Prince of Orange, a new boy in a school with vast complexities and numberless conventions, from which no holidays would give him respite. Suddenly bereft of the affectionate warmth of his big family, he found himself no longer one among the many children of parents not rich, waiting his turn for a favourite pony or a promised treat, but instead a unique personage, attended rather than companioned by two or three hand-picked playmates, addressed as 'Monseigneur', waited on by innumerable servants, clothed in astonishing finery. At Dillenburg, he had wriggled in and out of his own clothes, but in the Netherlands his gentlemen-in-waiting dressed him, and sometimes he performed the same service for the Emperor. Perhaps to an independent little boy this was the most extraordinary change of all.

William's portrait at this date shows a self-possessed child, with an open, good-humoured face. Auburn-haired, blue-eyed, neatly made, with a brown, clear skin, he had at least all the characteristics likely to make the change as easy as it could be, was physically confident, not in the least shy, had great charm, and was so used to being liked that he commanded affection by frankly offering and expecting it. He was fortunate too in his master, for the Emperor Charles V had a taste for family life which he had never been able to gratify; he was devoted to his wife, who had recently died, and to his children, of whom in his many political journeyings he saw almost nothing. To this lonely, tired and worried man, the confiding child from Dillenburg made an immediate appeal. His manners, if at first rustic, were naturally good, and at an extremely early age he seems to have acquired the art of sympathetic listening. The Emperor could talk to him seriously and get serious answers, grumble and see no sign of boredom on his face, or, in nostalgic mood, recapture, by watching him in the tilt yard or the tennis court, the pride of his own decaying strength. Indeed so much valued and favoured was the young Prince of Orange, that, when ambassadors had private audience with the Emperor and all other courtiers withdrew, Charles, with a turn of the head and a '*Prince, demeurez*', would give him leave to stay and hear all.

But Charles was never long in any place. During his absence the Court of Brussels centred about his widowed sister, Mary, Queen-dowager of Hungary and Regent of the Netherlands, under whose strict but loving supervision, therefore, William grew up. She too, like her brother, fell under his enchantment; childless, she came to regard him as her son, and freely called herself his mother. She was a woman of limited sympathies but determined character and high principles. The opulence of her Court was offset by discipline and regularity. If she had neither understanding for the aspirations of the people nor respect for individual opinions, she was at least fully aware of the responsibilities of her position. She governed the lively and rebellious Netherlanders as dictatorially as she could and more dictatorially than they liked, but on the whole she governed them well. Her leisure was occupied in collecting rare books, in commissioning pictures and tapestries for the luxurious hunting lodges which she had had built at Mariemont and Binche, in listening to modern music of which she was an enthusiastic patron – she played the lute herself – and in pursuing deer through the wooded chases of the Ardennes.

Throughout his adolescence the influence of these two, the Emperor and his sister, was paramount with the Prince of Orange. Nothing would have shocked them more than the later career of their ward; he, whom they had educated to be the loyal servant of the dynasty, became the champion of the rebellious people against the dynasty. Yet the very precepts they had taught him governed his decision, for, with all their limitations, the Emperor and his sister were imbued with a sense of duty towards their subjects, which they had only too successfully impressed on their ward. Where he differed from them was in an assessment of right and wrong which was moral rather than political and of which the foundation must surely have been laid in early childhood at Dillenburg. He differed too in the wider scope of his imagination. The easy and overflowing good-nature which characterized his youth, the unusual sensibility which made him recoil before the everyday brutalities of his time, were to broaden and deepen that sense of duty, which his guardians had taught him, into a constructive political faith. The divergence of his path from theirs began unobtrusively enough, possibly when as a young officer he excused himself from tracing a corporal of his who had indiscreetly – and presumably in drink – criticized the Regent. This was the action of a man moved more by compassion for the individual than respect for the law: from such acts was to spring that policy which ended in the liberation of a people.

He grew up a man of action rather than of words, not much given to analysing his feelings or formulating his theories, living directly and very much in the moment, liking people, perhaps too indiscriminately, acquiring practical knowledge of how to handle men and situations, not deliberately but because he had both the temperament and the taste for it. Such men leave little in writing by which the process of their earlier development may be traced. It is hard to say when the young Prince of Orange grew to love his adopted country. Not, consciously, for many years, since even when he was thirty he still spoke of his native Rhineland as 'ma patrie'; but perhaps unconsciously.

The Netherlands, the cities which he visited, the villages through which he passed on hunting parties, even the countryside presented a very different face from the rural uplands of Nassau. There he had been among peasants and countryfolk, a simple, retarded and – in that favourable district – a contented people. Here in the Netherlands he was among people already industrialized; the cities, not the countryside, gave their colour to society and stretched their tentacles everywhere. Industry, manufacture and trade ruled the economy of the Netherlands; already a great mass of the populace had sunk into a wage-earning class. There in Nassau the old feudal Europe persisted, its economy based on land and its society on the mutual obligation of lord and vassal. Here in the Netherlands all was capitalized – greedy, primitive and cruel, but wonderfully alive.

The young man's frank interest in human beings helped him to understand this changing society better than most of his fellow nobles. While he belonged by birth to a class whose feudal outlook was already out of date, he acquired early the ability to get on with the merchants and financiers who formed the middle-classes of the Netherlands, and to feel a profound sympathy for the people whose physical needs were always to be his first consideration and whose defencelessness stirred his conscience. All this came gradually and through the medium of individual contacts, for the theories which the young Prince learnt from his mentors taught him extremely little of the world in which he would have to live, for that world was too

new to have its text-books, and the correct teaching for a future statesman
was still feudal theory with a superimposition of Divine Right.

So, in nine years, the rustic William of Nassau-Dillenburg grew into
the accomplished Prince of Orange, whose name throughout western
Europe stood for all that was elegant, courtly and diplomatic. The next
portrait which has survived shows him at the age of twenty-two. The
plump child's face has thinned to a spare outline. The auburn hair, cut short,
is brushed back from a high forehead, the eyes under straight brows are
observant, even calculating, the sensitive gentle mouth has a judicial close-
ness. The confiding child had grown into a young man who never gave
himself away; he had charm and animation, was full of pleasant conversation
and fashionable jesting, but he had learnt to hide his feelings. 'He was
marvellously clever at gaining the hearts of those who spoke with him, were
it only once; so well did he understand how to accommodate his humour
to that of other men, and to enter into their interests.'[1] Significant, this, of
something more than mere social charm, for it was this outward-looking
sympathy, this ability to put himself in the place of others which was to
decide the formation of his political judgment. Close observers, however,
thought him proud and self-controlled, sensitive and easily hurt, yet expert
at concealing his susceptibilities. This controlled pride made his ready
sympathy all the more flattering, since it could not arise from ulterior
motives, for what need had the Prince of Orange to ingratiate himself with
anyone? Moreover his manners to all men were the same, and, if he gave
offence to any, it was to those of his equals who regarded courtesy as their
prerogative alone. The Prince of Orange was courteous to all.

Courtesy is a quality which, even after the lapse of four centuries, reveals
one of the inmost springs of character. For courtesy arises from an acute
sensitivity to the reactions of others, in which the desire to be liked is, whether
admitted or not, an important element. This amiable weakness, combined
with a genuine respect for others, and a singularly sweet disposition made
the Prince of Orange deservedly popular, but his popularity carried its
inevitable penalty: attractive to the many, the universally charming man
is strongly antipathetic to the few. William was no exception, and those
who either from suspicion or jealousy did not fall under his spell reacted
as violently from it. Certainly he had faults. He was suggestible, rather vain,
more anxious to please than to be truthful, sacrificing the standards of
Dillenburg without much compunction on the altar of good manners;
and astonishingly obstinate. When he wanted his own way he wanted it
with a tenacity quite at variance with his habitual easy temper.

[1] Strada, 125.

III

He was twenty-one before he resigned his position in the Emperor's bedchamber, and by that time was so heavily loaded with other offices of state that he clearly could not waste his time ceremonially handing the Imperial shirt. At eighteen he had been given his first army command, a troop of horse, at nineteen an additional colonelcy of foot, and at twenty he became, over the heads of older men and by Imperial favour, lieutenant-general of the troops in the Netherlands. Civil duties showered upon his not unwilling head: at sixteen he made his first essay in official entertainment when he received the Emperor's son, Prince Philip, at Breda with a public holiday, feasting and fireworks. He had a gift for this, too, and soon the Government were to delegate most of their official entertaining to him.

Long before he was grown up the Emperor had selected as a wife for his favourite ward, Anne, only child and heiress of the wealthy Count of Buren. They were married at the bride's castle with suitable splendour on July 8th, 1551; William was eighteen, Anne a month or two younger. It was an arranged marriage, and as successful as such marriages are when both parties to the contract are dutifully determined on its success. William was powerfully attracted by women, and much taken by the fragile prettiness of his wife. But they were both very young. Her interests did not extend much beyond preoccupation with social formalities, improvements at their various residences, and her own rather precarious health; she had not the depth of feeling, nor probably the intelligence, to make their relationship an inspiring factor in his life, though it seems to have been a pleasant enough partnership. Certainly, at nineteen, separated from her by his duties as a soldier, William found it cold and lonely in his camp bed, and particularly annoying to be away from his Anne on their wedding anniversary; 'I long for you every day more keenly', he wrote; 'if you were here you would certainly keep me warm at night.'[1] They were at first happy enough, being ignorant of greater love than they had found. It is idle to dispute, four centuries later, whether William was faithful; no evidence has survived. He was young, strong and virile, precociously adult like all his contemporaries; and if at Dillenburg he had learnt in the benevolent shade of his parents' happy marriage respectable standards of sexual morality, the common conduct of his fellow courtiers was a different example. At eighteen the censure of elders is preferable to the mockery of contemporaries. William's adaptability, later to be his strength, was in his young manhood a

[1] Japikse, 9-10.

weakness. He was as attractive to women as they were to him, neither a slave nor a tyrant to his body, but perhaps too indulgent a master. He liked an easy life. Now and again he was foolish, as when at a riotous bachelor party he proclaimed that wives were for founding dynasties, but for pleasure – no.

He had been married six years when he said this, and perhaps the relationship, based on too little, was wearing thin. Anne too may have found something lacking: he was charming, but what went on in his mind? She confided once to a friend that she knew her husband no better after six years than on the day they first met. An odd admission: unless intended merely to silence the friend, a chatterbox, who was impertinently inquiring into her husband's private opinions.

Shortly before his marriage William had taken over the management of his estates and set up his own household. Now, again, he had a home of his own, very different from the only other home he had known. His country house was at Breda, in the green plain of Brabant, a spacious market town before whose lofty Gothic church stood thirteen great sycamore trees where yearly the storks nested. From the city walls stretched away the flat land, overarched by the wide, translucent sky; here cattle grazed on the fresh pastures between the slow, broad streams and the sparse silvery birch copses, while prosperous farmsteads huge-eaved and red-roofed showed among orchard trees, with thickset peasant women clattering from the dark byres to the tile-floored dairies, their copper milk-pails swinging from the broad wooden yokes across their shoulders. Not that the Prince of Orange had much to do with copper milk-pails and farmyards, unless it was to stop now and again with a cavalcade of guests as he came back from a hunting party, paying with a scatter of gold pieces for a cup dipped in a frothing pail.

His castle at Breda, unlike the primitive pile at Dillenburg, was luxuriously appointed, standing fair and free in its great park and girdled in orchards widely celebrated. Here William could entertain to his heart's content, offering his guests some of the best hunting in the Netherlands, the run of a cellar and cuisine internationally famous, freedom from wearisome formality yet the best of service, and his own always good-humoured company. Here, in response to standing invitations, his relations from Dillenburg came to admire his good fortune, or to stay and share it. One of his sisters married in the Netherlands and his third brother Louis was already, with his elder's patronage, making his mark in the army. Nor had he forgotten his father, on whose behalf he had intervened with the Emperor in order to secure a long-disputed estate for the Nassau family. Once even his mother made the journey to Breda and saw, with amazement, the gold-threaded tapestries, the many servants in their expensive liveries, the glazed windows, the wax candles, the rich food piled in gold and silver dishes, the elegant modern chairs with their gilt Italian carving and plush upholstered seats, the fashionable pictures by Frans Floris of Antwerp, depicting females who might be goddesses but were certainly not ladies; and in the midst of these worldly splendours, a formidably fashionable young man in the richest Italian velvet, his hands flashing with precious stones, who lifted her not very smooth hand to his smooth lips and politely asked for her blessing.

More often he came to Dillenburg, staying for a night or two on his way to and from diplomatic missions in Germany, startling the courtyards and galleries with the size and splendour of his train, the noble horses and the glittering servants, delighting his young relations with elegant presents. He had changed. Even his language had changed, for when he left for the Netherlands he had had only, besides Latin, a guttural, inflexible German; but now he spoke French, the official language of the Netherlands and of the imperial Court. He spoke Dutch, too, the common idiom of his tenants in Brabant and of the troops he commanded; and a little Spanish, because there were Spanish officers and Spanish soldiers in the Imperial army, and the Emperor's son, Philip, spoke only Spanish. He had beautiful manners and the graceful insincerities of society. His chaplains were Catholic priests and he went to Mass as a matter of course; it was a nice point for Juliana whether she would have preferred him to show a more genuinely devout spirit, seeing that his professed religion was no longer hers.

A woman less loving and more worldly than Juliana would have assumed from all this that her son was wholly changed, and would have been wrong. Juliana, much as she disapproved of his religion and little as she understood the subtleties of his life, rightly dismissed the finery and the manners as mere surface phenomena. She believed in her son and, profoundly as she distrusted the worldly society in which he moved, she still felt that a household over which he ruled was a fit place for her younger children. Her husband, who wanted his sons and daughters to get on in the world, had never doubted it.

IV

William was master in his own house at Breda and lord of the surrounding country. At Brussels he was the servant of the State. Here, on that small eminence where the *Académie des Beaux Arts* now stands, was the magnificent

Palais de Nassau, built for his uncle in the Flemish Renaissance manner, with steep-pitched two-storied roofs and fantastic pinnacled towers. Here were kept the splendid horses on which he and his suite rode through the streets to welcome foreign embassies or to receive visiting princes. Here were rich carvings, inlaid woods and linen-fold panelling, macabre paintings by Hieronymos Bosch for whose work Prince Philip of Spain had set the fashion, and, in more ordinary Renaissance taste, suave marble groups of Hercules and Dejanira and the Judgment of Paris 'perfectly represented' to titillate the senses of arriving guests. Here, in the spacious banqueting hall, under the ceiling of coffered gilt, he entertained distinguished visitors, or in some smaller dining-room plied foreign envoys with strong wines and leading questions. Here he gave balls and banquets which were the talk of the country, set up fountains of wine in the courtyards, or surprised his guests with some quaint device, as when every dish on his table was made of transparent sugar, wrought into the twisted shapes of Venetian glassware. Here from time to time he challenged his fellow noblemen to a drinking contest which ended only when the victor, cocking a bleary eye at the swaying floor, saw his last opponent roll gracelessly over among the heaps of earlier victims snoring under the table. Here, in a small lodge across the formal gardens, with a tennis court adjoining, he counteracted with a bout of furious exercise the effect of too much good living.

The great estates of the Prince of Orange had come to him from his cousin René loaded with debt. His own way of living did nothing to alleviate the load. In a period of exaggerated luxury, and in the richest country in western Europe, he excelled all others for the splendour of his extravagance. It was not merely youthful folly, for the sixteenth-century nobleman was frankly expected to invest public life with colour and style. The populace, having very little public entertainment, looked forward to fairs, processions, or executions with avidity, and regarded it as little less than the duty of a great man to provide them with a spectacle; they expected the cavalcade of shining horses, the liveried pages and gentlemen attendants, the hunting dogs in leash, the hooded hawks on the wrists of the huntsmen, the gorgeous clothes and the embroidered canopies. What else were noblemen for? The taste may have been a silly one: it was very understandable. When the Emperor's son, Philip, came to Brussels it was no use his setting up night-shelters for the destitute, with a daily distribution of eight hundred free meals of bread and beer. Nobody but the destitute cared at all about that. He should have dressed his servants in cloth of gold and ridden through the streets with a smile on his face, waving his hat to the multitude. But the Emperor's son did not like processions, except religious ones, and in these he walked, hooded and unrecognizable, among the dingy penitents. The people felt that they were cheated.

Meanwhile prices went up, although the revenues from the lands of the nobility remained fixed. In order to live as was expected of him, a nobleman was bound to overspend his income. This was William's position. Generous, and young, with expensive tastes, and neither more nor less self-indulgent than is natural, he felt it his duty to give the people what they liked; but he enjoyed doing it and his standards were as high as his vanity could make them. He was frank about it: reproached for extravagance, he replied cheerfully, that he liked to make friends.

Yet in all this whirl of popularity, and luxury, in a world whose standards were only material and social, he maintained a sense of just proportion, for the greatest drain on his purse was the maintenance of his tenants' welfare, and the payment of the troops which the Emperor had placed under his command. His officer's salary of three hundred florins monthly 'was barely enough for the camp hands who set up my tents';[1] the balance of the men's pay, equipment, billeting, and food he met out of his own purse, and generously. Moreover, as Charles V was growing old, and his son Philip a poor host at the best of times, official entertaining fell more and more to his share. Embassies to the King of France or the princes of Germany were all in the day's work. If an effective representative was needed, the obvious choice was the Prince of Orange, who could be relied on to make an impressive show and to present no bill.

William was sixteen when he first met the Emperor's son, Philip. The King of Naples, as he was then, was destined to succeed his father in Spain and the Netherlands, though not in the Empire and Austria, which had been reserved for the Emperor's brother. Philip was the ruler for whose service in the Netherlands Charles had been educating his Prince of Orange; pleased with his own work he did not notice that Philip discovered an immediate antipathy to the younger man. Tongue-tied, shy and neurotic, Philip saw before him a youth whose evident self-reliance and popularity galled his pride. He was suspicious of the fluent manner, the unruffled humour, the quiet courtesy, while, with his queasy stomach and awkward build, he resented William's physical self-sufficiency. Temperamentally there was no bridge between them, for their good and their bad qualities alike clashed. Philip's sense of duty was mystical, William's practical; Philip's sensuality was shamefaced, William's frank; Philip's courage was all of the mind, William's of the body as well; Philip had the cruelty of the self-tormented, William the easy kindness of the contented mind;

[1] *Apology or defence of the Prince of Orange.*

Philip was intellectual, but not intelligent, William intelligent but not intellectual. One thing only they had in common—a dogged, persevering obstinacy. Under the bulbous forehead and the anxious blue eyes, the turned-up nose, and the loose, thick mouth, Philip's small, narrow determined chin was not unlike that of the Prince of Orange.

Nothing of this antipathy appeared on the surface. Both young men behaved correctly, though without warmth, and when his wife gave birth to a son, William asked Philip to be godfather. The favour was graciously granted, and the little Count of Buren, as the child was called after his mother's inheritance, was duly christened Philip William.

V

A few months later, in October 1555, the Emperor Charles V took the step for which he had been long preparing. Prematurely old at fifty-five, crippled with gout and plagued by many anxieties, he had planned to abdicate. His son Philip was twenty-eight years old, and already experienced in politics. He had absolute confidence in him. For himself he would build a charming rural retreat in Spain and there spend his last years in simple but adequate comfort, contemplating his latter end. So much his dream; though, as his ministers fully realized, he would of course still want to be consulted about everything.

Whatever actual relinquishment of power the abdication implied, it meant that Charles would be leaving his Netherlands for the last time. It was a sad and disillusioning moment, for Charles had been born in the Netherlands, at Ghent. There he had grown up, sown his wild oats, been acclaimed Duke as a boy of thirteen; there, in a significant hour, in the Cathedral of Sainte Gudule, he had been hailed King of Aragon and from the sand dunes of Flushing he had set sail to become in course of time the most powerful ruler Europe had yet seen. Time and again he had come back to his Netherlands as to his home. But now this decision to go to Spain for his last journey symbolized something which his people of the Netherlands had not yet fully realized. Spain had become the heart and centre of his dominions. His native land, the old and honourable Duchy of his forefathers, was a mere annexe to the foreign kingdoms he had had from his Spanish mother, and whither he was now going, to die.

Charles himself, insensitive to political atmospheres, realized neither the impression caused by his project nor the apprehensions felt in the Netherlands at the thought of his son's succession. He was more immediately concerned for the arrangement of the abdication itself. Interminable war with France smouldered along the Flemish border, and there, with the Imperial troops, was the Prince of Orange: he must come back to Brussels, the Emperor wrote, for he wanted to have him beside him at the ceremony. It was not exactly convenient, for it meant abandoning his post at what happened to be a critical moment, but Charles insisted, and, after arranging for Anne to have a good seat among the ladies in the gallery, William rode to Brussels from the camp.

So, on October 25th, 1555, at three o'clock in the afternoon, before the representatives of the Estates of the Netherlands, the nobility of his dominions, and various foreign envoys, the Emperor Charles V abdicated. Dressed in black, hobbling with one gnarled hand on a stick, he supported himself with his other arm on the shoulder of his dear Prince of Orange. Behind him came his son Philip and his sister the Regent Mary. When at length William had assisted him to his huge velvet-covered chair, and he had assembled his notes, wiped and adjusted his spectacles, his speech was long and deeply moving. There was a kind of ingenuousness in the way this powerful dynastic ruler reviewed and explained all that he had done in a reign of forty years, and with a touching dignity asked pardon for any wrong he might inadvertently have committed. 'Here', as an English eye-witness relates, 'he brake into weeping, whereunto I think he was much provoked by seeing the whole company do the like.' Other speeches followed, shorter and less impressive; lastly, Philip the heir, tongue-tied with emotion, fell on his knees before his father to receive his blessing. Raising him before he could finish the obeisance, Charles proudly presented him to the assembled room. When silence was restored an official read out the Act which conferred on him the heritage of the Netherlands. Now it was Philip's turn to speak. During the reading of the Act he had already resumed his seat; now, leaning forward in his chair, he explained in a few uncouthly spoken sentences that he found French difficult, and added that the Bishop of Arras would read his speech. The Bishop stepped forward, scroll in hand, and Philip sat back. It was one of those moments which history has crammed with extraordinary significance.

William was back with his troops on the following day and spent the rest of that autumn and winter fending off mutiny while the men struck for the pay which — not for the first time — neither Philip nor Charles could produce. If nothing more serious than a little looting took place, the King of Spain had to thank no one more than the Prince of Orange, whose popularity and tact, and probably money, alone held the army in check.

Meanwhile in Brussels Charles was giving instructions to Philip for the future. He warned him against sudden changes, urged him to respect the susceptibilities of the people and to employ none but Netherlanders, or at least no Spaniards, in the administration of the country. To ensure some respect for his wishes he ingeniously and typically made a whole series of important appointments immediately before he abdicated. He talked much of the special fitness and great promise of the Prince of Orange. Possibly even Charles was feeling a little anxious about his son's plans. His more outspoken sister, the Regent Mary, did not even conceal her doubts. She was still in her early fifties and a capable governor: Philip, harassed by the French war, by his interests in England whose Queen he had recently married, and by the ever pressing needs of Spain, had once asked her whether she would continue in the Regency after Charles's abdication. She was explicit and almost rude in her refusal to those sent to sound her; she said she was too old to learn her A B C again, or, in other words, she would not change her methods to suit the new King.

Philip had not shown his hand, but already the Netherlanders suspected him, noticing with distaste his fanatical devotion and his lack of sympathy for their temperamental noisiness. In England, a country with which they had close trading relations, the bloodiest religious persecution in that country's recorded history was in progress under the auspices of Philip's devoted wife, Mary Tudor. When the French war was off hi thands, did he intend the same methods for them?

Yet, for the Prince of Orange, and indeed for the whole of the Netherlands, things went on much as before. The brilliant victory of St. Quentin, won by the Netherlander Egmont, virtually finished the French war. William, though on active service in that campaign, had not been present; conspicuous on that glorious day was a young cavalry officer of nineteen, Louis of Nassau, his younger brother, whose small, well-made person and engaging smile now raised cheers in the streets of Brussels almost as enthusiastic as those for William himself.

Less spectacular and more difficult tasks fell to William's lot. Philip, himself so unpersuasive, used the persuasive talents of the Prince of Orange whenever he could; already the young man had an extraordinary reputation for managing the wealthy merchants on whose funds the Government depended. In the New Year of 1558 he was sent to raise a loan for Philip in Antwerp, and managed to extract one, not from the Flemings, but from the English merchants there. No sooner was this done than, in the early spring, he set out to attend a meeting of German princes at Frankfurt. Here at a drinking party he uttered those foolish words about marriage which his enemies noted for later use. The indiscretion fell at a bad moment, for news came in March from Breda that his wife, Anne, was ill; hastening home, he arrived on March 20th to find that she was already dying. What her illness was does not appear; pleurisy or pneumonia seem the most probable, but in the sixteenth century everything was either a 'fever' or a 'chill', or both. Four days later, early in the morning, she died.

Distress left William inarticulate. His answers to letters of condolence were brief and stricken. 'I am the unhappiest man in the world,' he wrote in reply to King Philip's stilted words of comfort.[1] Shock and the hurried journey through treacherous spring weather had made him ill, too. He had fits of trembling and a high fever, but recovered enough within a few days to attend to his affairs. Even while preparations for Anne's funeral went forward at Breda, he found time to write to Philip asking for a reprieve for one of his soldiers who had had the misfortune to kill a man in a brawl.

VI

Greater affairs of state left little time for mourning. King Henry II of France had sued for peace, and in September the Prince of Orange was inevitably among those sent to discuss terms with the French delegates at the pleasant seat of Câteau Cambrésis in the Ardennes—inevitably, because his tentative diplomatic interchanges with one of the French marshals, a prisoner lodged with him at Breda, had been the forerunner of the formal peace offer. The treaty, concluded in the following April, followed the usual lines of a dynastic treaty. There were minor frontier readjustments in Philip's favour, guarantees against future warfare and the usual marriages, optimistically planned to heal dynastic strife: Henry's young daughter, Elizabeth, was to marry Philip, recently bereaved of his elderly English wife. But there was more to the treaty of Câteau Cambrésis than its surface betrayed. It had come about, not merely through the total defeat or exhaustion of one combatant, but through the joint realization of both that they had common enemies against whom they must unite. For years Popes and prelates had tried in vain to make peace between the jealous princes of Europe, by dangling a Turkish bogy before their eyes; but, in spite of momentary anxieties, the Turkish bogy seemed a long way off. In any case, familiarity had bred a kind of contempt. The infidel hammered, sometimes alarmingly, at the gates of Christendom, but he was only at the gates, or at worst in the backyard. But now, Popes, prelates, laws and Inquisitions

[1] Japikse, I, 120.

notwithstanding, there was a different kind of infidel in the very heart of the building.

The Reformation happened when it did, not because the teaching of Luther was inherently more compelling than that of earlier reformers, but because it came at a moment when the aggressive European dynasties saw in ecclesiastical reform a means of consolidating their power and increasing their wealth, because the growing merchant and trading classes, who had no place in feudal Europe, found in it a faith more easily reconcilable with their outlook, because Europe was growing, economically and politically, so fast that the old structure of society had split. The old Church was built into that structure and split with it. For more than a generation Protestant-ism drove its wedges into the cracking structure of Catholic feudal Europe: great pieces fell away — England, Denmark, Sweden, half of Germany; great fissures struck across France and seamed the Netherlands.

It is impossible now, indeed it was always impossible, to disentangle sincere and self-interested motives among Protestants on the one side or Catholics on the other. At all times some men will be moved by deep spiritual motives incomprehensible to the materialist, unpredictable and inexplicable in terms of politics and economics. It adds something to knowledge to know the economic thrust behind the Reformation, but it diminishes knowledge to see that and nothing else. Some men made a good thing out of the new religion: others died for it in agony. Some men saw their interests bound up with the old Church, others perished rather than deny it.

In Philip of Spain, political conviction and religious zeal were so com-pletely fused that he could never himself have separated his motives. His conception of kingly duty rested on the inviolable union of Church and State. Both were holy. Henry II of France, a conventional Catholic, took a more practical view, but he too saw that the time had come for decisive action. For Protestantism in a Catholic country meant, to the responsible ruler, far more than the mere loss of his subjects' souls. It was an implied defiance of the royal authority, an activity directed against the divinely ordered State. Protestantism was tacit rebellion.

Of Philip's delegates at Câteau Cambrésis, the Duke of Alva was the one who felt most strongly on the religious problem. A disciplinarian and an authoritarian, he bitterly resented the impertinence of independent thought. His advice in dealing with opponents was always the same, for he belonged to that ancient school of thought whose slogan is 'Put 'em up against a wall and shoot 'em'. Only he preferred to burn them and the conventions of his time did not prevent him from saying so.

But the Prince of Orange was notoriously compassionate; fugitives had an odd way of evading his search, he rarely inflicted capital sentences and was sickened by torture. Also, of course, his relations at Dillenburg were Lutherans. It was unwise to forget the remote, heretical nest where this bird of paradise had been hatched. So it was Alva and the Bishop of Arras who discussed the religious question with the French delegates at Câteau Cambrésis when the Prince of Orange was not there.

William gave them plenty of occasions. The Netherlands are small, and it is nothing of a journey from the Ardennes to Brussels or from Brussels to the frontier; political and private business kept him on the move between the capital, his own estates, and the scene of negotiations – perhaps elsewhere too. He knew, of course, the drift of Philip's religious policy, disliked its ruthlessness, and was worried, too, by the growing antagonism between Netherlanders and Spaniards. The old Emperor had managed things more tactfully than his son, who made no effort to seem other than a foreigner; but even the Emperor, for military reasons, shortly before he abdicated, had drafted some Spanish troops into the Netherlands, to hold the frontier against French attack. These professional soldiers had made a lot of trouble, not always their own fault. William, as lieutenant-general of the army, knew that only too well. The commander-in-chief, the Italian Philibert of Savoy, no less aware of the gravity of the situation, had frankly told the King that the people of the Netherlands were saying that a Spanish war was being fought, for Spanish interests, on their soil. It was not true: but it was believed.

These were constant and growing worries; but William, at twenty-five years old, was enjoying life in spite of them. His spirits, damped by the loss of Anne, recovered quickly. It was sad, perhaps, that this young marriage had touched no deeper springs in either of its partners, but Anne, with all the opportunities they both had lost, had gone to her tranquil grave at Breda. There was no help for that. His children, Philip and Mary, were babies in the nursery, reverentially spoken of as *Messieurs les enfants* by their regiments of highly-paid attendants. His home exerted no strong call on him and politics but partly filled a mind still immature. He began to look about for a second Princess of Orange: socially and dynastically a new marriage was advisable. Being a widower did not suit him, as he wrote with disarming frankness to his younger brother John, 'pour le peu d'age que j'ai encore'. A wealthy and attractive suitor, he foresaw no great difficulty, but his first negotiation for a bride ended in comic withdrawal; he had wanted the young Princess of Lorraine, but her widowed mother, an amorous blonde of thirty-five, declared that she herself was the 'meeter match'.[1] William

[1] Kervyn de Lettenhove, *Relations*, II, 257.

retreated hastily. Meanwhile he amused himself: 'At that time', he later admitted, 'I had nothing so much in my head as the play of arms, the chase, and other exercises suitable to young lords.'[1] To the distress of his virtuous family in Dillenburg the 'other exercises suitable to young lords' chiefly engaged him in the winter and spring following Anne's death. The amourette was a Flemish girl, named Eve Elincx; nothing is known of her save that she was the Prince of Orange's mistress, and — according to some — daughter to the burgomaster of Emmerich; to judge by her later conduct, she was no professional courtesan. After giving birth to a son, acknowledged and educated by his father under the name of Justin of Nassau, — 'le petit de Mon-seigneur' appears first at six years old among the pages at Breda — she passed out of her lover's life, and out of history, as the respectable wife of a burgher called Arondeaux.

It is significant of the conflicting tastes and impulses unevenly balanced in William's education that he should have been dallying with his young mistress while at Câteau Cambrésis Alva and the Bishop of Arras were discussing the extermination of the Protestants in Europe. No hint as yet of the man who was to liberate a people.

By April 1559 the French treaty was concluded, and King Philip sent hostages to France for the fulfilment of his side of the bargain. At least they were called hostages, but were in fact honourable guests, with some of whom, at least, it was hoped the French King would further discuss this question of Protestantism. The three who entered a decked and jubilant Paris on June 16th were the Prince of Orange, Count Egmont, and the Duke of Alva. The city presented an appearance of expansive gaiety; even the paving-stones had been taken up in the Rue Sainte Antoine for the jousting, the Court had borrowed 1,100,000 crowns for the festivities, and Parisian caterers and tailors, armourers and jewellers were doing the best trade of the century. There was dancing and hunting; a radiant Court of young people, among whom the exquisite Dauphine, Mary Stuart, shone as the ascendant star, gave every occasion for a young good-looking widower to find a new wife. William was instantly taken with the little Duchesse d'Enghien, herself recently a widow and, at seventeen, particularly fetching in her elegant mourning; yet, hospitable as King Henry was, he could not permit one of the greatest heiresses in France to carry her fortune away to the Netherlands, and William received and took a hint to withdraw his suit.

The festivities continued with unparalleled splendour, yet all was not well in Paris, for at the recent meeting of the *Parlement* two lawyers had

[1] *Apology*

uttered shocking Protestant sentiments and were even now awaiting execution. Hunting in the woods at Chantilly with his guests, King Henry pondered deeply on this growing evil; he knew that the King of Spain had intended some of his hostages to discuss the problem with him and his only mistake was in selecting wrongly. He chose the Prince of Orange to whom to unburden his heart, speaking with enthusiasm of the plan suggested by Alva for the extermination of heresy by the united French and Spanish, but chiefly Spanish, arms; beginning in that plague-spot, the Netherlands.

William listened in stupefaction, yet betrayed by no discernible sign his indignation and dismay. He even interjected polite and non-committal remarks which would lead the King to tell him more. A hundred trivial hints and unformulated anxieties crystallized into certainty. Far away now seemed the fencing and the hunting and the parties, the 'other exercises suitable to young lords'; he remembered the Netherlands' laws against heresy, which he and others had long hated to enforce; he remembered 'those cruel deaths by fire, by the sword, by drowning', on which the new King was so painfully insistent. His mind dissolved in 'pity and compassion for all these good people doomed to destruction', and he felt, for the first time consciously, a surge of love towards the Netherlands, the country of his adoption, the country where he had grown up, towards that hardy, crude, stubborn and energetic people who so vociferously loved him. 'A country', he said later, 'to which I had so great an obligation'[1] — yet all the obligation he had was to be worthy of the applause he had so long unthinkingly accepted.

Nothing signalized that revelation: the woods of Chantilly were still green, the white wine still cool in the silver-rimmed goblets, the picnic baskets and the damask cloths lay scattered under the trees, the joyous notes of the horn, the gush and babble of the ladies, sounded as before. The revolutions of the human mind happen in secret and in isolation, while the sun moves across the sky, and the brooks run on, and other people are making love or wondering what there will be for supper.

But the Prince of Orange had reached his crisis. He had learnt social and political duty at the Court in Brussels, but he had learnt right and justice at Dillenburg. And suddenly the elements, fused so long in the easy acceptance and discharge of his responsibilities split, divided and pointed different ways. He had to choose between absolute obedience to his King and master, and his own sense of justice.

Years of self-deception were yet to come, years of struggle to reconcile his political loyalty with his moral judgment; years during which he was to

[1] *Apology.*

cheat himself with the hope that Philip would forgo his terrible decision. But when, twenty years later, he looked back over the road he had travelled, he saw with unhesitating clearness where the first signpost had been. There, at Chantilly, at midsummer, in his twenty-seventh year. As between his overlord the King and the people of the Netherlands, he chose the people; as between political loyalty and moral right, he chose right. Dillenburg had defeated the Imperial Court.

CHAPTER II

THE GATHERING STORM
1559-1565

I

WHILE the King of France unburdened his mind, the Prince of Orange had remained – metaphorically speaking – silent. He had not given himself away, not entirely out of discretion, but because the turmoil of his feelings had hardly yet settled down into any definite view. He was, in a sense, to remain silent for seven years longer, acting as the loyal servant of King Philip and hardly himself admitting that he might have to betray that loyalty in the end. He was, fortunately, good at hiding his feelings; sly, his enemies called him, '*schluwe*' in Dutch. Grandiosely rendered into Latin as 'taciturnus' it came back absurdly into all the languages of western Europe as 'silent'. The surname earned during these next years – William the Silent – could hardly have been more unsuited to this affable young man, yet it was not without truth, even in its mistranslated form, for these were the years of suppressed and divided feelings.

While William was recovering from the shock, the midsummer jousting in the Rue Sainte Antoine came to a sudden end. King Henry, stubbornly running a tilt although everyone else was tired out, was wounded in the eye by a splintered lance and died ten days later. His successor, Francis II, a child of sixteen, could hardly play the part his father had had in view. Alva's plan would be shelved.

Philip's marriage to the eldest French princess was solemnized in heavy gloom, while the Queen-Mother's tears dripped quietly on to her black bosom, and the Duke of Alva made a dismal proxy for the bridegroom. The bridegroom himself was busy in the Netherlands, planning his return to Spain, and thither in the late summer hastened the Prince of Orange, to receive the parting instructions of his master.

From every point of view, this summer of 1559 was full of foreboding to William. Up to this time he had had everything his own way: the old Emperor had petted and put him forward and, if he had incurred minor anxieties and some expense in the public service, he had been flatteringly selected for all the most honourable and responsible offices. He, for instance, had carried the Imperial crown to Charles's brother and successor, he had received Philip's cousin, the Archduke Max, when he came to Brussels, and, when Charles had died in Spain, it was he who had stood forth, superb in black, under the huge catafalque in the cathedral of Saint Gudule, to utter the last vibrant challenge: 'Le Roi est mort, vive le Roi!' But, since the death of Charles and the disappearance of this last fetter on Philip's conduct, he found himself opposed, thwarted, kept out. The indiscretion of the French King had shown him not only where the Netherlands stood, but where he stood himself. How many faint slights, equivocal expressions, small political setbacks fell into place when he was faced with this one startling and incontrovertible fact — that he had been deliberately shut out of his master's councils in a matter which concerned his country.

In the last four years Philip's cool dislike had hardened into a definite mistrust of William. Oversensitive and resentful of the least criticism, the King was not an easy man to serve. Lacking the self-assurance to modify his opinions by experience, he clamped his mind together with unalterable principles. Temperaments so diverse as those of the King of Spain and the Prince of Orange found expression in political attitudes irreconcilably opposed. Philip was all theory, William all practice. Philip believed intensely in his divine selection and mission as a ruler, preferring a centralized and unified state to the separate privileged seignories and cities which were the legacy of the Middle Ages. At best his ideas were lofty and constructive, aiming at the joint organization of Church and State which would, through a conscientious bureaucracy, care for the bodies and souls of all his subjects. But the realities of the world meant too little to him. His eyes, fixed on the distant goal, overlooked the suffering by the way.

William cared little for political theories or religious dogma. He acted rather as the turn of events, the characteristics of individuals, or the immediate needs of the people seemed to warrant. He had an instinct for the situation as it was, a mind infinitely flexible, open to impressions and experience, above all an imaginative understanding of human beings, their practical needs and their unreasonable visions. The force which guided his actions was his own character, not imposed theory. Europe, for instance, might gain in order and coherence by the rigorous submission of all Philip's subjects to his sovereign will, or the total extermination of heretical sects, but William could not see beyond the immediate sufferings of the individual involved. To Philip laws and theories were good or bad in themselves, to William only in their effects. While Philip believed in uniformity and rule, William preferred variety and individual discretion. The laws against heretics, for example, were loosely administered in the Netherlands, where the sects enjoyed much private sympathy. Philip instructed his ministers to enforce the laws, but William considered this unwise and acted, in his own districts, as he thought best. Occasionally, even, he warned the accused in advance, so as to be sure of avoiding the embarrassment of having to arrest them. This kind of action undermines the bases of the authoritarian State. But William thought less of the State than of the human beings who were part of it.

II

In 1559 the political aspect of Philip's policy was more immediately disturbing than the religious. The people of the Netherlands had seen their country become a part of the Habsburg dominions when their Duke Charles succeeded to the throne of Castile and Aragon, the Duchies of Austria, Styria and Carinthia, the County of Tyrol and all the rest of it. Charles, Duke of Burgundy, although he acquired so many irrelevant titles and became to the rest of Europe the Emperor Charles V, remained always to them *their* Duke. Not until he sailed away finally to Spain and his son Philip succeeded, not even until Philip himself prepared to leave for Spain, did the people of the Netherlands fully realize that they had not annexed the Spanish monarchy: on the contrary the Spanish monarchy had annexed them. For some years doubts had been growing; they had murmured about Spanish troops, and wars undertaken for Spanish interests, but only in this summer of 1559, when Philip was on the point of going, came the dreadful certainty.

The Netherlands as William knew them defy modern terminology. They were neither a State nor a nation, but a tangle of counties, duchies, and seignories which had been amassed over generations into the hands of a single ruler, confusingly styled the Duke of Burgundy. Each of the seventeen provinces had its separate privileges, its greater and lesser nobility, its Courts of Justice, while in their midst the cities exercised independent rights of their own, with their law-courts, guilds, trade-boards, municipal councils and time-honoured constitutional charters. Charles V had tried, without conspicuous success, to centralize and amalgamate some of these, but apart from a few general laws promulgated of recent years — the so-called *Placaten* against heresy, for instance — there was no unified system and the sole authority of the central government consisted in its right to appoint the leading officer of each province — the Stadholder — and the Grand Pensionaries, as the chief magistrates of the cities were called. The Stadholder was commander-in-chief of the local levies, chairman of the provincial Estates or Parliament, inspector of dykes and social services, chief justice in his own district. Invariably a nobleman of standing, the Stadholder did not – for obvious reasons – usually hold office in that part of the country where his personal influence was paramount. William, for instance, with the bulk of his lands in Brabant, was Stadholder of Holland, Zealand and Utrecht. The central government also controlled the army, but had to wheedle the money for its payment out of the Estates General.

As for national unity there was none. The Netherlands which Philip ruled are split to-day between four separate countries: Holland, Belgium, Luxembourg and France. They extended to take in Dunkirk, Arras and Cambrai in the west, and the present Grand Duchy of Luxembourg in the south. In William's time they were in theory a part of the Holy Roman Empire, a quaint political fiction of which no one took any practical notice. There was not even any unity of language: in ten of the seventeen provinces Dutch was spoken, in six of them French. The seventeenth, Flanders, was divided between the two. French was the language of the Court and government, a fact which had as yet provoked not the slightest resentment among the Dutch-speaking majority.

Intense local patriotism and trade rivalry between the cities kept the Netherlands in a continual excitement, but the character of these disorders was undergoing a sinister change during the last years. The capitalist revolution had transformed the Netherlands earlier than any other European country. Where they had once been a land of rival cities, each a self-contained society with guilds, privileges and apprentices, the Netherlands were now, at least in the south, an industrialized country, with a huge and growing proletariat, and a controlling class not of merchants but of manufacturers and financiers. Already the coal and iron mines of Liége, Namur and Hainault cast their sordid shadow on the land. At the heart of all was the huge town of Antwerp, a city which held a position such as has never been held before or since by any other town. For nearly a century, from 1500 until 1580, this cosmopolitan city controlled exclusively the money-market of the known world, and the whole varied interchange of goods and wealth. Every nation had its concession within the walls, every important loan in Europe was negotiated here.[1]

The north was still rural, given over to dairy produce and livestock, the breeding of 'great beeves and ewes' and the making of cheese. But here, too, along the coast, fine cities were growing up based on the fishing and carrying trades. Middelburg was already 'a famous and goodly city', Amsterdam, the greatest of the northern ports, was the corn staple for all Europe, as the graceful city of Dordrecht was the staple for Rhine wine.

[1] See Pirenne, *Institutions*, I, 275-6.

But this extraordinary little strip of land, the Netherlands, with a population of three million and over three hundred walled cities, was not only the seat of the most advanced trading and manufacturing centres of Europe, but also of its oldest, proudest and wealthiest nobility, a nobility who regarded the grandees of Spain as penniless upstarts. The antagonism between the Netherlanders and the Spaniards was not, in its initial stages, that between a race of traders and a race of soldiers and aristocrats: not on the Netherlands side at least. The nobility were the first to resent the intruders; the Spaniards were foreign to them by the remoteness of their culture, by their too recent civilization which, as the Netherlands nobility saw it, had risen from obscurity to the dominating position in Europe in the last half century. The reserve of the Spaniards, mistaken for pride, was becoming a by-word in Europe; but it was as nothing compared to the pride concealed under the more jovial exteriors of the Netherlands nobility. Because of their very pride, their supreme self-confidence, they had taken long to recognize what the connection with Spain was doing to their country. They could not believe it.

History is lived forwards but it is written in retrospect. We know the end before we consider the beginning and we can never wholly recapture what it was to know the beginning only. The War of Liberation of the Netherlands was in the end the struggle of a small and chiefly mercantile people against a great imperial power; but it did not begin that way. The Spanish monarchy, with its possessions in the New World and Italy, had, of course, greater resources and power than the Netherlands, but the full extent of these was not at first fully understood. The Netherlands revolt was ultimately sustained by the tenacity and genius of the middle-class; but in its early days such nationalist feeling as there was centred round the nobility. Moreover, the people of the Netherlands were very far from seeing themselves as a small, oppressed people deserving of pity. On the contrary they regarded themselves from every point of view as the first nation of Europe, both for the greatness of their nobles, the splendour of their Court at Brussels, and the perfection of their arts and manufactures. Theirs the best miniature painting, the finest stained glass, the richest tapestries, the most beautiful pictures, the best Church music; theirs – at least in their own opinion – the high flower of French poetry, the most ambitious architecture, the finest cities, the greatest ports, the palm of knightly chivalry. Were they not the centre and market of the world, 'terre commune à toutes les nations?' Had not their Duke punningly sneered at Paris: 'Tout Paris dans mon Gand'? Had not the names of Netherlands provinces slipped into the languages and literatures of all Europe to stand for those wares of which they produced the finest and the best? Arras for tapestry, Cambrai for fine linen and Holland for the durable kind, Malines and Valenciennes for lace, Edam for cheese.

Such then were the Netherlands, the most politically chaotic, the most culturally and industrially advanced, the most highly populated district in all Europe: a land with a vast and active proletariat, weavers, dockhands, miners, labourers — we know their gargoyle faces and uncouth bodies from the paintings of Breughel — with an energetic and flourishing middle-class, merchants, lawyers, doctors, teachers; with a proud and ancient aristocracy. A land drawn outwards by a hundred activities, by the international connections of its nobles as by the financial ventures of its traders and the cosmopolitan interests of its seamen and shipowners. Finally, a land with no semblance of unity, in which the nobility had been quarrelling with the merchants, the burghers with the artisans, the cities with the countryside, and the trades with each other for as long as anyone could remember. A bundle of arrows with the inscription 'L'union fait la force' was a very favourite device of the Netherlands — as pretty a piece of wishful thinking as one could wish to see. Yet it was not, in time of crisis, untrue. For this disunited country was paradoxically united in its love for its own disunity. That was the element of union, the common respect of all for the time-honoured particularities of their neighbours.

III

The overlordship of the Spanish crown had hitherto brought with it little outward change. The provinces of the Netherlands maintained their various independent privileges. Their separate Estates, or Parliaments, met in their separate capitals; they sent smaller delegations to the Estates General at Brussels, which was not so much a Parliament as a convenient gathering to which the Duke — or in these later times the King — or his representative could explain his policy and ask for subsidies. The delegations, after referring the question to the separate local Estates and fully debating it there, came back to the Estates General with their answers. If the answers were unfavourable, the Government had to begin all over again. The country was small, flat and well-roaded, but this shuttling to and fro was a great consumer of valuable time and a source of grotesque irritation to a man like King Philip. But he had learnt in the last four years that he would not be able to reduce the Netherlands to a pattern of order by direct action. He must work slowly and by indirect means, undermining first one section and then

another. It should not, after all, be difficult in a society so divided. His first
move was to confront the Estates General in this summer of 1559 with a
request for a nine years' subsidy. It was very ill received. Philip had hitherto
done nothing to alter the impression, growing throughout the country,
that their funds were being used to fight a war on behalf of Spanish power in
Europe. Peace had only made matters worse. For why did the King want
more money now? His Spanish troops were still billeted on the country, yet
he dared to face them with the statement that he was going away, that he had
made provision for withdrawing his troops, and that he wanted a subsidy to
last for nine years.

A nine years' subsidy would mean the temporary abdication of the
Estates from such power as they exercised. It would mean virtually that the
King had nine years in which to deal with the nobility, the army, justice and
religion without being held up by the necessity of asking for funds and
submitting to criticism before he could get them. At first the Estates General
refused the obvious trap; but Philip was tenacious. He was, after all, their
hereditary sovereign and his father's son. It was not his fault that he had to
abandon their country for Spain. A refusal of funds might entail setbacks to
his general policy which would redound neither to the credit nor the
prosperity of the Netherlands. All these arguments could be marshalled
against the Estates to counterbalance their doubts. Furthermore, a nine
years' grant did not absolutely preclude their re-assembly: a new war, a
sudden crisis, a special need, and they would be called again. Nor were they,
after all, the sole guarantors of the interests of the Netherlands. There was
the Council of State consisting of the Stadholders and the native nobility,
the Knights of the Golden Fleece who had special rights of criticism, the
self-governing towns and provinces who would not willingly tolerate any
tampering with their independence. Indeed, there was scarcely a member
of the Estates General who had not his finger elsewhere in the administration
— was a burgomaster or a pensionary or one of the innumerable legal
officials attached to the local Courts of Justice, at the very least an inspector
of dykes and sluices, or a small country gentleman with perhaps a command
in the army. The Estates, local or general, were not by any means the only
effective check on the King's will; they were one among many and not the
most important.

William came back from France while the Estates were still in session and
found himself at once, suspiciously, the object of Philip's attention. For some
years past he had been reputed to have great influence with the delegates,
and indeed he threw open his house to them with a freedom scarcely emu-
lated by the other nobles. He could certainly handle them; but to what effect?

Philip was not sure. In earlier years he had once or twice asked William to use his influence; but, if the Prince did his best to explain the King's case to the delegates, he made an irksome habit of explaining the delegates' case to the King. This time Philip's attack was both clumsier and more direct: he appointed William to the Council of State and offered him, jointly with Egmont, the command of all the Spanish troops. It was really a little too obvious and William more or less said so. The appointment to the Council of State was simply a bid for his unconditional support, and a meaningless one at that, for as he well knew, King Philip took not the slightest notice of his Council, preferring to consult only with two or three trusted ministers. As for the army command, it was an ingenious method of compromising him into supporting his policy of keeping the troops in the country.

Yet absolutely to refuse the King his subsidy could hardly be done. In the end William and Egmont with some other nobles directed the Estates towards a middle course which, as William later wrote, should have served to show the King how far he could safely go. The nine years' subsidy was granted, but with it went a remonstrance, signed by the greatest men in the Netherlands, asking for the removal of the Spanish troops and clearly setting forth the time-honoured constitutional rights of the land. A graphic anecdote records that while Philip was reading over the remonstrance, William was at chess with Egmont in the latter's house, where a Spanish gentleman found them and rated them for playing when their lives were in danger. The King, he informed them, was even now arranging with the Bishop of Arras to get rid of all those who had signed the petition on the earliest convenient occasion. The story bears the stamp of invention, yet it conveys in a compressed and caricatured form the atmosphere of suspicion and fear already brooding over the Netherlands. Egmont, we are told, only laughed, but the Prince of Orange looked grave.

In August Philip took leave of his unloved Netherlands, an irritated and disillusioned man. Acting in character to the very last, he discovered at Middelburg, while waiting for a favourable wind, that some arrested heretics then in prison in that town had been examined with insufficient rigour; writing to the authorities he insisted on the application of torture. Meanwhile the nobility had gathered to speed him on his journey, with dutiful expressions of goodwill. Philip saw no reason to gloss over his recent annoyances and when the smooth-tongued Prince of Orange began, with that deprecating manner which he so acutely distrusted, to explain away the behaviour of the Estates, his habitual self-control cracked ominously. With an expression and tone unmistakably spiteful, he checked the soothing words; without help from higher quarters, he said meaningly, the Estates would never have given any trouble. So clear an indication of personal mistrust could not but be noted by those who heard; the words themselves were veiled enough, but the manner and the occasion made the meaning clear, and gave rise within a surprisingly short time to a dramatic if legendary rendering of the scene. Philip, it was said, had clutched suddenly at William's sleeve and hissed in his face, in Spanish: 'Not the Estates, but you, you, you.'[1]

IV

This outburst and other rumours he had heard decided William to say farewell at once and not to go on shipboard with his more obsequious or effusive colleagues. He had no mind to be carried off to Spain by an inspired accident.

The challenge had been given for the long duel between the King of Spain and the Prince of Orange. The underlying political, religious and economic issues, which gave it historical importance, do not alter the essential fact of this personal duel, in which were reflected the aspirations and necessities of an epoch. Philip's outlook completely represented the rigid super-imposition of the State on the multitudinous conflicting interests of men; William's outlook – or rather lack of it – was the epitome of the haphazard, practical, popular developments which at every turn contested the growing power of the authoritarian machine. Sooner or later these two points of view were bound to clash; sooner or later the Netherlands were bound to challenge the encroaching Spanish monarchy, and the Protestant minority the established Church. But the timing and the motions of the conflict were set by the two protagonists.

The distinction between disloyalty and legitimate opposition is narrow. Certainly for years to come William strove to act with loyalty in the face of Philip's uncomprehending mistrust. William strove in vain to make him see things as his peoples saw them; he had opposed, criticized, and tried to modify the King's actions neither from ill-will nor from any desire to undermine the royal authority; but, knowing that the Netherlands would never, in the long run, submit to this new autocracy, he sought to prevent the coming breach. But to Philip the merest hint of opposition, particularly from a minister of the Crown, was tantamount to treason and he blamed William for creating the very conditions which, in fact, he was trying to alleviate. The first part of the duel, which lasted from the King's departure in 1559 to the sending of Alva

[1] Aubéry du Maurier, 7; Gachard, III, 146-7.

to govern the Netherlands in 1567, was fought, therefore, with all the advantage on Philip's side. Believing the Prince of Orange to be a traitor, he was waiting only for a favourable occasion to denounce him, made no attempt to understand his conduct, and was outspoken to his confidants as to his ineradicable distrust. His determination to get rid of him, together with the other great men of the Netherlands, never altered and he worked steadfastly to that end. He could be, and was, entirely unscrupulous in all that he said and did where William was concerned. William on the other hand saw himself still as a responsible minister striving to dissuade his master from an impossible policy, and to prevent the inevitable breach between King and people. He might oppose Philip, but when it came to outbursts of violence against him he was the first to still them, the first to condemn the use of force and to implore the use of reason.

William was attempting the impossible. Deeply perturbed by what he had learnt in France, put on his guard by Philip's open hostility, he knew the Netherlands for Philip's legitimate heritage and Philip for their legitimate sovereign. Such a thought as deposing the King did not cross his mind. That would have been a breach of every duty in which he believed. But it was a different matter to keep watch against the encroachments of Spanish theories and a Spanish personnel in the government, to stand by the letter – or rather the whole alphabet – of the Netherlands' privileges. If King Philip thought that was treason, King Philip was wrong: in theory and in fact William was thus bound in all he did by a definite code of loyalty. Compromised often enough during this period by the conduct of his friends and indeed by his own popularity and the cries of the mob, he did not, ever under the strongest provocation, deviate in his personal conduct from this standard.

Philip left a curious situation behind him in his Netherlands for he was covering his policy of gradual erosion by a surface apparently normal, placating those whom he wished to destroy by bestowing on them honour and place. It did not create confidence; rather it created a situation so perplexed with mutual distrust that no ordinary Government would be possible for no one could accurately assess the King's suspected but hidden intentions. The two noblemen whom Philip most feared, Count Egmont and the Prince of Orange, he elevated to two of the most important Stadtholderates; Egmont to Flanders and Artois, William to Holland, Zealand and Utrecht. He had also forced upon them the unpopular command of the Spanish troops.

Philip had appointed as Regent during his absence his half-sister Margaret Duchess of Parma. A daughter of Charles V by a young woman of Ghent he had been born and educated in the Netherlands, and although she had been long absent in Italy, first as the wife of a duke of Florence and later as Duchess of Parma, she was felt to be a native princess. She was very Flemish to look at, solidly built with a large-featured, sensible face and a competent mannish stride. A woman of frugal, respectable habits, she was liked by the people, while she commanded some respect from the nobility by her magnificent horsemanship, and evoked their sense of chivalry by an essential womanliness — she stitched at her embroidery frame through council meetings — not altogether belied by her unappealing features and considerable moustache. Yet intelligence and good nature were her best attributes; she lacked unhappily what she was most to need, character and dignity. Philip left no final authority in her hands. Every important decision had to be referred to him in Spain, which meant a delay of nearly a month even if the mails were not held up, and if he answered immediately. In a country where events moved rapidly and much depended on using the advantage of the moment, this was to hobble the government.

Margaret's position was not at first fully appreciated by her ministers, but they did immediately recognize that the most unpopular feature of Philip's rule was to be extended into the regency. This was the existence of an unofficial inner body within the Council of State. Of old the central governing body of the Netherlands had been the Council of State, with its various offshoots, the council of finance, the council of war, and an occasional inner council set up to deal with specific problems. The Council of State was composed of the Stadholders, the chief officers of the army, and what we should now call the heads of departments, experienced civil servants drawn from the learned classes. This advisory body discussed, either with the Regent or the King when he was present, all problems of policy and administration, important decisions being put to the vote. The results of its deliberations were laid before the Estates General, when the next subsidy came to be voted. This very loose system — the King, or Regent, the Council of State, the Estates — was the classic embryo form of popular government. As long as the connection persisted between the three parts — the Council controlling the ruler by advice, the Estates making their opinion felt by granting or withholding money — there was an effective check on autocracy. But Philip had tended to reduce his consultations with the Council to a mere formality, taking advice in private from his own inner clique of adherents. Leaving, he gave Margaret definite instructions to discuss certain matters only with these selected ministers: the *conseil secret* or the *consulta*, as the group was commonly called. Finance, justice, police, above all administrative appointments and constitutional questions, were thus whisked out of the hands of the great nobles of the Netherlands, and referred exclusively to a group of Philip's satellites.

The Council of State was, from now on, a mere formal assembly to which the decisions of this inner ring were revealed simply as instructions. Philip had thus reduced the great nobles of the Netherlands to mere executive officials, and the first bastion against the encroachment of the Spanish monarchy was already breached. The chief men on the inner council were the Bishop of Arras, later elevated to the rank of Cardinal under the title of Granvelle, Count Berlaymont, the insignificant Stadholder of Namur, an obsequious and impoverished time-server, and Viglius van Aytta, an efficient civil servant of no original ability. All three were Philip's men.

But was it likely that the great nobles of the Netherlands would accept the situation without a struggle? There were others beside the Prince of Orange ready to protest: the flamboyant Egmont, forty years old, an experienced minister of state and a famous soldier with the glorious victory of St. Quentin to his credit; the cross-grained Horn, Admiral of the Netherlands and Stadholder of Gelderland and Zutphen, an older man than Egmont with a continuous record of conscientious service and no mean opinion of his merit; Horn's younger brother, the impulsive Montigny; the querulous Bergen, the fiery little Hoogstraten, the self-important Mansfeld. These were all great men, wealthier than any grandee of Castile, and with traditions of service to Philip's predecessors in the Netherlands which went back, in their opinion, further than the whole history of Spain.

Many of them shared another and more holy bond with their sovereign, which he, by excluding them from their due influence, seemed to disregard, or at the least to slight. This was the Order of the Golden Fleece. The wily Duke Philip the Good had founded the Golden Fleece for the ostensible purpose of setting Christendom free from the Turk. Although this object was never achieved — or attempted — the other rules of the Order remained in force: by these, the Knights were privileged to be called together whenever the ruler of the Netherlands, their president, needed advice, and were bound by their solemn oath to speak freely, under privilege. Things could be and were said to the sovereign of the Netherlands, in the chapters of the Golden Fleece, which were often very harsh to hear, but which were of inestimable value in shaping their policy. But of later years Charles V had introduced some foreigners into the Order, bestowing it rather as an honourable gift on distinguished allies, a purpose for which it had never been intended. Philip II had adopted the same custom. Presiding at his first chapter a few weeks after his father's abdication, he had, however, conferred the Order suitably on those of the Netherlands nobility whom his father had recommended for his ministers, the Prince of Orange, Count Egmont, Count Horn, the Duke of Aerschot, Count Berlaymont. The difference was that Philip never really understood the Order to be more than a decoration or a reward. Its proper function escaped him entirely. Although the Knights exercised their privilege of criticism with growing exasperation during the next years, the King failed to appreciate either their advice itself, or their right to offer it.

V

Only a few weeks after Philip's departure, family affairs demanded William's attention. In October 1559 the Count of Nassau, his father, died, leaving his second son John to succeed him in his lands, and many children still under age. William could not immediately hasten to the support of his mother, who took her husband's death hard enough. In her grief she found the young Count of Schwartzburg both efficient and sympathetic; an old pupil of the Dillenburg school, he had appeared as soon as he was of age as a suitor for the hand of William's sister Catherine, and it was in his position as son-in-law elect that he dried the widowed Juliana's tears and guided her large and youthful family through the crisis. William, held back by official duties in the Netherlands, was both touched and relieved at these attentions to his mother; which made a bond between him and his future brother-in-law which was to withstand the battering of the years.

Not for some months did he himself manage to revisit Dillenburg. By then his next brother John was fully established in his father's stead, and the orderly routine of castle and school was re-established. Even his reason for staying with his family was a happy one, for Catherine was now to marry Gunther of Schwartzburg and William had been specially asked by his mother to procure in Brussels a suitable ring for her to exchange with her bridegroom. Such rings were not to be had in Dillenburg. Marriage was altogether in the air: many guests had been invited for the wedding, among them the Princess Anna of Saxony who was there by request and for a purpose. In the interim William's search for a wife had remained unsuccessful; the entrancing young widow of the boy-king of France, dead after a year's sovereignty, had been deaf to his oblique and indirect suggestion. Mary Queen of Scots and Queen-dowager of France had set sail for her own kingdom, untrained and unprepared, at eighteen to wear the most dangerous crown in western Europe. Not for her to be Princess of Orange, not for him to be King of Scotland.

Disappointed, but not disheartened, for he had indeed been flying too high, William made discreet preliminary overtures to the Elector of Saxony for his niece Anna; and as it was thought best that they should at least see each other she had been asked to the Nassau wedding. 'The Fräulein', wrote one of Anna's ladies-in-waiting to her aunt the Electress of Saxony, 'will never be persuaded to do anything she is not inclined to.' They knew in Saxony that it would be quite useless to go on with the negotiations if Anna took it into her head to object to the bridgroom: and how they hoped at the Electoral Court that she would not object, for Anna was a handful. It was a relief when her inspection of the elegant Prince of Orange at once fired her vanity and her desire. William, on his side, was more or less prepared to accept any reasonably well-looking girl for the value of the political alliance. Anna was a lumpish blonde of fifteen with a high colour and slight curvature of the spine. She would do.

To follow up the first impression William sent his brother Louis to Dresden to woo the lady, and shortly after came himself. This time he was allowed several interviews with Anna who was delighted with him. Had it depended only on her, he could have taken her back with him at once, but her guardians were careful of political and social details. The only child of the great Elector Maurice of Saxony, the niece of the reigning prince and the granddaughter and ward of that Landgrave Philip of Hesse whose determination to marry two wives at a time had unloosed the Reformation across half Germany, Anna was an important match. She was also, from the King of Spain's point of view, a very dangerous wife for the Prince of Orange, for she would bring him into significant contact with the forces of organized German Protestantism. William must therefore proceed carefully in order to reconcile Philip to the marriage.

Pondering these things, he returned to the Netherlands. A day's journey from Dresden, at Leipzig, no less than three love letters from Anna caught up with him, all written within a few hours of his departure. He was preoccupied with other things – he had been collecting opinions and forecasts of the religious crisis in Europe, and of Philip's policy – and he had not time to respond to Anna's excessive passion. His brother, and now constant companion, Louis drafted him a suitably gallant reply which he copied out and sent back to her, not taking her too seriously.

VI

Back in Brussels he reported to the Regent Margaret part of what he had heard in Germany. It was generally believed among the princes, he told

her, that Philip was planning an armed attack on the Lutherans in the Netherlands, with the help of the French; generally believed and generally feared.
There was probably a good deal of truth in his report, for rumour was busy
with Philip's future plans. But William was fairly deliberately making the
most of what he had heard, for he believed it essential to warn Philip that his
designs were known not only in the Netherlands but abroad. He hoped
that if nothing else would stop the King, the fear of an embroilment with
the German princes might do so.

The next move was to compel Philip to honour the word he had given
to the Estates General in the summer of 1559 when they granted his subsidy.
He had then agreed to recall all Spanish troops, but now, more than a year
later, nothing had been done. With Egmont's help, William determined to
force Philip's hand, and together they threatened to resign because their
connection with the Spanish troops was, they said, destroying their credit
with the people and making it impossible for them to carry out their duties
as Stadholders. At this even Granvelle advised Philip to give in, and in
January 1561 the troops left for Spain. Philip's agreement was ominously
quiet for he was clever enough to see that he might steal a march on the
Netherlanders by disarming their worst suspicions. When the time came it
would not be very difficult to send another army.

Yielding over the army, he was not yielding over another and more
significant part of his policy — the Church. The religious policy to be pursued in the Netherlands presented some complications, for the King could
not count here, as he could in Spain, on strong support from a majority of
his subjects; the body of Catholic opinion in the Netherlands was utterly
indifferent to the problem. The first wave of resurgent Catholicism had
barely yet broken over their country and their faith was still a genial Renaissance convention with nothing of crusading strength. The nobility were
particularly lax and regarded the priests as mere sources of dispensation from
the occasional inconveniences of the faith. A prelate who took his office
seriously, complained of a lady who had asked for a licence to eat meat in Lent
on account of her delicate health, but, he protested, 'they tell me she was dancing the night before'; other applicants troubled him yet more: 'I do not like
to grant licence to those not in real need, particularly not to the Count of
Everstain, who is young and strong and gets drunk daily.'[1] Nunneries and
monasteries became the refuge of unmarriageable daughters of the wealthy,
or of superfluous sons, and the standard of Catholic life, always prone to take
its tone from the monastic, sank to a lower level than at any earlier time in
the history of the Netherlands. As mercantile or professional careers offered

[1] Granvelle, VI, 27.

wider opportunities to the intelligent, the Church no longer had the pick of the country's brains. Intellectually and morally its standard fell.

As early as 1520 Charles V had attempted to arrest the dangerous progress of heresy in this demoralized country, and from this time onwards he had issued those proclamations which under the name of *Placaten* were to gain a sinister fame. The initial persecution had the effect of frightening off the intellectual dabblers in novelty, the nobility and the learned classes. Protestantism went down instead among the people and became, in its extremer forms, mingled with the eternal outcry of the oppressed. While the respectable doctrines of Luther made steady surreptitious progress among the merchants, wilder and more emotional sects flared up among the people. Of these the Anabaptists with their communist creed and uncompromising devotion to their tenets drew upon themselves the greatest odium. Their initial excesses and subsequent piteous tenacity served to divert attention from the Lutherans. These multiplied, as it were, behind the smoke-screen of the Anabaptist pyres.

The *Placaten* filled an odd position in the political structure of the Netherlands. Heresy, previously a crime only against the Church, was made by them into a civil offence. Moreover these were almost the only laws which ran from end to end of the Netherlands without legal variation. The religious policy of Charles and his son Philip was thus in a very practical sense a step towards the centralization of the Government. But it was something more, for the mechanism by which the *Placaten* were carried out was the Inquisition, an international institution. In 1524 the Inquisition was formally introduced into the Netherlands; twenty years later, in the very year when the young Prince of Orange first came to his adopted country, a Papal Bull had given the Inquisitors power to testify before lay Courts in heresy cases. This cleared up the contradiction between lay and ecclesiastical jurisdiction; it was now clear that the Inquisitors were to act as cross-examining counsel and expert witnesses, and to prepare cases for the lay Courts, while the government itself prosecuted and burnt. Yet in spite of the joint encroachment of Church and central government some of the provinces, notably Brabant, Gelderland and Holland, and of course the powerful city of Antwerp, protested that their charters totally and effectively excluded the Inquisition. This was an assertion of political, as much as of religious, independence.

In their origin the Inquisitors had been papal officials and the Inquisition a mediaeval institution which had for centuries contested heresy with marked success. Only in later years as the spiritual significance of the Pope waned had it come to lean heavily on the State for support, and only in Spain had it undergone that radical transformation into an instrument of State unity and State control, a kind of spiritual Gestapo; though related to and derived from the old papal Inquisition, the Spanish Inquisition belonged in spirit to the centralized and authoritarian world which had nothing to do with the Middle Ages. Those who paid attention to such things in the Netherlands were gradually beginning to wonder whether the Inquisition in their own country was to undergo transformation in the Spanish fashion, and when in 1550 Charles V proclaimed that henceforward Inquisitors were recognized Imperial functionaries whom every citizen was bound to assist, the shadow of the Spanish Inquisition had reached their country.

In this same year another name was added to the list of writers whose works were prohibited in the Netherlands: John Calvin. The prohibition was itself evidence enough of the way in which this strong, dynamic and organized sect, the sect which was winning whole districts of France and which had its organized theocratic republic at Geneva, was gaining ground in the Netherlands. Calvinism was tougher and more tenacious than Lutheranism, it knew no compromise with established Church or established State, and where it took root it flourished, ineradicable and prolific as the dandelion.

Meanwhile Charles's persecutions awoke more sympathy for their victims than seemed healthy for the Government, which was not surprising, for the only strong religious feeling in the Netherlands was that of the sects, and the sight of men gladly suffering for a strange faith had a powerful effect on those who had never felt any desire to suffer for their own. Later on King Philip was to prohibit the public burning of the unrepentant; only those who wept and recanted might die before the multitude, the resolute and ecstatic perished with none but their executioners to see.

Within a year of his accession, and against the advice of his councillors, Philip took another step, that of introducing a new religious order into the country: the Society of Jesus. The Jesuits were the shock-troops of the counter-Reformation, of the renewed and purified Catholic Church whose rigid doctrines were being evolved during these years at the long sessions of the Council of Trent. Even before his father had left the country, Philip had worked out with his advice a comprehensive plan for the re-casting of the Netherlands Church. Kept secret until after Philip's own departure, it was promulgated in the form of a Papal Bull eight weeks only after the withdrawal of the Spanish troops. The four sprawling bishoprics of the Netherlands, which bore no relation either to the linguistic or political boundaries of the country, and some of which overflowed into Germany, were to be converted into eighteen well-defined and approximately equal districts under the primacy of Malines. Appointments to abbacies and other preferments were assumed by the Crown, and were to be made in future on merit and sanctity alone. All this was highly respectable, and indeed it was difficult to quarrel with so excellent a plan, as far as the Netherlands Church or the welfare of the people's souls was concerned. The outcry was partly at least personal and interested, and almost wholly political. The nobility, who had long regarded the plums in the Netherlands Church as the perquisite of their younger sons, were incensed at this assault on their privileges. What was to become of younger sons and superfluous daughters if they could not be preferred to canonries and convents? The middle-classes felt the same annoyance in a lesser degree; they too had had their pickings in the Church. But they were concerned at the veiled threat to their own easy-going way. Protestantism — in its Lutheran form — was a live issue among these people, and the Netherlands Church, maintaining a pleasantly casual relationship with the laity, had winked at these mild heresies; but, if stern-faced young men of proven orthodoxy were to be put into every ecclesiastical vacancy, this would cease.

Yet the most significant thing about the plan was that it had been evolved without any consultation with the chief men of the Netherlands and promulgated by a Papal Bull. The Church was a big landowner throughout the country, and its clerics filled important administrative posts. Although in fact no suggestion was made that any Spaniard should receive preferment, although the first primate was to be Granvelle, who came from Franche-Comté and was, therefore, not technically a foreigner, yet the plan was unquestionably something imposed from the outside — by the King of Spain and the Pope. And it looked very like the sort of thing which, fifty years before, Cardinal Ximenes, the Grand Inquisitor, had imposed on the Spanish Church. So at least the members of the Council of State anxiously protested. With that word 'Grand Inquisitor' fears, nebulously forming for more than a decade, took definite shape. Was this to be the groundwork for a Spanish Inquisition in the Netherlands? It looked like it.

The Church plan made Philip's withdrawal of the army appear the empty gesture that it was. All show of actual force had been removed, but already he had delivered two well-aimed blows at the independence of the provinces. He had eliminated the nobility from his councils and assumed direct control of the Church.

VII

William, striking the balance nicely between his loyalty and his misgivings, told the Regent Margaret that although she might rely on him to carry out the King's orders he anticipated very considerable opposition from all classes of the population. He added that such a policy of rigorous exclusion was particularly unsuited to a country which lived by its foreign contacts, many of them Protestant.

William's opinions came as no surprise to Philip who was already indignant at the news of the marriage negotiations with Saxony. He was convinced that the wedding festivities, to be held at Leipzig, would provide the occasion for a general conspiracy between the German princes to undermine his power in the Netherlands, and he was not in the least reassured by one of William's altogether too diplomatic letters, representing the marriage as wholly advantageous to Philip, since it would be a reconciling factor in the relations of Germany and the Netherlands. Unfortunately he could not forbid the match. While writing a letter of somewhat tempered congratulation to the bridegroom he was privately urging the Regent to throw every obstacle in his way. In particular, she must insist that the new Princess of Orange was to become a Catholic. Margaret put the point to William as emphatically as she could, reminding him that he had promised that his sister should become a Catholic when she married into the Netherlands. The promise had not been kept. William, reacting to the atmosphere of mistrust, was disingenuous. He not only informed Margaret that his bride would conform, but added the astonishing news that his brother Louis was receiving instruction, and volunteered an elaborate explanation of his own misconduct in eating meat on Friday. Margaret was only partly re-assured, and Philip not at all.

But whatever subterfuges and social deceits the extreme delicacy of the situation in the Netherlands forced on William, he behaved on the whole with loyalty and discretion. He was for instance withstanding the exaggerated demands of his bride's relations for a full guarantee in writing that Anna was to have free and open exercise of her religion. He refused to give them any such document and would concede no more than what he knew he could perform – namely that his wife should worship in her own house as she chose and be exposed to no attempts at conversion. His wife's religion was to remain her own private affair: he had said to the Regent, truthfully enough, that in public life she would conform. More he could not promise, and did not.

In the end Philip could do nothing but send insincere congratulations to the bridegroom, and instruct Margaret to buy the usual ring — not costing more than three thousand *écus* — for the bride. William had been prepared for Philip's disapproval; he was less prepared for the disapproval of some of the bride's relations. Anna's grandfather, the Landgrave of Hesse, opposed the marriage fiercely. He disliked the idea of marrying his grandchild to a Catholic prince living at a Catholic Court, and backed this disapproval by arguing that William, who, in spite of his minute sovereign principality, was incontrovertibly the minister and servant of the Netherlands government, was not good enough for the daughter of an Elector. Besides, as William had a son by his first wife, Anna would not be the mother of the heir. One after another William charged these barriers until at last he gained his end. He was young, headstrong, and, quite apart from the politics of the matter, he wanted a wife. Nor was he displeased with the little he had heard and seen of Anna. He had indeed heard and seen much too little. She was kept very privately at Dresden, and Louis on his diplomatic visits to her uncle's Court saw and communicated with her only in brief, breathless interviews; he can hardly have had the chance to carry out William's suggestion to 'squeeze her hand from me and tell her I wish I was in your place.'[1] Still less can he have been able to assess her character.

An awkward adolescent, brought up in seclusion with little love — for no one could forgive Anna, the only child of the incomparable Elector Maurice, for being a girl — Anna threw herself headlong into the role of long-sought bride. She had declared her passion with immodest heat and haste as soon as she first saw William, and kept up since then a playful line of badinage at second hand, through Louis, persistently declaring her adoration for 'the black traitor' as she romantically named the mysterious Prince of Orange whom her relations did not want her to have. Anna's conduct was not that of a well-balanced girl; she was indeed self-absorbed to an abnormal degree, weak, assertive and cruel.

Determined to prove worthy not only of Anna but of the pretensions of her family, William made stupendous preparations to fetch his bride. He began by asking all the chief noblemen of the Netherlands, but this was too much for Philip, who forbade the guests to accept for fear of what they might see or hear in Germany. As an English agent wrote home, 'There is commandment by the King that no man bearing office shall go with him . . . because they shall not be infected with any of the heresies that is used in that country'.[2] The next thing was to get the Dillenburg family ready for the event. Juliana was altogether pleased with the prospect. 'May you soon

[1] *Archives*, II, 94.   [2] Burgon, I, 390.

have your Fräulein Anna happily in your arms', she wrote, 'and may you
have every happiness and contentment', but a little later she was worried
because her son wanted two of his younger sisters to be present to greet his
bride and Juliana found to her dismay that they had no clothes. They *had*
had best frocks for Catherine's wedding, but had grown quite out of them.[1]
It would end, of course, in William dressing them anew in finery from
Brussels.

At last all was ready and William made his formal entry into Leipzig with
a train which would satisfy the most exacting bride, eleven hundred in all,
with liveried servants and glittering pages, and gentlemen-at-arms, not to
mention packhorses and wagons laden with gifts for Anna. It was August
1561; he was twenty-eight years old and at the height of his physical powers
and good looks, and Anna, gorgeously dressed and in the first flush of youth,
made a not unworthy bride. The Saxons celebrated the marriage in the old
style, even to the public bedding of the happy couple in a vast four-poster
canopied with their joint Arms. Apart from this jocose formality, the
arrangements left little time for the Prince and his wife to be together. For a
week banqueting went on into the small hours, and the jousting lasted all
day, William tactfully permitting the Saxons to win, although the Elector,
a heavy faller, broke an arm in the lists. The little accident cast no shadow
on the festivities and for six nights no one went to bed sober. Was it after a
glass or two that William unwisely told the Electress, Anna's aunt, that now
she was his wife the Princess should dance instead of sew, and amuse herself
with novels like *Amadis de Gaule* rather than religious tracts and sober
sermons? The Electress, who had been trying to warn the husband, rather
late in the day, that his bride needed a firm hand, was outraged. Dancing
and French novels would be the undoing of Anna. History was to prove
her wisdom, but no shadow yet darkened the young marriage and when
William carried his ecstatic bride back to the Netherlands he was, both
politically and personally, well pleased with the alliance.

VIII

The King had now been away for two years and the great nobles of the
Netherlands had fallen into two groups, William, Egmont, and Horn
permanently on guard against any infringement of the Netherlands privileges, and the Duke of Aerschot with Count Aremberg acting as the King's
and Granvelle's supporters. Aerschot, a year or two older than the Prince

[1] Japikse, 222; Jacobs, 441.

of Orange and after him the richest man in the Netherlands, was ambitious, haughty and conservative, with little interest in anything except his own position, while Aremberg, a loyal feudal nobleman of the old school, was a brave man of limited sympathies and outlook, who felt a stronger duty to the Crown than to his countrymen. Unquestionably the advantage of intelligence and personality lay with the opposition, and this in the early days of the struggle was to be important. William was still the idol of the multitude, although Egmont ran him fairly close. Egmont, a florid, jovial soldier, typically Flemish in his manners and tastes, with a hearty laugh and an easy manner, had won the heart of the people when he gained the victory of St. Quentin, and had maintained his popularity ever since. The third member of the opposition, Count Horn, Admiral of the Netherlands, was the least attractive of the three, a crabbed, prematurely aged man, but with a gruff way of speaking his mind which was not without its appeal to the populace. These three were supported with considerable enthusiasm by Horn's brother Montigny and the young Hoogstraten, and with rather more reserve by the Counts Megen and Mansfeld. The opposition seemed formidable and Margaret did not face with equanimity the prospect of carrying out the King's unpopular religious policy, with the most influential men in the country grouped against her. Without a murmur of positive disloyalty, they could make their will felt simply through the administration still in their control. So far, the King had neither the power nor the means to replace them. Should they go further and give any open signs of their dissatisfaction with the central government, serious trouble with the people might follow. Already the heresy hunt had provoked angry mobs at Valenciennes and Bruges to storm the churches.

The only stalwart pillar of Philip's policy was Cardinal Granvelle. Aerschot and Aremberg had neither great ability nor popularity: Berlaymont was a nonentity and Viglius van Aytta good only for executing orders. Granvelle, on the other hand, was an able politician, far-seeing, wary, quick to notice advantages and to use them, deeply experienced; he had a diplomatic manner, a cultivated charm and even a sense of humour. Trained under the Emperor Charles V, he was essentially a man of the Renaissance; not strictly virtuous, an Epicurean, interested in the arts, he scandalized the prudish by collecting classical statues and modern pictures: the Church for him had been a career, not a vocation. A strangely unsuitable servant for Philip II, he advocated religious reform chiefly for political reasons. His one weakness was an acute class-consciousness, which made him — a member of the lesser nobility — very much alive to slights from his often openly arrogant fellow ministers. Yet often as he winced under rudeness, he found the courtesy of the Prince of Orange yet more galling. Rudeness at least he understood, but William's politeness seemed mere mockery. He it was who had first called William 'sly', and his dislike bred a defensive contempt which led him persistently and fatally to underestimate William's ability.

While Philip was planning in his slow and thorough way to dislodge the Netherlands nobility, they countered the surreptitious campaign by combining for the removal of Granvelle. The defeat of this one man would serve a double purpose. It would give the King clear warning of their determination to defend the ancient status of their country and privileges of their class, and it would rob him of his only efficient instrument for executing his policy.

Rumours of a conspiracy against the Cardinal had begun before the Prince of Orange went to Germany. For the past year, William had drawn ever more closely to Egmont, and the older man, naturally lazy and rather optimistic, simpler and less suspicious, soon gave in wholly to the persuasive influence of the younger. Nevertheless Egmont was dangerously suggestible, prone to believe anything that was put to him with apparent good faith, and the last thing he heard in preference to the one before the last, so that it was necessary to keep him constantly primed against the friends and agents of Granvelle.

The atmosphere had not improved while William was being married in Germany. The ubiquitous presence of spies, at this time a commonplace of political life, heightened the nervous tension. Not a person of importance but had his spies in the houses of his enemies or rivals, not a great house in Brussels without one or two of these agents among its staff. Paid in proportion to the frequency and value of their information, they naturally magnified all they heard, constructed freely on a scant foundation, rationalized and gave political significance to any plausible rumour. At a time when truth was hard to get at, when no news services existed and the most important events gained currency in the end only by word of mouth, the confusion wrought by these agents could be very considerable. Certainly at this time William was informed with some semblance of probability that Granvelle had considered with the King of Spain the advisability of his removal, if necessary by assassination, and while he was fully aware of the propaganda value of such a rumour in working up feeling against Granvelle, he was also partly convinced himself.

Granvelle, no less conscious than William that the rumour could be used against him, determined to silence it in the only possible way. Confronting the Prince of Orange one day at Court, with Egmont at his side, he frankly discussed the whole question, declared his innocence, his cordial friendship and his indignation at such a libel. William had no choice but to accept his denials, but in his heart he remained unconvinced.

Soon after, he persuaded Egmont to join him in a preliminary joint letter to the Regent Margaret, setting forth their unwillingness to continue longer on the Council of State, since only Cardinal Granvelle's advice was treated with respect. As he anticipated, Margaret implored them to stay, for she could hardly risk the impression which their withdrawal would make on the people. Granvelle himself, fully aware of what was going on, denied in a letter to Philip that anything serious was afoot, though it was impossible, he added, to know what went on in the mind of the Prince of Orange. As for an alleged masquerade lampooning him, which was supposed to have been acted at one of the Prince's parties, he could not find out that such a thing had occurred. Playing for time, while he planned less drastic means than assassination to rid himself of his chief enemy, he went on to report that the Prince of Orange had – on a credible estimate – debts amounting to nearly a million florins and could get no more credit; perhaps the extravagant young fool had already dug and fallen into his own pit, for rumours had gone about at the time of the German marriage that he was going to sell his property in the Netherlands to meet his creditors, and retire abroad. If these hopes proved too sanguine, perhaps the King would offer him the governorship of remote Sicily? Thus Granvelle. But he hoped too soon.

Huge as was the morass of William's debts, he was far from sinking. He was tenacious, and in the last years he had grown in political perspicacity and moral determination. As the chief opponent of the King's policy, he showed his hand ever more frankly. In this spring of 1562 the first religious war had broken out in France, and it occurred to Philip, who wanted to see nothing so much as a united France ready under his leadership to join in an European crusade, that, if he could send troops from the Netherlands to the assistance of Catherine de Medici, the Huguenots might be finally crushed. Both the Regent Margaret and Cardinal Granvelle protested that the suggestion would have the worst effect in the Netherlands, but Philip was obstinate and they had no choice but to place his requests before the Council. William, with unusual directness, stated that the power to command did not lie with the King; it was against the law and customs of the Netherlands to send out an army without the consent of the Estates. As William was the commander-in-chief, that was evidently the end of Philip's plan.

The civil war in France gave William enough to ponder. Civil war, the breakdown of the mechanism of the State, seemed to him the worst of evils, the crowning condemnation of any Government misguided enough to let it happen. But civil wars, particularly when the root causes are the same, are apt to spread. All the more ardently did he hope to prevent the King's uncompromising religious policy from leading to 'a dangerous access of civil war' in the Netherlands.[1]

He had in fact been himself directly affected by the French disaster; a serious Huguenot rising had occurred at his sovereign city of Orange with which his deputy-governor had had to deal. It involved William in correspondence with the Pope, who was not only his Holy Father but also — owing to the papal lands at Avignon — the neighbouring landlord; while protesting his devotion to the Church, William strove to check the excesses of his French subjects of both religions, a thankless task, and a ticklish one, for he knew that Philip of Spain must be watching his conduct at Orange for the light it would throw on his future conduct in the Netherlands.

Meanwhile emigration induced by the King's religious policy was bleeding Flemish industry white, while local administration was breaking down, because nobody would carry out the religious laws. Disrespect for one group of laws is the beginning of disrespect for all authority, and both Margaret and Philip recognized the gravity of the situation, though with different results. The nobility still seemed to Philip the first barrier to be disposed of, to Margaret the first group to be won over. In June 1562, she called a meeting of the Golden Fleece, falling back on this time-honoured method of informally discussing with the leading men in the country the more serious problems of government. The Knights of the Golden Fleece, in solemn session, advised her to call the Estates General, and to send one of their number, Horn's brother Montigny, to Madrid, to explain to the King that his policy must be altered. This was outspoken enough for a public meeting with the Regent; in a private session at Hoogstraten's house, under the chairmanship of the Prince of Orange, they agreed that Granvelle must go. They did more; they condemned as impolitic the King's religious policy. William, already heavily committed to a policy of opposition, now went even further, and when the Estates General met in Brussels, not only did their delegates make a habit of treating the Palais de Nassau as a permanent committee room, but, as the Regent indignantly wrote to Philip, William was for ever intervening at their sessions to give direction and point to their demands.

William was doing nothing illegal. As a nobleman of Brabant, he had a right to speak during sessions of the Estates General, and for the rest, he had always entertained lavishly on official business, he had always encouraged his fellow nobles and the members of the Estates to make use

[1] *Apology*.

of his house, and he had always liked to hammer out problems of policy in private, informal discussion. Naturally and inevitably he had become the actual if unacknowledged leader of the opposition, both inside the Estates and outside, and was virtually turning the tables on Margaret and the *consulta*, by transferring the direction of Netherlands policy to his private house. In the undeclared struggle between Philip and William, William was unmistakably winning the first round.

Meanwhile, news came from Germany that the Archduke Maximilian was to be elected as his father's successor in the Holy Roman Empire. The election and coronation of the heir would take place at Frankfort, a couple of days' journey from the Netherlands, and within easy reach of William's family at Dillenburg. What more natural than that he should ask to go as representative of the Netherlands government? What more natural, yet what more disturbing to Philip? For Philip and his cousin, the Archduke Max, disliked each other almost openly. Max was a highly intelligent young man, with startlingly modern ideas and strong Protestant sympathies, who at one period had all but changed his faith, strong family representations alone holding him back. Philip did not want the Prince of Orange, who had always got on a great deal too well with Max, to have any chance of renewing the acquaintance. Still less did he want him to meet a crowd of German Protestant princes in friendly, unbuttoned mood, and plan mischief for the Netherlands, but he could not precisely forbid him, since he was, so inconveniently, a sovereign in his own right and had so many relations in Germany. But he could and did indicate both directly and through Margaret that he did not wish him to go. Nevertheless, he went.

Naturally at Frankfort the situation in the Netherlands was discussed and William took occasion to say that Philip's recent attempt to assist Catherine de Medici had been a preliminary to a campaign against the heretics of the Netherlands. There was nothing very indiscreet or unusual in his saying this, for no observant spectator can very well have thought anything else. All the same, Philip was not anxious to have the Prince of Orange speculating aloud on his policy to an audience unsympathetic to it. Moreover his two leading opponents, Egmont and William, were now both married into German princely families: Egmont to a sister of the Elector Palatine, William to his Saxon Anna. This was a sign that the Netherlands nobility might, if occasion arose, take a stand on the old fiction that their country was part of the Holy Roman Empire.

William's visit to Frankfort was brief, for in November 1562 he had to be back at his house at Breda, for the lying-in of his young wife. Anna gave birth to a daughter who lived only long enough to be christened with full

Catholic ritual. Margaret sent polite letters of condolence to the young mother and informed Philip that, whatever secret sympathy William might have for the heretics, his outward behaviour was unimpeachable.

Deadlock, however, continued in the Netherlands, for Granvelle was still, impervious to all hints, in smiling control of the Council, and Montigny had come back from Madrid with nothing but vague messages of goodwill from the King. The nobility waited three months to see if this goodwill would find expression in the recall of Granvelle, and, when it did not, William, Egmont and Horn wrote in March 1563 a stiff letter demanding his withdrawal, on grounds of public expediency. April, May, June went by and Granvelle remained on the Council; in July the storm broke. The Prince of Orange, leading a deputation of the Knights of the Golden Fleece, delivered what was in effect an ultimatum: Granvelle must go or they could no longer guarantee the good order of the Netherlands. At the same time the Estates of Brabant (prompted surely from above) categorically refused to pay any further subsidies until Granvelle withdrew. Margaret suggested a new embassy to the King, but William would not hear of it, pointing out that the last embassy had done no good. Until the King gave in, he and Egmont and Horn would leave the Council of State. It was in fact a strike of the chief executive powers, and Margaret wrote imploring Philip to recall Granvelle — as far as she was concerned, she had already capitulated.

Granvelle and the King still refused to be intimidated, though when the Estates General were summoned in August, even the Cardinal thought it prudent to withdraw from Brussels, at least until the concourse and excitement were over. Egmont and the Prince of Orange had suddenly dressed all their servants in a grey livery covered with crimson fool's heads. This oblique mocking of the Cardinal, too oblique to sound very convincing to those used to the outspoken cartoons and political abuse of our own time, was immediately understood by a people brought up in a tradition of side-long puns and hidden meanings. The Regent complained at once, and the Prince, expressing amazement that anyone should have taken the crimson fool's heads for Cardinal's hats, immediately changed them for a quiver of arrows. The reference to the device of the Netherlands, the arrows which were the separate provinces, bound into a common unity, jumped to every intelligent eye.

Meanwhile, at the Palais de Nassau, the usual concourse of delegates came and went, and the opposition nobility dined and wined freely, their tongues growing looser as the evenings wore on. Montigny recounting his experiences at Madrid loudly declared that he was sick to death of the obsequious attendance at Mass in the Netherlands.

Margaret's letters to Philip grew more insistent. Even Granvelle was for yielding — temporarily at least. Little as the King relished a surrender to political blackmail, he was beginning to see that he could not hold out without provoking serious trouble. And, although he wanted serious trouble in his own time to provide an excuse for drastic changes, he did not want it before he was ready.

It had been a game of bluff and counterbluff, a waiting game for two years, to see how far the Prince of Orange would dare to go. Now it was apparent that he would go just as far as was necessary to get rid of Granvelle. In the winter, with calculated indiscretion, he merrily told the Estates of Brabant, or as many of their delegates as happened to be dining with him, that they had no cause to worry about further disorders in the Netherlands: Granvelle was going to restore tranquillity by cutting off his head. The Cardinal's rage at the renewal of the old accusation was all the more violent in that it described what must by this time have been his most ardent wish. In the present mood of the country, two or three more remarks of this kind from William, and Granvelle would have to seek safety abroad of his own accord.

This, precisely, was what William planned. In a way it would save the King's face, for he would not have to yield personally, and had Granvelle been less angry, less obstinate and less brave, the situation might have solved itself without a further wound to Philip's already inflamed vanity. But in the end Granvelle would not act, and Philip had to. Avoiding open surrender, he chose the middle path of suggesting that the Cardinal make a private excuse for leaving the Netherlands. Margaret, under instructions, sent for William, hinted that things could be arranged, and asked him to return to the Council. She found, not for the first time, that the agreeable Prince of Orange could be as obstinate as a mule. He would come back, he said, when the Cardinal had gone, and not before.

There was no help for it. On March 5th, 1564, immediately after his interview with Margaret, William was writing to his brother Louis: 'Certain it is that our man is going; God send that he goes so far as never to come back again'.[1] Certain it was; discovering a sudden craving to visit his aged mother, Granvelle left the country, never to return, on March 12th, 1564. On March 18th, after an absence of eight months, William, Egmont and Horn resumed their places at the Council table.

[1] *Archives*, I, 214.

IX

This first victory had been won by William almost single-handed. He had persuaded and given the lead to his colleagues, dragging a bewildered Egmont and a captious Horn by the sheer force of his personality; he had known how to restrain or unloose the feelings of the delegates of the Estates, had managed by subtly interjected hint, or thoughtful persuasion, to marshal forces which Granvelle might otherwise have diffused and rendered harmless. For a first essay in political manœuvring it was brilliant. No wonder Granvelle left the Netherlands with a bitterness in his heart against the Prince of Orange which lasted to his death.

William was satisfied with the victory, but he did not over-estimate it. There had been nothing like official surrender on Philip's part, and not a hint of changed policy. Unhappily, a new and uncontrollable element was making itself felt among William's friends. His house was becoming, rather through accident and good-nature than through any deliberate design, a Protestant centre. His Saxon wife, although publicly conforming to Catholic ritual and official ceremonies, was permitted to worship privately in her own Lutheran fashion. Thus there was an excuse for the presence of Lutheran preachers in the Prince's house, discreetly in Brussels, but openly at Breda. Moreover his brother Louis, as a German prince, was free to practise his religion openly, and, when in the summer of 1564 William's mother arrived on a visit from Dillenburg with some of her younger children, the great house at Breda resounded on Sundays, and probably on weekdays too, with the stirring melodies of Lutheran hymns. Philip was, of course, informed and wrote commanding Margaret to scold the Prince of Orange into keeping his relations in better order. The Regent shook her head over the King's blind optimism. Did he not realize that she needed all the support which the Prince could give her in the ceaseless battle with the Estates for extra subsidies? Would it be politic to offend him at this moment? Evidently not.

But William was anxious; he was not in his own view a Protestant politician, and he saw the religious question merely as one among several important constitutional problems. Moreover he had seen enough of the world to know that no Church had a monopoly of good men. Bred a Lutheran until his eleventh year and in constant touch through his family with Lutheran opinion, he had a natural sympathy with their views, although personally Catholicism suited him very well. He was not a very devout man, entirely uncontemplative, willing to leave the things of the spirit to each man's

private taste. He did not in the least understand fanaticism, and he deplore
violence, whoever used it. Hating cruelty, believing that practical gover⟨n⟩
ment and the prosperity of the people are the true aim of statesmanship,
was impossible for him to understand, still less to support, religious extren⟨i⟩
ists. The justification for burning men alive, as the Calvinists had do⟨n⟩
at Geneva and the Inquisition was doing everywhere, was the belief that on⟨ly⟩
by so horrible a measure could men be dissuaded from going to damnatio⟨n⟩
But William could never fully believe that God was either so cruel or s⟨o⟩
unreasonable as to damn men for their opinions. He was man of the wor⟨ld⟩
enough to know that not one man or woman in a hundred ever fully unde⟨r⟩
stands what he believes or why he believes it. 'How many men and wome⟨n⟩
have we not seen', wrote Montaigne at about this time, 'who have patient⟨ly⟩
endured to be burnt and roasted for misunderstood and vain opinions whic⟨h⟩
they have borrowed of others.' It was, to William, a spectacle heartrending⟨ly⟩
piteous, and he could not believe that it gave God the least satisfaction. Th⟨e⟩
turn now emphatically taken by the revivified Catholic Church towards
more rigid and cruel enforcement of doctrine was entirely antipathetic t⟨o⟩
him. Hardly less antipathetic were the doctrines of Calvin with the⟨ir⟩
insistence on eternal damnation for the great majority of mankind, ye⟨t⟩
among all his Protestant relations and friends Calvin's doctrine was gainin⟨g⟩
converts. The milder teachings of Luther were being totally submerged -
or, worse, were coming into collision and provoking open war among th⟨e⟩
Protestants. William was too observant a politician not to see that Calvin⟨-⟩
ism, the strength of the French Huguenots, was likely to be the more seriou⟨s⟩
force in the future, but he would have preferred to see some kind of recon⟨-⟩
ciliation between the two, for only united Protestantism would be able full⟨y⟩
to withstand the new Catholicism.

The religious question remained for him a secondary one in th⟨e⟩
whole business. Even when Henry II had told him of Alva's plan, his firs⟨t⟩
reaction had not been one of outraged religious feelings (he was a Catholi⟨c⟩
so how could it have been?), but of outraged humanity. It had seemed t⟨o⟩
him an unprovoked attack on a decent and trusting people. It had seemed t⟨o⟩
him an immoral act *politically*, contrary to the sworn duty of a King, whos⟨e⟩
function is to protect his people. He had decided then, not to champion th⟨e⟩
Protestants, but to eliminate Spanish influence in the Netherlands, two ver⟨y⟩
different things. Seeing at once, and quite rightly, that the plan was i⟨n⟩
essence political, and that, however sincere the religious fervour whic⟨h⟩
prompted it, its result would be the subjection of a relatively free people t⟨o⟩
autocracy, and of the Netherlands to Spain, he had directed his whol⟨e⟩
policy since that time specifically against Spanish influence, and Philip'⟨s⟩

tempts to absorb or disintegrate the privileges of the Netherlands. Religion had entered into his actions merely as a secondary consideration, as part of the inalienable right of human beings to their own opinions.

Few of his supporters saw the situation in so dry and cool a light. Men like Egmont and Horn resented the attack on them personally, as privileged and respected nobles of the Netherlands. They were a small group and William had exploited their not very wide or constructive political ideas the interests of something greater. He had hitherto done much the same with the diffused forces of the Protestants and Protestant sympathizers. But with Granvelle's withdrawal, some of the younger nobles took the bit between their teeth, and William, try as he would, found it impossible to prevent their turning a sound political issue into a dangerous religious quarrel. Yet, unless he turned out his brother Louis, to whom he was growing ever more deeply attached, he could not prevent these hotheads and heretics from using his house as their unofficial headquarters.

King Philip for his part was not displeased to see the troubles in the Netherlands take this turn, for if his constitutional position was weak his religious position was very strong. Should the Protestants be foolish enough to play the part of political trouble-makers, patriotic opposition to his policy from the Catholics – the sort of thing he had had to face over the reorganization of the bishoprics, and the predominance of Granvelle – would be stifled. Philip would be able to disguise the impending onslaught on the independence of the Netherlands as a straight fight between the old faith and the new; thus in a country predominantly, if unenthusiastically, Catholic, he would cripple any kind of 'national' opposition, and establish Spanish armed control of the Netherlands under cover of defending the faith.

This was what William foresaw and strove to prevent. This was the catastrophe towards which the Protestant extremists were enthusiastically steering the Netherlands.

From the moment Granvelle left, they began to get out of hand. Protestant sympathies – Lutheran and Calvinist, but mainly Calvinist – swept the lesser nobility like the fashion of a new doublet, and with as little real meaning. It was smart; it was advanced; it was popular with the people – poor devils, some of whom genuinely believed – and young noblemen like to be popular. But it was an odd kind of religion showing itself chiefly in sneers at official Catholicism, or such gross ill-manners as coming drunk to Mass when the Regent was present.

Margaret watched these manifestations with growing anger. But she had more immediate and serious worries. The Estates, encouraged by Granvelle's departure, were now asking for a careful revision of the King's

religious policy. Their anxiety, on the most practical grounds, was justifiabl
Emigration to England and Germany was robbing the country of its be
workers. Colonies of them departed yearly, encouraged by other goverr
ments, to impart their valuable techniques to foreigners and rivals. Margar
saw the point and explained it to Philip: this was not properly a religiou
issue, for even the priests, canons and abbots in the Estates were anxious fc
a reconsideration of policy.

Philip read her protests with indifference. He had already taken h
decision, as she realized, when, in August, she received a startling instructio
to promulgate the rulings of the Council of Trent to the Netherlands. N
one on the Council of State, not even Philip's most loyal servants, thougl
the moment well-chosen and the reaction throughout the country was higl
unfavourable. Catholics and Protestants alike resented this categoric
command. Except to a few religious enthusiasts the definitive re-statemer
of Catholic practice and dogma at the Council of Trent meant nothing. I
the Netherlands the wealthy and well-born had for years paid the mere
lip-service to the Church while the poor were well content with lax an
ignorant priests chanting their old *mumpsimuses*. The revived spirit of tl
Counter-Reformation was as strange to the Catholic majority as it w:
hateful to the Protestant minority, and equally 'foreign' to both. But wors
than this Philip's command ran directly counter to their privileges, for it w:
the introduction of new laws without consultation with the Estates. Yo
Philip knew well what he was doing, for though the Catholics might grumbl
only the Protestants would act; he was forcing the Protestant minority t
show their hand. The move did not quite succeed. Thanks to the loyalt
of the Stadholders, thanks to the restraining influence of the Prince of Orang
nothing that could be called rebellion greeted the King's new rulin
although the Estates of Flanders immediately petitioned against the Inquis
tion, and the Antwerp mob stoned the executioners during the burning of
relapsed heretic monk. Valenciennes and Bruges, so disturbed a year befor
remained quiet.

But on the Council of State, the inevitable trio, William, Egmont an
Horn, insisted on referring the matter back to the King before further ste
were taken to enforce his orders. They even put forward a suggestion tha
he should visit the country in person; after all, he had been gone over fiv
years. The suggestion seems to have been genuine, and certainly vindicate
William against the charge of premeditated treason. If Philip came,
might be possible to dissuade him personally from a policy which not on
of his councillors in the Netherlands really favoured. Since Granvelle ha
left, the unquestioning loyalists Berlaymont, Aerschot, Aremberg, an

Viglius had dropped into a kind of casual acquiescence which lacked nothing so much as enthusiasm.

Philip replied that he would visit his Netherlands at no distant date, and asked the Council to send him in the meantime one of their number to explain their objections to him. They selected Egmont, and, in the winter of 1564-65, in a series of lengthy sessions, hammered out their grievances and their apprehensions into a remonstrance for the King's reading.

During the session of December 31st, 1564 William spoke at length on the situation as he saw it. Five years of observation and experience were behind the suggestions which he offered for the consideration of the King. While he asserted with some vehemence that the constitutional rights of the Netherlands must be respected, he urged that the King's religious policy lacked realism. A country surrounded by states in which Protestantism was tolerated, could not be expected to submit to a policy of drastic repression. This was practical common sense, but, unusually for William, he strayed suddenly into theory. 'However strongly I am myself a Catholic,' he said, 'I cannot approve of princes attempting to rule the conscience of their subjects.'[1]

The statement came out with no special emphasis, but the anxious Viglius, disturbed at all the Prince of Orange was saying, was chiefly disturbed by this, for here was an assertion of the rights of the individual, which undermined the whole theory of the King's authority. It was too late, by the time William had finished speaking, for any answer to be made that night. And on the following morning, after hours of fruitless wakefulness, Viglius still had no argument ready with which to oppose the Prince of Orange. His body came to the rescue of his defeated mind: he had a stroke before the Council met.

And so, armed with his instructions, Egmont went to Spain and Philip, receiving him with unusual graciousness, read the names signed in order at the foot of the remonstrance, and privately noted what heads must fall in the Netherlands.

[1] Hoynck van Papendrecht, I, I, 41-2.

CHAPTER III

PROLOGUE TO TRAGEDY

1565-1567

I

WILLIAM never had much hope of the success of Egmont's mission. Th
King yielded in one place only to attack in another — gave in over the army
but forced through his reform of the bishoprics; withdrew Granvelle, bo
immediately imposed the rulings of the Council of Trent. He was retreatin
only to advance. Looking back in years to come on the gradual steps whic
had led to catastrophe, William was to say, with truth, that he had told th
King and those who supported his policy that they were 'spinning a rope t
hang themselves'.[1] But no one else in this spring of 1565 saw the outcom
so clearly. Egmont's buoyant confidence and the news which soon arrive
from Madrid that the King was treating him with extraordinary favou
raised a mirage of hope on the political horizon. William remained sceptica
'The end will show all',[2] he said significantly to Louis, when he reporte
the welcome Egmont had had in Madrid.

The gay young Prince of Orange had changed in these last years. A
thirty-two, he had already lost his resplendent youth. His portraits no
showed a grave, almost a melancholy, face, and indeed it was his broth
Louis, at twenty-seven, who chiefly kept the great houses at Brussels an
Breda alive with gaiety. Those who knew most about William's private li
may have ascribed his changing outlook to a cause which was not politica
and may have been right. Deeply as William was involved in the questio
of the Netherlands, politics alone had not robbed his laughter of its lightne
nor drawn the lines of sleeplessness about his tired eyes.

For the whole of his adolescence and early manhood, he had had every
thing he wanted. Then political difficulties had gathered about him, deman
ing from this easy-going, easy-natured young man courage, patience an
judgment, for which his earlier experience had not trained him. They ha
been forthcoming. But now a personal tragedy spread dark decay ov
what was left of his youth, rotting alike his personal confidence and h
peace of mind.

His wife, Anna, had been pleasant enough at first, a little awkward i

[1] *Apology.*   [2] *Archives,* I, 369.

her manners perhaps, a little arrogant and haughty in the cultured and easy society of the Netherlands — it was recorded that she had boldly out-stared the Regent when she was presented — but she was, after all, only seventeen. Then, gradually, something went wrong between the Prince of Orange and his wife, and the secret evil, forcing its way through surface formality, was clear to the world: so clear that Anna was generally spoken of as William's 'domestic curse'. No gossip is more delightful than the inside story from the bed-chamber of the great, and, popular as was the Prince of Orange, few people could resist the temptation to embellish and pass on anything which they happened to hear from the whispering corridors of the Palais de Nassau, or the tattling purlieus of Breda. Soon housewives in backstreets from Delft to Antwerp were shaking their heads over the troubles of the Prince of Orange — how his wife was unkind to his children, how she had been rude to the Regent, how oddly she had behaved at Count so-and-so's wedding, how she had contested precedence with the Countess of Egmont, how haughtily she treated her husband. Four years from their marriage the passionate girl whom William had fetched from Saxony was an unmanage-able vixen, frequented by a gang of lewd companions, who varied hysterical gaiety with fits of drunken melancholy, locking herself in her room with all the curtains drawn for days at a time, rocking herself to and fro and crying by candlelight, and then as suddenly running off to Spa with her noisy friends, and shrieking that her husband was planning to poison her when he asked her to come home.

It is impossible to say why this had happened to Anna. Her character had always been bad, for no redeeming virtue is recorded of her, and even the bitterest propagandists, who stopped at nothing to blacken William, could find no word to whiten his wife. Her first two children, both daughters, had died within a few days of their birth; the third, a son, christened with great rejoicings and a torchlight procession at Breda this February of 1565, seemed more likely to live. But the earlier disappointments, or possibly some physical derangement, not understood at the time, may have hastened what was to be the gradual disintegration of Anna's reason. Brought up austerely and with no affection, she had the less resistance towards the temptations which the Netherlands offered to a young, sensual creature. Probably William began by being too indulgent; it would have been natural to him to lavish amusements and luxuries on his ingenuous bride. The unaccustomed pleasures went to her unsteady head and she could not be temperate in her enjoyment of them. Later, when William tried mildly enough to put a brake on her indulgence, her vanity, inflamed by too much repression in childhood, flared into violence. Was she not a princess of Saxony and had she not honoured him by becoming his wife. Then, or earlier, he should have quelled her, for, if one thing emerges from the scattered records we have of Anna, it is that she dearly loved a scene she would have liked him to beat her. Foiled, she vented her frustration in unkindness to his children and furious public scenes. On at least one occasion she startled Count Horn and a company of dinner guests at the Palais de Nassau by screaming across the table at her husband a string of injuries beginning with his social inadequacy to her exalted rank and ending with his inadequacy in a more intimate capacity. Her private tempers were a daily cross, yet 'what happens secretly', wrote William, 'can well be borne ... but verily I found it hard enough to hear her speak such things in front of everyone'.[1] Anna's conduct made it impossible to draw a veil of decency over their deplorable relations. In vain for William to behave, under her persistent attacks, with a forbearance worthy of a better cause, or to answer the Regent's probing questions with the discreet pretence that his wife was ill. Anna herself, her own worst enemy, advertised her follies as a woman and her failure as a wife everywhere.

William at length appealed to her family to restrain her. Faced by reproachful messengers from her relations, Anna staged a spectacular repentance. It did not impress her husband, who had seen this tearful self-abasement before, and all to no purpose. How little indeed her conduct improved was evident from the fact that he sent his eldest son precipitately to the University of Louvain in the summer of 1565, and asked the Regent Margaret to receive his eldest daughter as one of her ladies-in-waiting. The boy at twelve years old was only just of an age to make the change in his education seem reasonable, the girl at eleven was so young to enter the Regent's household as to provoke comment. Anna's shortcomings not merely as a wife, but as a stepmother, were evident from her husband's decision that his children would be happier and under better influences anywhere but in his own home.

Robbed thus of the society of his elder children and of the comforts of his private life, William turned wholly towards politics. If, at this period, they became his very existence, that was as much due to the darkening of his personal horizon as to the darkening of the political skies. Warm-hearted, susceptible to human relationships, setting much store by human affection and human contact, the private tragedy released and re-directed his energies. He lacked the toughness, the hard impersonal temperament which characterize the natural statesman: strange contradiction that his softer qualities, good nature and compassion, helped by this private tragedy, were pushing

[1] *Archives*, II, 32.

him inevitably towards the lonely, hard and dangerous part of national saviour.

II

On April 30th, 1565, Egmont was back in Brussels, bursting with satisfaction. He had travelled all the way from Madrid with the Regent's son, the young Prince of Parma, who was hurrying to Brussels to be married, and perhaps to be given some post in the army or about the Court. He brought with him a glowing account of his reception in Madrid. King Philip, seeming more human in the sympathetic surroundings of his native Spain, had been exceptionally charming, so charming that Egmont had not troubled to insist on any definite political promises. Not only had Philip spoken in the most understanding way about the Netherlands, but he had sent messages to the Prince of Orange in particular, asking in the friendliest way whether William would send him, as a special favour, the chef of whose genius he had heard so much. Egmont, who was greedy, had evidently talked to Philip of other things beside politics.

William was not in Brussels to see Egmont's return, to hear his first joyous and vague report to the Council of State, nor, a week later, to witness his mortification when official instructions came through from Philip. Re-stating his religious policy with incisive force, the King suggested a new educational policy to stamp out heresy in the Netherlands, and conceded only that the Regent might call a council of bishops to discuss practical details. This time even Egmont was incensed, more especially Egmont, for Philip's instructions were dated three days exactly after his own departure from Madrid and revealed with insulting clearness how the King had fooled him.

Trapped between the King's instructions and Egmont's indignation, Margaret appealed to William; whatever his opinions he had reassuring manners and would exert a steadying influence on the Council and perhaps on the furious Egmont.

It was the middle of May, notoriously a time apt for disorders. Previous Mays had seen outbreaks of image-breaking and the release of Protestant prisoners by excited mobs in Valenciennes and Mons, in Bruges and Antwerp. William feared more serious trouble yet within his own provinces, Holland, Zealand and Utrecht; for one of the periodical quarrels between the Scandinavian countries had broken out, the Sound was closed to traffic, and the repercussions of this blockade on the carrying trade, and, above all, the corn exchange of the northern provinces, were extremely serious. The docks at Amsterdam were quiet, the barges on the canals empty. Dock-hands and labourers faced a starving summer. In the circumstances, William wrote to Margaret, he could not possibly leave his Stadholderate until he had arranged for the distribution of food to the destitute and seen by what other means the situation could be alleviated.

The incident throws a significant light on William's political outlook. The greater issue must be postponed until the immediate necessities of the people were met: so he had always argued, and so, to the end of his life, he still argued, seeing the State exclusively as the means for serving the people. Let the Council and the King's policy wait until the people of Amsterdam had been fed. Only when he had the emergency services working more or less smoothly did he at length return to the council table.

There was little he could do to help Margaret; if he remained outwardly more calm it was only because, unlike Egmont, he had never expected anything else from Philip. If he refused to give any open expression to his opinions, it was because he had none which could be safely or profitably expressed. The committee of bishops, suggested by the King, duly met and — since the bishops were chiefly men of his own appointment — duly approved the royal decision to impose the rulings of the Council of Trent on the Netherlands. Closely supported by the indignant Egmont and the mistrustful Horn, William refused to endorse this decision. Whatever the bishops might think, they, as Stadholders, were unwilling to take the responsibility for the consequences of carrying out the King's policy.

Baffled, Margaret wrote again to Philip for instructions and the summer heat settled on the Netherlands with nothing decided. Besides the distress in the north, emigration continued from the south. The outlook for the future of the country had never seemed darker and the air was heavy with rumours. In Brussels itself a spurious gaiety reigned, for two society weddings — that of the Prince of Parma and of Horn's brother, Montigny — kept the luxury trades busy. The Prince of Parma's delightful presence enlivened the Court and warmed his mother's heart for a while; but soon his ill-manners made trouble with the native lords, while painful family scenes occurred with his too-loving mother. Wrangling with her husband over the marriage settlement and waiting for Philip's long-delayed instructions, frayed her irritated nerves. She was reported by the autumn to spend much of her time crying in her own room.

Philip's letters, when at last they came in early November, gave her cause to cry; not that tears would avail anything. It took her a week to collect strength to face the Council, for his instructions were even more uncomprehending than before: he insisted on the execution of his religious policy without further delay, adding, with an ingenuous attempt to soften the blow, that he had sent a shipload of corn to the poor of the Netherlands.

Even the devoted Viglius felt misgiving; loyal, limited, half realizing the peril of the State, Viglius in his office of chairman of the Council sought vainly to gain time and pacify the opposition, suggesting that yet another deputation should be sent to the King. His Majesty had perhaps not fully understood the present dangerous situation. . . . But the King's opponents themselves would not hear of it. Philip had received two embassies and innumerable letters; he must learn now, they hinted, by bitter experience that his policy was — as William once described it — 'neither Christian nor practical'.[1] The crisis could be postponed no longer. There was some relief perhaps in feeling that at last the gloves were off, and as the meeting broke up William said in an aside to his neighbour which Viglius heard with dismay: 'We shall soon see the prologue to a high tragedy.' His voice, to the anxious ear of Viglius, sounded light and truculent.[2]

After a bad harvest, winter was already at hand; Philip's shipload of corn would not go far among the hungry. Famine and unemployment sharpened the political sensitivity of the people. Their economic unrest and physical discomfort were bound soon to find a violent outlet, and religion had become the bursting channel for the outcry of the oppressed. 'It is folly', wrote William, 'to enforce the *Placaten* when corn is so dear.'[3]

The gloomiest prognostications seemed justified. At Antwerp and all over the south whole colonies of artisans were emigrating to England; even wealthy burghers were selling out and making ready to go. Submission to the King's religious policy meant economic suicide for the Netherlanders; even the King's own supporters feared it, and throughout the entire middle-class and among the younger and more modern nobility — Catholic or heretic — the determination to stop the King's folly was hardening into action. Meanwhile sporadically the populace moved. Prisoners seized by the officers of the Inquisition were forcibly released, and papers libelling the Regent and the Government were scattered in the streets and pinned in every public place. Appeals to William and Egmont to stop the Inquisition appeared on the doors of their houses in Brussels, and another was thrust into Margaret's hand as she walked to Mass. 'Brabant awake!' was now the cry, and popular rumour did not hesitate to name William among the expected leaders. One of the boldest of the manifestos, plastered one night in all the public places of Antwerp, was commonly ascribed to his brother Louis of Nassau. And where Louis of Nassau stood, there in the view of the people must surely stand their beloved Prince of Orange.

[1] *Archives*, I, 440.   [2] Hoynck van Papendrecht, I, I, 45.   [3] *Archives*, II, 19.

Perhaps it was this unfounded faith that William or Egmont would step forward to save them from the King which prevented the immediate breaking of the storm. But, in the rising clouds of political vapour, it was becoming impossible for anyone clearly to distinguish friend from foe or one direction from another.

Margaret, meanwhile, cheated herself with the hope that she could win over the Prince of Orange; wrongly convinced that he could be gained by playing on his ambition and vanity, she was right in believing that the opposition would lose its greatest strength in losing him. But William would not play, and she noticed with growing fear the reckless indiscretion of his brother Louis, and Egmont's ever closer connection with them both. To break down this alliance was her next hope and, when it was rumoured in Brussels that William had been offended by some discourtesy of Egmont's at a dinner party, Margaret strove to enlarge the imagined breach. She chose the left-handed manner of publicly snubbing William's Anna while favouring the Countess of Egmont. The repercussions of this behaviour in the privacy of the Palais de Nassau may be imagined. 'The Countess of Egmont sits with Madame while the Princess of Orange is kept standing,' wrote a malicious observer; 'the Prince is dying of rage.'[1] But it was not so much rage as one further unbearable irritation to add to the squalor of his private life. Anna had by this time forgotten her promises of good behaviour and her disorderly conduct was again the talk of Brussels.

The two great weddings which had been preparing all the summer were celebrated with amazing splendour in the autumn, Montigny's first, with a tourney in which William rode a tilt with the younger men, his last jousting; Parma's a few weeks later. The Flemish nobles were willing enough to attend wedding festivities, for even if they regarded the Spanish-speaking son of the Regent with suspicion, a banquet was always a banquet. Foremost among the younger set was the handsome Louis of Nassau, who combined the attractions of a young and already distinguished soldier with those of a wit and a ready speaker. Indifferent to women, he was at his best at the noisy bachelor parties for which the two approaching weddings provided a suitable excuse. His inseparable and admiring companion was the red-headed Henri de Brederode, some years his elder, but valiantly keeping in with the rising generation; an aggressive restless exhibitionist with rowdy tastes and enough good nature to earn a superficial popularity. In the same set were the Counts of Culembourg and Bergen, Horn's brother Montigny himself, the intelligent Hoogstraten, fierce for his lack of inches, William's special friend among the younger men, and innumerable lesser nobility and

[1] Granvelle, I, 43.

ountry gentlemen who enjoyed the hospitality of the great and liked to be in
he fashion. In this winter of 1566 fashion and the opposition were one. Not
ll these men were serious politicians, and few perhaps felt much personal
iterest in the religious question. Louis of Nassau was a sincere anti-Catholic
: not an austere Protestant, and there were two brothers, John and Philip
Aarnix, Counts of Thoulouse, who had recently come back from Geneva
onvinced that their souls' and their country's salvation depended on the
arsh, fighting creed of John Calvin. Yet on the whole the ideas which
ound this group together were ill-thought-out and mostly negative:
iey blamed the King for disregarding their privileges and their rank and for
ighting the advice of their great men, rather than for the active wrong of
is policy.

There is always something fascinating in the idea of conspiracy, with its
levation of unrest and egoism, of personal discontent and frustration,
ito a sacred political cause. The men who drank and talked far into
ie night that winter in Brussels, and who carried their ostentatiously con-
iiratorial gatherings to the pleasant outlying watering-place of Spa, when
ie spring came, and in the hawking season, to each other's country estates,
onstituted rather a threat to Margaret's government than a hope for the
Ietherlands. Philip's supporters, the few loyalist nobles and the even fewer
enuinely devout Catholics of the Netherlands, mainly churchmen, regarded
ieir Confederation with anxiety; 'ne scay ce qu'ils dient, entre eux — Heaven
nows what they are talking of among themselves'.[1] Speculating on what
ras said, the loyalists attributed to the talkers a good deal more sense than
iey actually had.

The danger to the government was not from this group of young nobles
iemselves, but rather from the fusion of religious feeling — and Calvinist
:eling at that — with the vague, growing resentment of the middle- and
vorking-classes which had its root in economic insecurity. Some connec-
on between the nobles and the merchants existed through the debts which
.most all of them had contracted among the financiers of Antwerp. But
ie connection, though real enough, was not the only reason for the growing
nity of interest between the classes, for the economic structure of society is
erpetually modified by psychological factors, and in 1566 we are still too
:ar to feudal Europe to think in terms of princes and nobles taking orders
om the financiers of the city. Not economic pressure alone, but the fatal
ieptitude and cruelty of Philip's policy was uniting the whole people of
ie Netherlands against him, from the soft-living Prince of Orange
i the Palais de Nassau to the calculating business men of Antwerp and

[1] Granvelle, I, 24.

Dordrecht, and the hungry, smoke-grimed labourers in the foundries o
Liége.

Meanwhile William had reached a decision. His brother's outspoke
opposition to the Government, his wife's Lutheranism and notorious ill
conduct, had irreparably compromised him. But he felt no confidence i
the new group of extremists with whom Louis persistently consorted
doubting whether he had the influence to control them and fearing that an
action they intended would be futile and perhaps, in its ultimate repercus
sions, dangerous. Rumours were already circulating that King Phili
was about to send an army to the Netherlands, to enforce his policy. If thi
were so, he would need an excuse, and that, precisely, was what th
irresponsibles were giving him.

Early in the New Year of 1566 William sent for Louis to Breda, invitin
at the same time Egmont, Horn, Brederode, Bergen and Culembourg
Whatever persuasion the extremists employed on this occasion to gain hi
support for their scheme of compelling Philip to change his policy, h
remained unmoved. In his view they over-estimated their own strengt
and under-estimated the King's, playing for ephemeral success at the pric
of lasting defeat. Useless to tell William that a German soldier of fortune
Eric of Brunswick, was collecting troops in neighbouring Cleves wit
the King of Spain's commission; useless to repeat the rumour that Phili
himself was preparing to send an army. He was fully aware of these fact
but saw in them a reason for more, rather than for less, caution. In his view
the protests of a group of noblemen, however strongly phrased, wer
scarcely an effective measure of defence. Louis, then, or later — but probabl
then, for Louis never guarded his tongue — spoke of raising troops in th
Protestant German states, so as to be ready for whatever Philip migh
attempt. This was flat treason, and William would not contemplate i
Not yet. Not until the King's own attack justified it.

The only course of action which William seems to have suggeste
appeared to Egmont and Horn unnecessary, and to the others pointless. Thi
was an appeal to the Emperor Max, Philip's intelligent cousin, asking him t
take notice of the fact that the Netherlands were, in political theory,
part of the Holy Roman Empire, and therefore had a right to the regiona
privileges granted to Protestants, or at least to Lutherans, under the Augsbur
settlement of 1555. But this idea hardly met the demands of Louis, Brederode
or the Marnix brothers, for in the first place the Augsburg settlement onl

permitted the exercise of the reformed faith in lands ruled over by reformed princes, and therefore would have made no difference to Philip's Netherlands; in the second place the Augsburg settlement recognized no reformed religion except the Lutheran. And what use was that to the Calvinists of the Netherlands? What William's ultimate intentions were it is hard to say. He found Calvinism increasingly unsympathetic, and perhaps he hoped by forming some alliance with the German Lutherans both to strengthen the Netherlands against Philip's impending attack and to swing the Protestant balance back to the Lutheran side. But he failed either to dissuade Louis and his friends from their projects or to impose his own views on Egmont and Horn. The extremists went their headstrong way all too fast, while the conservatives, Egmont and Horn, were too sorely perplexed to go any way at all.

The meeting had been wholly unfruitful and, though they parted with some promise of further discussions at Hoogstraten's country seat later in the year, William seems to have made up his mind to the defeatist course of withdrawing altogether from an intolerable situation. At any rate, on January 24th, 1566, he sent in his resignation to the Regent, stating frankly that it was against the constitution of the Netherlands to give State support to the Inquisition on the Spanish model, while to do so at a time of acute corn shortage was highly impolitic. He further advised her to wait before taking action, until the King himself came to the Netherlands, as he had promised to do. In the meantime, he asked her to find 'someone to take my place who better understands the people and is more skilled than I am at keeping them in peace and tranquillity'.[1]

'Someone who better understands the people and is more skilled than I am ...' was a tall order, as well the Prince knew when he wrote those bitter-ironic words. Little was left now of the Emperor Charles's favourite. Margaret's vacillations, her pathetic appeals to him and Egmont for help just at those times when the King's policy most strikingly over-rode their advice, at last perhaps the personal cruelty of her rudeness to his wife, had turned him against her. She was no longer gracious 'Madame', the queenly Regent, but 'a passionate woman armed with the visor of a King's power',[2] the instrument of Philip's cruelty and deceit towards the defenceless Netherlands. But he was still only a conscientious, compassionate, perplexed man in a wearisome quandary, not by a long way yet the sure-handed protagonist of a cause. The faults of his education undermined him. Hating the loneliness and the opposition which he felt rising against him, the criticism and the suspicion, he wanted to throw in his hand, and escape from the scene of

[1] Gachard, II, 106-110.   [2] *Apology*.

political failure and social humiliation. No sooner had he written to Margaret than he went to Antwerp and painfully interviewed those merchants whom he had approached eight years before in the King's name. Now it was for himself, and not for the first time. His debts ran to a million florins and he could hardly leave the Netherlands without settling the worst of them. Hence this painful week of argument with the financiers of Antwerp.

One thing certainly happened in that week: two things may have happened. First, he discovered that his credit would cover no more heavy borrowing, a fact which in itself might have been sufficient to make him alter his plans. But did something else happen at those interviews? No group of people was more concerned at the situation in the Netherlands than the wealthy burghers and responsible citizens of Antwerp; the decline in trade and the crazy uncertainty of the money-market owing to Philip's policy was part of their reason, but it was not the whole of it. They were a thoughtful, independent class, self-reliant, proud of what they had achieved, the liberties their forefathers had gained from past rulers, and the high reputation of the Netherlands throughout the world.

William had always made friends of these men, while to some of them he was indeed fairly heavily indebted, but the relationship neither began nor ended there. He had always respected their experience and judgment as a class and their individual qualities as men. During the sessions of the Estates General they had eaten and drunk at his table, using his house as their club: it is impossible to suppose that neither he nor they mentioned politics during the interviews of this January week in 1566. Was it the discovery of their trust in him which decided him to change his plan, and acquiesce in Margaret's plaintive request for him to reconsider his resignation? Certainly one of Antwerp's leading citizens, the Pensionary Wesembeeck, visited him at Breda during the next weeks more than once and seems from this moment to have become one of his most trusted councillors. They had much in common: by temperament both were moderate men, both wanted an understanding, not a break, with the King, both sympathized with the Lutherans, and both suspected and disliked the violence of the Calvinists. But Wesembeeck, while he was firm in his loyalty to Philip until the eleventh hour, was never in favour of surrender, still less of flight.

For the next eight weeks, William sought in vain to check the extremists, without losing their confidence, by building up some kind of defensive policy to which they could safely divert their energies. Unhappily, as he well knew, there was no feasible defensive policy; his plan broke down on the sheer lack of it. Louis and his friends came and went at Breda, but nothing was decided, and, as William at every meeting grew more hopeless of preventing their excesses, they, mistakenly, grew more convinced of his ultimate support.

The nobles of the Confederation, as it came to be called, had by this time drafted to their satisfaction an open letter, couched in the form of a petition to the King of Spain, asserting formally that he must alter his religious policy for his Netherlands; specifically, that he must withdraw the inquisition, which was an innovation against their privileges. There were few intellectuals among the Confederates, and the authorship of the *Compromis*, as it was called, can be ascribed without much doubt to John and Philip Marnix. John, the elder and more impulsive of the brothers, may have had less to do with it than the studious Philip; a misfit among the gay young men, this inhibited, deep-feeling, grave student, with the acute mind of a lawyer and the heart of a fanatic, moves through this crisis of the Netherlands impersonal as a disembodied intelligence; his the mind that drafted and the hand that wrote the documents which shaped a nation's history. The *Compromis* was his and the Netherlands' first step to maturity.

Meanwhile the document collected signatures — the petty nobles, some of the army officers, and one or two of the great; significantly not one Stadholder, not one Knight of the Golden Fleece, set his hand to that paper. William, Egmont, and Horn held aloof; but this coldness of the three most effective and popular opponents of King Philip was partly neutralized by the appearance of Louis's name, in his rash, flowing hand, second among the signatories. Many, who would not otherwise have dared to put their hands to the *Compromis*, did so because they took Louis's signature for a guarantee that William approved the plan.

Towards the middle of March, Egmont, who had, since January, avoided visiting Breda, received an invitation to join the Prince of Orange and his friends for some days' hunting at Hoogstraten. He arrived at about eleven one morning, to find, as well as William, Louis, the energetic Hoogstraten, Horn and, among others, a German professional soldier who seemed to be giving expert military advice. They were apparently discussing the best way of presenting the Confederates' petition to the Regent. William, seeing that the document existed and was already known by common report, favoured some kind of formal recognition of the Confederation by the Stadholders and, possibly, even a qualified approval of the contents of the petition. Egmont, alarmed by the presence of the German professional soldier and by Louis's flighty talk of recruiting volunteers in Germany, refused to have anything to do with the scheme, and did his best to make the occasion merely a festive one. According to his account, 'ne se traicta

autre chose que faire bonne chère' at that merry meeting. It seems a little
improbable even for one of the Prince of Orange's entertainments, but in any
case Egmont left by nightfall and reported all he had seen to the Regent.[1]

Horn joined Egmont in obstructing William's policy. These two were
brave men and with a higher sense of responsibility than the great majority
of the Confederates; but falsely secure in their ancient ideas of mutual loyalty
and obligation between sovereign and vassal, they could not see the true
meaning of the King's policy. Intent on convincing Philip of their own
loyalty, they did not understand that he conceded no merit to loyalty alone
He wanted co-operation. Nor could they follow William's argument that
since the Confederation existed, it was better to control than to disregard it

Meanwhile, in Brussels, Margaret watched the signs with nervous
agitation. Seeing the greater nobility as her only bulwark against the
encroaching tide of discontent, she called a chapter of the Golden Fleece
and wrote imploring William to come to Brussels to help her. Next she
indited a dispatch to Philip, the most outspoken she had yet dared to send
telling him frankly that, unless he was prepared to use force, he must abandon his religious policy. As if to emphasize her fears, one of her councillors
came in while she was writing to announce that about five hundred of the
gentry, with their following, were converging on Brussels, ostensibly to
present a petition to her. The Confederates, with or without the support of
the great, had decided to move.

William had withdrawn to Breda, to a household made more than
usually desolate by the death of his and Anna's only son, a child eighteen
months old. Here he received Margaret's appeal and answered briefly that
he could not, at this time, leave his sick wife. At the same time he was
preparing a general letter to the Lutheran princes of Germany warning them
that a major crisis was approaching in the Netherlands and urging on them
the duty of moral support in case the King continued in his rash policy
This was barely out of his hands when a second and more insistent letter
from Margaret forced him to abandon all else and hurry to Brussels.

Here, on March 27th, 1566, Margaret appealed to the Knights of the
Golden Fleece to speak their minds openly under the ancient privileges of
their Order. Perhaps she had hoped that her forlorn condition would
appeal to the gallantry of her hearers, but the Order of the Golden Fleece
had changed since the courtly days of its inception, and the anxious
statesmen of the Netherlands saw no occasion for a display of chivalry. Nor
in truth did Margaret effectively fulfil the part of the maiden in distress for
whose sweet sake every knightly sword would flash from the scabbard

[1] Reiffenberg, *Interrogatories*, 18-19; Philip II, I, 398.

The tears which trickled unbecomingly down her rugged cheeks provoked no more than general embarrassment and a kind of hectoring contempt.

William, who at least remained courteous, stated in a long speech that the King's best hope was to withdraw the *Placaten* against heresy and restrain the Inquisition. As for the petition which the Confederates had prepared, he asserted that it contained no disloyalty to the Government; its authors were anxious rather to prove their sincerity by concealing nothing of what they felt. Cross-questioned by Margaret he grew reticent, asserting that the King intended to have his head in the end and he dare not speak more clearly, lest his words be twisted against him. She turned from him to Hoogstraten, who with the uncompromising directness of youth and confidence told her that whatever he knew about the *Compromis* of the Confederate nobles he was under no compulsion to repeat. Next came Horn's turn; loudly lamenting the King's ingratitude to his best servants, he recapitulated his past services to the Crown while for twenty minutes somnolence gathered over his hearers. Margaret could hardly fail to gather from this meeting that the King had forfeited the goodwill of those very noblemen on whom three generations of Netherlands rulers had relied in safety. She realized that she herself was included with the King when the Knights, instead of escorting her politely to the door, at length rose and filed out, leaving her mortified and alone.

Two days later, Margaret called the Council of State. Surrounded by suspicion and distrust, feeling no confidence at all in the judgment or ability of Philip's supporters, the councillors Berlaymont and Viglius, she now threw herself on the generosity of the Prince of Orange, believing that her only chance of staving off popular revolt, until the King either came himself or sent an army, lay in his assistance. Deliberately and unscrupulously she played for it. And he, knowing her, as he must have done, to be nothing but the King's instrument, did what she wanted. It was he, and he almost alone, who through these critical months opposed the bulwark of his personal popularity between her government and the people.

Why he did this is still a mystery, yet perhaps comprehensible from our knowledge of the man, his character and his traditions. Like Egmont and Horn, he regarded loyalty to the King as a fundamental duty. In that, he belonged to the highest feudal tradition. But he was an admirable administrator, conscientious and practical, and he had the administrator's horror of avoidable disorder. It is possible that, in spite of all disillusion, he cherished the ineradicable hope that a compromise might yet be reached — not, indeed, by clumsy attempts to frighten the King — but rather by a demonstration of firmness and loyalty. Tenacity and patience were the bases of his greatness,

and perhaps he showed them at their highest power in this last effort to save
the King who had rejected in turn his every opportunity. Moreover, he
distrusted the Confederates, not as individuals, but as a group. He saw
clearly that these excitable and inexperienced men had neither the solidarity
nor the perseverance to make them politically formidable. A conglomeration
of humours tossed together by the chances of the time, they would as easily
be tossed apart again. Even the unanimous outcry against the *Placaten*,
which, for the first time in the history of the Netherlands, was causing the
mob in Antwerp and in Amsterdam, in Valenciennes and in Delft, in the
stolid north and the excitable south, to shout the same slogans, did not seem
to him to represent a force vehemently enough united to justify rebellion.
If rebellion could ever be justified — on that point, William felt the iron
control of his education. Both in Dillenburg and in Brussels, he had learnt
the lesson of feudal loyalty. Rebellion could only be reconciled with right
when the sovereign himself violated his duties. Typically, William refused
to countenance rebellion until Philip himself appealed to arms.

He made his position clear to Margaret at the Council meeting of March
29th. 'In all things there must be order', he said, 'but it must be of such a
kind as is possible to observe . . . to see a man burnt for doing as he thought
right, harms the people, for this is a matter of conscience.' In such circumstances, he went on, the judges did not carry out the laws, and the authority
of the government fell into disrepute. Rather than see the King's authority
thus undermined, he suggested that some kind of intermediate plan, some
moderation be applied, until the King himself should come.[1]

IV

On April 1st, 1566, Brederode himself bounced into Brussels, accompanied by Louis of Nassau. Each had a following of two hundred horsemen,
armed with a couple of pistols apiéce, so little attention had even Louis paid
to William's advice. Not three weeks before he had written explicitly:
'The more peacefully you come, the better. It will serve your turn the best.'[2]
The brothers, so far from working in conjunction, were politically at cross-
purposes, William too gentle and too deeply attached to Louis to forbid
his rash actions, and Louis impetuously determined to entangle his great
brother with the Confederates, whether he would or no.

So Louis and Brederode clattered through the streets with their train,
looking more like a hunting party than a threatening army, and poured

---

[1] Gachard, III, 368.   [2] *Archives*, II, 75.

uninvited into the courtyards of the Palais de Nassau. For, of course, they were going to stay with the Prince of Orange; with whom else? 'They thought I wouldn't dare to come', cried Brederode, not specifying further that mysterious 'they'. 'Well! Here I am and may be I shall leave in a very different fashion.'[1] Reported to Margaret, the silly boast had an unpleasant ring.

Louis and Brederode were not the only guests who had, as always, depended on William's hospitality. Count Horn, and the young Mansfeld had arrived first. Son of Peter Ernst of Mansfeld, a crotchety, self-important old soldier, Stadholder of Luxembourg, who had been flattered by the attentions of Louis and Brederode almost into supporting their policy, the young Mansfeld was beginning to have doubts. Horn still more so; as soon as he saw his fellow guests, he was inexplicably taken ill and had to have all his meals sent up to his bedroom.

Later that evening the more sensible and moderate men, William, Mansfeld and Horn sat together, discussing the situation, suggesting and rejecting one line of action after another. Should they, for instance, resign from the Order of the Golden Fleece as a gesture? It hardly seemed worth it, since the King would probably not even understand the implied reproach to himself.

The official centre for the Confederates was the house of the obstreperous and extravagant Culembourg. Here, during the next three days, the *Compromis des Nobles* received its final form. Here, in an atmosphere of unsuitable hilarity, the signatures were finally affixed. And here Louis, a little drunk, but withal in earnest for the cause of religion and the Netherlands, climbed on a garden table in the mild April dusk and harangued the excited throng. But the Confederates could not confine their business entirely to Culembourg's house, and, though William seems to have refused official hospitality to Louis' wilder friends, they slipped in and out through the backdoors and side doors and garden gates, and swarmed all over the Palais de Nassau, where Horn came upon them confabulating in corners, and took them up short for the things he heard them saying. They laughed boorishly in his face.

At last, on April 5th, 1566, a Friday, their *Compromis* was ready and Margaret willing to give them audience. They set off through the streets, Brederode leading, perhaps two hundred gentry and petty nobility in all — so much had the rumoured five hundred dwindled — accompanied by the enthusiasm of the Brussels mob. Margaret was in no state to receive them; she had worn herself out for the last fortnight, sitting in Council sometimes from seven in the morning until eight at night, presiding at the meeting of

[1] Philip II, I, 406.

the Golden Fleece, practising her charm (poor woman, a hard task for one so lacking in it) on the Prince of Orange. She had visibly aged, and her nervousness would have been pitiable had it not been exasperating. She lacked the conscious femininity and above all the physical characteristics to capitalize her all too genuine fears. As usual her eyes were unseasonably wet. Irritated, the councillor Berlaymont strove to rally her. 'Quoi, Madame', he said, 'peur de ces gueux?'[1] 'Ces gueux', 'these beggars'; in this way he mocked the procession of Netherlands gentry. It gave the Confederates the popular name they yet needed to establish them firmly with the mob. Within the week, Margaret was to hear 'Vivent les Gueux!' at every street corner.

She need have had no immediate fear, for she had all her councillors about her, including William, Egmont and Horn, while Brederode left the greater number of his following in the street, entering her presence with a mere delegation. Fervidly protesting his loyalty, he handed over the famous *Compromis*, and Margaret, uttering a few formal words of acceptance, dismissed him from her presence. The whole ceremony was over in a few minutes.

Quite what anyone had expected to happen at this climacteric moment is hard to say. But now the petition was in the Regent's hands, like any other petition; and there was nothing to be done for the next few days, except wait for her answer, and have a good time.

Brederode had already made arrangements for the good time. Using the willing Culembourg's house he had invited three hundred guests and made lavish provision of food and drink, especially drink. The Confederates had already heard the contemptuous words 'ces gueux', and now scoured Brussels in high spirits for as many round wooden beggars' bowls as could be collected; these they substituted for the gold and silver goblets on the dinner tables. Brederode, filling his to the brim with wine, drank a toast to the whole company, shouting, 'Vivent les Gueux!'

The same evening William was dining gloomily with Egmont, Horn and Mansfeld when they were interrupted by one of Margaret's agitated requests for their immediate attendance at a Council meeting to discuss the answer to the *Compromis*. She wanted Hoogstraten too. He was not with them, and someone remembered that he was where one would expect him to be — at Brederode's party. While Mansfeld hastened to the palace, William, Egmont and Horn rode round by way of Culembourg's house intending to have Hoogstraten fetched out. According to Horn, it was only when they reached the door and heard the noise which Brederode's guests were making

[1] Strada.

that anyone suggested going in. The evening was already far advanced and William thought it would be wise to break up the party before the guests could do any damage. There was no saying what trouble a horde of drunken young nobles might not start, if someone did not disperse them efficiently to bed.

So, in a moment of mistaken inspiration, the three greatest men in the Netherlands, the three whose names had been consistently linked together as Philip's opponents, dismounted at Culembourg's gates and marched into his crowded banqueting hall. Brederode's guests, as it happened, were not fighting drunk, merely at peace with the world, seeing a dimly glorious future through a haze of wine. They were changing hats and laughing weakly, with an unsteady clatter of occasional cheering, as they toasted each other in their beggars' bowls. Some wits were wearing them round their necks in the manner of those pitiable objects they had so often seen whining at street corners. The beggars' bowls dangling against the velvet and satin doublets of Brederode's guests were a good joke.

But they were not beyond recognizing the three visitors, and jumping to conclusions. Brederode made for them at once, with shouts of welcome. While Hoogstraten, fortunately more or less sober, was being called from his place, bowls of wine were pushed into the hands of the three great men. If they would not join the party they could hardly refuse to drink a health. As they drank, the whole room burst into vociferous, if unsteady, cheers. 'Vivent les Gueux!' they shouted; 'Vive le Prince d'Orange! Vive Egmont! Vive Horn!' But again and again 'Vivent les Gueux!' Horn, who had not the least idea what this new ribaldry meant, thought it a revolting party, but William and even Egmont thought it worse than that. As soon as Hoogstraten had joined them, they put down their bowls and left the room, not pausing to thank their host.

They had been there, as Horn was later to say, for the space of two 'Misereres' — perhaps five minutes — and they had neither sat down nor joined in the unseemly shouting. Yet on the following day it was known all over Brussels that the Prince of Orange, with Egmont and Horn, had joined the Confederates at their banquet and drunk the toast of 'Vivent les Gueux!'. In this form Margaret heard the story and drew her own conclusions.

Three days after the presentation of the *Compromis*, Margaret gave the Confederates her answer. A new deputation was to go to Spain to explain the situation to the King, and in the meantime she would suspend the extremer measures of the religious programme and evolve, as she put it, using William's word, a policy of 'moderation'.

It was not a good answer, although it was good enough to postpone for a few more weeks the outbreak of open revolt. Nobody thought the depu-tation to the King would have any effect, least of all Montigny and Bergen, the two noblemen selected for the task. They even feared that Philip would revenge himself on them personally for their opposition to his policy, an anxiety shared at this time by many of their fellows. Small wonder, then, that they hardly relished the prospect of visiting Madrid. Bergen, indeed, while playing pêle mêle in the Park, hit himself violently with his own mallet, fell down with groans of well-simulated agony, and announced, after he had been carried home, that he was far too ill to go anywhere; but Margaret was not deceived.

William, Egmont and Horn, too, were dissatisfied with the answer and, at a stormy meeting of the Council on April 9th, 1566, threatened resigna-tion, but at length gave in to Margaret's entreaty to wait at least for the outcome of Montigny's mission.

On the following day, Brederode left Brussels with his followers. Outside the gates of the city they fired their pistols into the air, then turned their horses' heads for Antwerp. From head to foot they were now all dressed in the grey-brown colour of begging friars, and their beggars' bowls were slung round their necks: evidently they were bent on mischief, but who was going to stop them? Margaret did not know, unless the Prince of Orange would help.

Excitement grew from day to day. Knick-knack makers throughout the country did a brisk trade in beggars' bowls, of all sizes and shapes; they dangled from ladies' earrings, they adorned the velvet caps of dandies. The Duke of Aerschot, boldly rather than wisely, tried to rally Catholic opinion by starting a counter-movement for wearing a medallion of the Virgin. But medallions of the Virgin had not the appeal of originality, and there was no effective counter-cry to the 'Vivent les Gueux!' slogan, now as common in the streets of Brussels as 'Hot pies' in winter. As the spring advanced, the Calvinists and their sympathizers grew bolder, for the government, with its old 'murderation', as the new policy of moderation was called, did too little either to satisfy or to control them. Exiles flooded back from East Anglia and the Rhineland — whither they had fled for religion's sake — to hearten the oppressed brethren at home, and soon they varied their war-cry with the open chanting of hymns or psalms in the vernacular, while at night toughs held up innocuous passers-by at the pistol point and made them shout 'Vivent les Gueux!' till they were hoarse.

William had left the capital for Breda, to attend to his local duties, and Louis was now in sole possession of the Palais de Nassau. He saw no reason why its hospitable roof should not shelter some at least of the sectarian preachers and their flocks. It was much more comfortable than the dark cellars or draughty fields where they usually met. With a mild attempt at discretion, he let the services take place in the small hours. They were well attended, by the curious as well as the devout; and it was a jealous wife, wanting to know for what mistress her husband left her bed night after night, who found the secret out and babbled the story to all Brussels. By this time there was no stopping the rumour that the Prince of Orange was himself secretly a member of the Confederation.

Serious trouble began first in Antwerp. The huge cosmopolitan port, honeycombed with privileged foreign concessions, where every religion was practised, had long been the source of Protestant inspiration for all Flanders. In the last years many of the persecuted had moved thither, in order almost openly to take advantage of the special conditions, while emigrants waiting there for transport to England, Germany, or Denmark formed an unstable group, ardent in their religion and with little to lose. Here Calvinism was especially strong, the great cosmopolitan port being the perfect centre for their organized and surreptitious advance. But the real danger at Antwerp was the huge population of dock-hands and shipyard workers, the hungry, fluctuating unemployed of a wealthy port. And in the midst of Antwerp, its sharp steeples pricking the enormous sky, stood the cathedral, crammed with gorgeous reliquaries, decked with rich hangings, its altars surmounted by precious candlesticks and jewelled tabernacles, its clustered pillars encrusted with carving and gilded ornaments — a symbol of that unregenerate splendour of Catholic worship which so incensed the Calvinists, and a temptation to the angry, the hungry, and the poor.

If there is to be trouble there will be trouble in May. The damp northern winter is over; gaiety and life and lust are in the air. Men are suggestible, excited, and feel suddenly strong. And this was the moment which Brederode and his hundred and fifty had chosen to go to Antwerp. Powerless and distraught, Margaret watched the approaching storm. No one in Antwerp doubted that it was about to break: no burgher but went armed, until the armourers had sold out all their stock. Then suddenly, the Calvinists came into the open, storming the town council for permission to preach freely, and when this was refused, streaming out to meetings in the neighbouring fields, two, three and four thousand strong. All attempts to prevent the assemblies were vain and tumults grew daily within the town. A rumour that Government troops were being sent to break up the meetings caused the people to assemble indignantly outside the town hall. Urged to disperse, they shouted 'We want the Prince of Orange!'.[1]

[1] Haecht, I, 66-7.

Margaret had had the same idea. She had no one else to trust. The army was particularly unreliable, for many of the lesser officers had actually signed the *Compromis*, and when she appealed to the chief commanders to know whether they would guarantee the loyalty of their men in putting down disorder, their answers were not reassuring. Even William, with unnerving frankness, said that he could guarantee nothing. Nevertheless, William or no one could quiet the disorders at Antwerp, and to Antwerp Margaret asked him to go.

Her letter found him at Breda where Anna was expecting very shortly to lie in. Her pregnancy may have been some excuse, though it was no justification, for her increasingly offensive behaviour. In her morbid, self-tormenting way she brooded on William's passing gallantries to Brederode's good-humoured wife, but Louis was the chief object of her jealous rage. Unable to perceive that her own conduct drove her husband to the warmer sympathy of his brother, she insinuated everywhere that William had a secret understanding with Louis, who acted only under inspiration.

Neither her pregnancy nor her spiteful indiscretions made it easy for William to leave her, yet he had no choice but to obey the Regent's command, and set off for Antwerp early in July 1566, taking with him no troops at all, and only a small train of his own servants. The news of his coming went before him into the excited city, and, three miles beyond the gates, he came upon Brederode with his hundred and fifty gentlemen-at-arms, caracoling about on their horses and letting off their pistols into the evening air, like the outriders of a circus. As soon as he came up with them they began to shout 'Vive les Gueux!' and continued to do so all the way into the town. Along the road crowds of enthusiasts took up the cry and, when William entered the city, his progress through the packed streets became little less than a triumphal procession. He himself refused the ovation. Far from smiling at the people, he shook his head reprovingly as the shouts rose, raising and lowering his hand in an unmistakable attempt to subdue them. Even Brederode, who, riding at his side, was doing his best to encourage the demonstrators, was quelled when William, turning on him with unusual asperity, said 'Have a care what you do, or you will live to regret it'.[1]

Never before had he played his own personal popularity with such reckless determination against the intemperate will of the majority. He was still the servant of the King; he still hoped — for he could hardly still believe — that the good conduct of the Netherlanders might soften Philip's heart, and he was convinced of the futility of anything the Confederates could do.

[1] Gachard, II, 136-7; Wesembeeck, 19, 249.

Perhaps, strongest of all the considerations which carried him through this fearful summer was the need he felt to restore to the ordinary man and woman the amenities of life, for, although a noisy minority will enjoy political disorder all the time, and a majority will enjoy it for some of the time, in the long run, as he well knew, the people of Antwerp wanted to get on with their everyday business. The greatest commercial centre in the world could not, without dislocating its own vital system, indulge in this sort of excess.

Disregarding the irresponsible Brederode, William at once selected for his lieutenant his friend the Pensionary Wesembeeck, whose sound good sense and reasoned patriotism he knew by personal experience; he had been a frequent visitor at Breda all that spring, a man who, like William, represented a moderate middle path between Catholic and Calvinist extremes. To Wesembeeck he entrusted the business of explaining his measures to the town council and advising on the best way of carrying them out. As for putting down disorder, preventing the assembly of Calvinist mobs in the outskirts, saving priests, monks, nuns and devout Catholic sympathizers from indiscriminate molestation and the daily dread which was making their lives unbearable, he had his own ideas. Margaret, watching anxiously from Brussels, expected him to proceed with a strong hand, but he was wiser. 'To go about it by way of force, Madame, is not possible,' he wrote.[1] He knew from practical experience the root of the trouble: dear food, declining trade, too little work. All these evils were, in part at least, the result of Philip's policy, in part the result of English competition in the cloth trade. William could not find a fundamental cure, he could only alleviate the situation until order was restored. He first made work for the unemployed by launching, with the assistance of the municipality, a programme of public works. Next, he issued proclamations calling on the people to give up the tumultuous assemblies outside the town, or at least to attend them unarmed, for no violence was intended to them by the government, which was even now planning a policy of 'moderation' by which they would be permitted to worship in a seemly manner within the city itself. Such clumsy attempts as theirs, he added, to frighten or force the government could do them only harm.

As for himself, he attended Mass with ostentatious solemnity. It was a nice question whether this display of his own official Catholicism would cost him his popularity or undermine that of the extremists. It had, as he had hoped, the latter effect: Catholics were reassured and waverers brought back to a more sensible frame of mind by his example. By the middle of

[1] Gachard, II, 136.

August he reported to Margaret that everything was normal, and the quays, for some weeks past empty of trade, were resuming their activity. As earnest of his faith in the good behaviour of the city he sent for Anna to join him. Even while obeying she found means to aggravate his troubles, for she stopped at Brussels to carry off her little stepdaughter from the Regent's household. Quite apart from the discourtesy to Margaret, William was unwilling to have his young child exposed either to her stepmother's tantrums or the possible dangers of Antwerp. He sent her back, with apologies. His life was not without incidental embarrassments, sometimes from the most unexpected quarters. A silly old abbot who entertained him to dinner in his monastery on Trinity Sunday, must needs, after a cup or two of wine, give the toast 'Vive les Gueux!', repeating the phrase in between hiccups forty or fifty times, despite all efforts to suppress him: the scene, recounted to Margaret, went for another proof of William's sinister political machinations.

Before setting out for Antwerp, William had urged the Regent to call the Estates General, thus to restore public confidence and give an outlet for opinions which were explosive only when suppressed. Margaret was afraid to do so. She had information that the Confederates at a recent gathering at St. Trond had actually given Louis of Nassau a commission to recruit troops in Germany. Whatever the truth of that rumour, they had certainly petitioned her again in the most impudent fashion, demanding that their Confederation should be formally placed under the protection of the Prince of Orange, Egmont, and Horn. Margaret, agitatedly trying to prevent this threatened alliance between the lesser and the greater men, called a meeting of the Golden Fleece to discuss the crisis.

Summoned to Brussels, William was unwilling to leave Antwerp while its continued order depended on his presence. The Feast of the Assumption of the Blessed Virgin was approaching, a signal, perhaps, for more Calvinist outrages, and, on August 14th, 1566, William received a petition from a group of merchants, asking when, precisely, Protestant services would be permitted inside the town. In something of a quandary he decided to leave Hoogstraten in charge at Antwerp, since in spite of his association with the Confederates, he felt him to be responsible and trustworthy, while his vigour and charm would work with the people. Margaret, who regarded Hoogstraten as little better than a traitor, categorically refused to give him authority. Since no one else could be found, William postponed his departure. The immediate question was whether in existing conditions the cathedral clergy dared to risk the procession with which annually they celebrated the Feast of the Assumption. On this occasion they carried through the streets of the city, the sacred black Madonna, that tiny, ancient figure, almost buried in stiff petticoats and embroidered bodices of gold and silver lace, crowned, sceptred and jewelled, which was the holiest relic in the cathedral. It would have seemed an admission of cowardice to forgo the ceremony, and relying on William's presence as a guarantee of order, the cathedral clergy held the procession, the Prince and Princess of Orange and Louis of Nassau looking on from the balcony of the town hall. Here and there, not in William's sight, guttersnipes jeered at them as they passed. 'Mollykin Mollykin', they mocked the tiny black figure in the midst, 'this is your last walk!' But nothing worse happened, and on the following day William left for Brussels, not without misgiving.

v

All the summer the storm had been gathering, swollen by the fears of the Regent and the hints of the Confederates, bursting in a deluge on the Netherlands when the Knights of the Golden Fleece were summoned to Brussels. Once these responsible men had left their posts in the provinces there was no one to restrain the people; indeed the lesser gentry of the Confederacy slipped immediately into the place of leadership left temporarily unguarded. Beginning on August 19th, 1566, the day on which William rode out of Antwerp, the cataract poured over the Netherlands, North and South, East and West, for five long summer days. At the Hague and Utrecht, at Amsterdam and Veere, at Oudenarde and Poperinghe and Valenciennes, and on the island of Walcheren, they stormed the churches, tore down the hangings, smashed the statues, shattered the glass, broke open reliquaries and tabernacles and drank the holy wine. At Vianen, Brederode's gang marched to their work to the merry music of pipe and tabor, and methodically stripped every sacred building to the stones. At his country seat, Culembourg had the altars cleft with hatchet blows, ordered his servants to bring tables into the wrecked chancel, sat down to dinner with his friends, and amid shouts of laughter fed the wafers from the ciborium to the parrot on his wrist. In William's own Stadholderate the Utrecht mob sacked four churches and two convents, driving monks and nuns into the streets to the mercy of the mob, while at Delft a party of furious viragoes broke into a monastery and beat up the monks, and at Amsterdam the mob carried a local monastery by assault, in face of the protesting burgomaster and members of the town council, some of whom were hurt in the struggle. The terrified clergy of Antwerp hid the little black Virgin in a side chapel, but a mass of apprentices found her out, tore down the iron screen, seized the unoffending black doll, rent off its finery and hacked it to pieces. Word went out through the slums and quaysides and all that night, to the flare of torches and the lurid light of bonfires, the cathedral and the great churches of Antwerp were put to sack.

Meanwhile, a libellous sheet blew about the gutters of Brussels and appeared plastered on walls and gateways. 'Awake, Brabant!' it ran. 'No bastard may hold office in Brabant. Is the bastard and the wife of a traitor to be your Regent? Has she not betrayed the land? Drive out the whore!'[1]

Margaret mistakenly saw in the general outburst and the personal attack on herself the combined machinations of the great nobles and the lesser men. Thinking this, she was lost. For she might still have trusted William, or Egmont, or Horn, but now she dared not; frantically she wrote to Philip for help, for the great men were all of them 'against God and the King'. Her letter crossed with one from him, bidding her secretly to raise thirteen thousand men in Germany. Before he had news of the Calvinist frenzy he had already decided to enforce his policy at the sword's point.

But whatever Margaret knew — or thought she knew — whatever orders Philip gave, the immediate danger remained. Margaret, convinced that William and his partisans intended to seize her and force her to do their will, had her fastest horse saddled to flee by night to Mons, a city alleged to be quiet. Caught and stopped by some of her councillors, she came trembling back to her palace in Brussels, and thence, at the height of the rioting on August 24th, 1566, issued the *Accord*. By this proclamation she lifted the ban on Protestant preaching indefinitely, promised a full reconsideration of religious policy, and implored the rioters in return for her concessions at least to give back the churches; they would be allowed to build new ones of their own.

Later, when she wished to break her word, Margaret said that she had issued the *Accord* under pressure; but it was not pressure from William and his friends, rather from her own fears. She had a plain, open countenance, but the workings of the brain behind it were erratic and twisted. The *Accord* was issued in pure perfidy. She never intended it to be anything but a quick way out of an impasse.

It had taken close on seven years to bring the tension between Philip and the people of the Netherlands to a crisis. Events had moved with a terrible slowness. Now they hurried to disaster.

Taking Louis with him, William hastened back to Antwerp. His first act was to punish the rioters, selecting from among the many culprits three only of whom to make examples. All three were foreigners; thus did he do rough

<hr/>

[1] Philip II, I, 450-1.

justice and prove himself in earnest, without provoking the rage of the citizens. By the first week in September, he had managed to clear the Calvinists out of the churches, though only by giving them meeting places in the city and promising them that they might at once start building conventicles. Delighted, they bombarded him with invitations to lay foundation stones, an honour which he invariably declined. Margaret was already plaguing him with querulous letters, asserting that she had not intended the *Accord* to be so generously interpreted; to which William could only answer that, if she knew a better way to get the rioters out of the churches than by giving them some of their own, she was wiser than he. But Antwerp was not his only anxiety, for there had been serious disorder in his own Stadholderate. He planned, therefore, to spend the autumn touring the provinces of Holland, Zealand, and Utrecht while making Antwerp his official headquarters for the winter, thus to restore and maintain confidence by his own presence.

Meanwhile the tide had sharply turned. So far the extremists had had it all their own way, but now Margaret was building up a party among the loyalists, the supporters of the Counter-Reformation, and the personal enemies of William, Egmont, and Horn. She was encouraged by a split in the ranks of the Confederates; there had always been two parties among the King's opponents, the *Gueux d'Etat* and the *Gueux de religion*, the political objectors and the religious fanatics. The August frenzy brought the latent disagreement to a crisis. The *Gueux d'Etat*, seeing a chasm of disorder opening before them, turned in fear and disgust towards the Regent and respectability. The split among the Confederates widened irreparably when Mansfeld's daughter eloped during a visit to Brederode and his wife. Mansfeld and his son took the matter as a personal insult, quarrelled with Brederode, and swung over furiously to the Regent's party. Moreover, the violent excesses of that fatal week in August had sickened the majority of moderate-minded citizens. The reaction throughout the country was sensational and almost immediate.

Early in October William, with Louis and Hoogstraten, had invited Egmont and Horn to a meeting at Termonde. The situation of the reputable opposition was now — as William saw it — desperate indeed. It was generally known that Philip was sending an army to subdue the Netherlands, nor did William doubt that all of those who now gathered at Termonde were marked for doom. An intercepted letter, said to have come from Philip's ambassador in France, declared as much; this document, turned over by the nobles met at Termonde, was in fact a forgery. But forgery or not, its contents were no more than a reasonable forecast of King Philip's policy which time was to confirm.

What precisely William planned at this Termonde meeting is hard to detect; not apparently the armed revolt of which Louis and Hoogstraten were the champions. It is significant that Brederode, the most active of the militant group, was not there: William did not wish him to be there. Probably he still clung to the belief that the Emperor would help. All this time he had had his hand on the pulse of Germany, keeping the Lutheran princes well-informed of the darkening situation in the Netherlands and asking — not indeed for armed help — but for moral pressure. If he and Egmont (and naturally Horn who followed Egmont) stood firm together, they could appeal for the protection of the Emperor Maximilian and the support of Saxony, Hesse, Nassau, not to mention the Elector Palatine. William's wife was niece to the Elector of Saxony, Egmont's was sister to the Elector Palatine. Would Philip dare to override the privileges of the Netherlands if the great men of the Netherlands could command such allies?

Everything therefore turned on winning Egmont's support. The efforts which Margaret and Philip alike had made to divide him from William showed how much they feared this coalition. But Egmont would be hard to persuade. Vain and trusting, he believed in his heart that Philip would not turn against him. His faith and his judgment were those of a great and generous feudal *seigneur*; he had done his duty always to his people and his overlord and he still trusted that his overlord would treat him according to the mutual bonds of fealty. William, alive to the changed atmosphere of a world no longer feudal, spoke a language Egmont did not fully understand.

The meeting place at Termonde seems to have been a small hunting-box with only two rooms, a kitchen and a dining-hall. While the servants set the dining table with choice foods brought from Antwerp, the guests stood about talking. William had to see Egmont alone: perhaps he wanted to be alone himself. Slipping out into the kitchen, which was empty since all the provisions had been brought ready prepared, he waited for Egmont's coming. There were no chairs. He sat down on the meat-block, and here Egmont found him — guided by the unexpected shout through the open door which greeted his inquiry for the Prince of Orange, 'Here I am in the kitchen, sitting on the meat-block!' — and here in these unconventional surroundings the two men had their vital and tragic interview. For Egmont would not change his mind. He could see nothing but the narrow precepts of his feudal duty and would not believe that such precepts no longer governed the world of 1566. It was not for him a question of saving the Netherlands from the encroachment of a foreign tyranny, for in his heart he thought of Philip as Duke of Burgundy, and truly believed that he would act — where his Netherlands were concerned — only as Duke of Burgundy. 'Alas, Count

Egmont', said William as they came back to the hall, 'you and your like are building the bridge for the Spaniard to cross over into our country.'[1] There were ears enough in the crowded room to hear him, and the phrase he used was current in Antwerp soon after.

When they rejoined the others, dinner was nearly ready and there was time only for a little general political talk, for which Egmont showed no willingness. As soon as the meal was served serious discussion ended: so at least Egmont afterwards declared, and so it may have been. For the business of the meeting was already concluded and what else was there to do but eat, drink and be merry?

VI

Thus with nothing concluded, William and Egmont went each his own way, to their respective Stadholderates, William to impose the *Accord*, Egmont to make a last vain attempt to prove his loyalty by hanging a few heretics. It was Louis who, throwing discretion to the winds, galloped off to join Brederode and Culembourg, and began to organize revolt. Margaret soon heard disquieting rumours and wrote insistently to William, to know what his brother and Brederode were doing. What could he reply? He knew something, certainly, for Louis was pestering him to join in the projected rising. But was he bound to betray what he knew to a government which was itself betraying its subjects? This time he thought not. He would do what he could to prevent the futile rising, but in the meantime he would assume a mask of ignorance.

For months now William had been trying in vain to control Louis. Theirs was an odd relationship, for, while William's age and experience made him in reality the master spirit, Louis' affection had nothing of obedience in it. Impetuous and reckless, with a touch of the possessive in his passionate attachment to his brother, he was convinced that he could force William's hand and was compromising him deliberately, as he thought, for his own good.

Meanwhile William toured his three provinces, going from city to city, from Utrecht to Amsterdam, to Haarlem, to the Hague, calming the fears of the officials, smoothing out the difficulties of the *Accord* between the new religion and the old. In these few weeks he succeeded in achieving the settlement of his own desire, with respect for the rights of all who would respect the rights of others. When the local Estates of Holland met at the end of the

[1] Haecht, I, 112.

year they celebrated the return of law and order and showed their gratitude to their Stadholder by voting him a gift of 55,000 florins. He refused, fearing that Margaret would think it a bribe. Nor in fact did he share the grateful confidence of the deputies; sincerely as he had worked at the settlement, he knew that it was doomed, for Margaret was openly declaring that she had granted the *Accord* under pressure, she had reassembled the forces of militant Catholicism about her and was recruiting troops at Philip's command in Germany. Philip had rejected the suggestion that he should call the Estates General, and the Spanish army was on its way.

Grey and worn with the anxiety of the last months, William ceaselessly exhorted the Regent to moderation. 'Make as little use as you can of force', he implored her, 'for terrible may be the consequences if the people are driven to desperation.'[1] He himself was being driven to desperation by Margaret's mistrust and Louis' persuasions and his own fears. In and out from his house at Breda hurried the different messengers, while he hesitated between justified revolt or hopeless loyalty. In February, Egmont came with Horn and Hoogstraten and Brederode. In this cold midnight hour, William tried once more, and tried in vain, to enlist Egmont's help. Failing this he exhorted Brederode to abandon his ill-conceived plan. As well might he have argued with an enraged bull: Brederode would have his revolt.

Margaret's spies knew that there had been guests at Breda. They told her too, more imaginatively, that William was fortifying his young son's castle at Buren. Margaret called the leading members of the Order of the Golden Fleece and suggested that they should call their brother to account; but when the summons to appear before the chapter of the Knights reached him, he was back in Antwerp, and, legitimately enough, refused to leave. The feverish excitement of the previous summer reigned again in the great port, and if tumult was to be prevented, he must stay. His two lieutenants, Wesembeeck and Hoogstraten, at whose entreaty he had cut short his tour of the north, were determined that he should not leave them.

Margaret now took drastic measures to forestall revolt; in February 1567 she required all her leading ministers to take a new oath of loyalty to the King. The rumour that Alva was on the march for the Netherlands was already widespread, and she strove thus to blackmail the nobles into a guarantee of acquiescence. Aerschot and Berlaymont took the oath immediately, Egmont with but little delay. William and Hoogstraten refused.

Margaret had no need of this refusal to convince her of William's 'treachery'. Her ubiquitous spies informed her that the Princess of Orange was packing up and preparing to go to Germany at her husband's instruc-

---

[1] Gachard, II, 319-20.

ons, and long before Margaret received any formal intimation of the child's
ithdrawal from her household, it was rumoured everywhere that little
1ademoiselle d'Orange was to go on a visit to her grandmother at Dillen-
urg. And then, in March 1567, Brederode raised the standard of revolt in
Iolland, and John Marnix in the south. The rebellion was doomed from the
utset, for it lacked leaders who could have stirred the populace to rise. And
ven had it had those leaders, had William himself rebelled, what chance had
ich a rising against Alva and his well-disciplined army, even now approach-
ig from Spain, overland, down the valley of the Rhine?

Not in this way could salvation come to the Netherlands. Salvation
ould come, and William had already pledged himself to bring it, but it
ould come only when, with foreign money and foreign alliances, the
rince of Orange was strong enough to challenge the King of Spain. So
1uch he had decided by March 1567. At Christmas, not only Louis but his
ext brother John, the reigning Count of Nassau, had joined him briefly,
nd the three had talked privately and long. Since then William had sold
late and jewels as quietly as he could and smuggled the proceeds away to
is family at Dillenburg. Anna was to leave for Germany with her own
aughter, and her stepdaughter was to be withdrawn from the Regent's
ousehold. Everything depended on William's getting out of the country
nd setting up out of Alva's reach a centre of resistance to Philip's military
yranny.

Meanwhile Brederode had taken possession of Amsterdam, where his
ebels were exhausting their energies in riotous living. It was fairly evident
o anyone of ordinary perspicacity that a revolt led by Brederode was likely
o come to an ignominious end in the taverns. Moreover William's careful
nd thorough pacification of the north had worked too well; the people did
1ot want any further change. The southern band of rebels, under John
Marnix, were more determined, if not more formidable. They made for
Antwerp, while inside the city William waited. In this hopeless hour he
ought only to prevent unnecessary and inevitable slaughter, to prevent
valuable lives being lost in a struggle which could end only in defeat.
Premature revolt could only bleed the youngest blood away from the
Netherlands, blood which it would need in the years to come.

Within three miles of Antwerp gates, on March 15th, 1567, the ill-armed
rebels were rounded up by government levies. Inside Antwerp they had
news of the battle, and the small band of government troops within the city
could do nothing against the menacing people. The wife of John Marnix,
her hair loose, ran screaming through the streets that her husband was being
murdered. William had ordered the gates to be closed, but two thousand

men, armed with swords and pistols, forced them open and poured out towards the scene of the battle; too late to help Marnix, they would have gone only to certain destruction. Galloping out to head them off, William, with Hoogstraten at his side, threw himself in front of them, imploring them to go back. 'Stand by me', he entreated, 'I will live and die with you; you run but on your deaths; their cavalry will kill you.' The foremost men threatened him with fists and levelled pistols, calling him 'traitor'. 'If you find me so', challenged William, 'then kill me!' They could certainly have done it, but the power of his popularity was still too great with them. 'In great danger divers times to be slain', as an English observer recorded, he forced them slowly back within the gates. His troubles were not over, for, deprived of their battle, the angry mob turned on the garrison, and breaking through the helpless troops, stormed the arsenal. There was only one thing to be done, since resistance would have been in vain. Facing the mob from the steps of the town hall William cried: 'You want arms? Come and take them.' He let them into the arsenal. He let them set up the cannon across the streets to defend the city. He saw their spokesmen and arranged for their volunteers to share the city watch with the government garrison, taking alternate positions. During the long sleepless night he toured the walls and batteries, then in the small hours roughed out with the leading burghers a temporary settlement. Morning found him, grey and haggard, facing the mob from the steps of the town hall, Hoogstraten at his side, white and sweating, but steadfast. William wore, over the flashing breastplate, the crimson scarf of an officer in the government forces, the forces into which he had temporarily incorporated the Antwerp rioters. Here, from the steps of the town hall, he read out the proclamation, by which the people became, jointly with the troops, the defenders of their city; further he guaranteed freedom of religion, and exhorted all save those selected for the task to lay down their arms. As he rolled up the paper and faced the people, he shouted, 'Vive le roi!' After a second's hesitation, they did the same, and, if here and there a 'Vivent les Gueux!' might be heard, it did not matter much.

Pressing from street to street through the people, white with fatigue and anxiety, the proclamation in his hand, going on foot to show his confidence, William read the paper from four other centres of the city, and each time gave the loyal salutation, 'Vive le roi!' In the end the mob dispersed, grumbling, perplexed, but harmless, leaving the cannon deserted on their improvised emplacements. 'The Prince very nobly hath travailed, both night and day, to keep this town from manslaughter and from despoil ... for that I saw never men so desperate willing to fight.'[1] Thus wrote an

[1] Burgon, II, 208; Haecht, I, 191-3.

English merchant. Gladly indeed would William have kept all the Netherlands from manslaughter and from despoil. But it might not be. The
bloodshed was yet to come, inexorably, and he himself at the fount of it.

The pacification of Antwerp, this last prevention of useless murder, was
his final service to his one-time master. Now he sent in his resignation to
the Regent and sold or packed the last of his movable goods. He had
raised a great sum of money in Antwerp and some of those who advanced
him the money knew what it would be for.

On April 10th, 1567, he wrote to Philip himself, tendering his resignation,
and on April 11th withdrew from Antwerp. The chief men of the city came
to take their leave of him; it was a sad parting with tears on both sides. 'We
may well say "Out of the depths have I cried to thee, O Lord"', he said to
them. Seventy or more of the burghers rode with him out of the gates,
while the people crowded about him, bewildered, wanting to know the
truth of all the rumours. Was he, too, abandoning them? He dared not
tell. 'Where are you going?' they called, catching at the horse's bridle,
clustering about his stirrups. The light manner, the social smile, struck a
ghostly note as he laughed and said, 'To Dillenburg for the hawking season'.
But the questioners were not to be fooled. 'A Prince of Orange', they
remonstrated, 'a man who has been so powerful, to content himself with
hunting after birds . . .' He knew what they meant; but he answered never
a word, only urged his way gently, irrevocably, through them, and went
out of their gates.[1]

He turned his train towards Breda, but on the way, at Willebroek,
Egmont intercepted him. Sent by the Regent, he had come to implore
William to stay. To stay for what? To be trapped by Alva? To stay so
that no man fit to bring help should leave the Netherlands alive? The two
friends did not meet alone; two of Margaret's people had accompanied
Egmont and saw to it that he had no word with William in private. Sinister
and tragic, this last meeting between them: Egmont deluded, anxious, yet
trusting; William foreseeing the future, undeceived, and silent.

Alone, therefore, and with a dark future before him, William rode in to
his house at Breda and said his last good-bye to the sheeted rooms and empty-
ing corridors. He did not forget the people, his tenants, but told them as
plainly as he could what lay before them and advised them to submit in all
outward ways to the Duke of Alva when he came: nothing was to be gained
by unnecessary martyrdom. When the time came to act, they would know.
He would not forget them.

His daughter, Marie, joined him from the Regent's household, and so,

[1] Haecht, I, 211; Granvelle, II, 373-4.

with his fretful Anna, and the two little girls, he left the fair seat of Breda o
April 22nd, 1567, riding towards the German frontier, as sad a procession a
ever set forth in the spring to pay a visit of courtesy to relations. For tha
was the reason alleged for his departure and he dared say no more lest h
should be stopped. Indeed, to allay suspicion he had deliberately left
hostage in the Netherlands. His only son, the Count of Buren, remained a
his studies at Louvain. On his way abroad he passed through the quie
university city, where only a year before he had strolled in the park with hi
son and watched with fascination a fountain on the topmost jet of which
light glass ball was held in constant, jumping motion. Here, for the last time
he saw Philip William, now fourteen years old, attractive, with his father'
slender build and irregular features. William had been twenty with a grea
career before him when this son was born and christened after Philip of Spain
his godfather; now at thirty-four all hopes and plans had perished, and th
future was obscured. He could not stay long, for time was pressing and
Alva drawing near, and, when he had said good-bye to this child of hi
carefree youth, a part of his life had been shut off for ever.

CHAPTER IV

THE LONG NIGHT

1567–1572

I

THE cherry and plum blossom was out along the valley of the Dill, the Rhineland soft and bright in Maytime green, when William, with his wife, his two young daughters, and a train of a hundred and fifty servants rode up to the castle at Dillenburg, twenty-three years after he had left to become Prince of Orange. Nothing very much had changed. Juliana still ruled the household, the school was fully attended and the courtyards rang to the high voices of children. William's second brother John, a little, stout, truculent man, was now the reigning Count. His children welcomed their two little cousins, 'Mesdemoiselles d'Orange', who were soon involved in the simple routine of the common schoolroom, a startling change for thirteen-year-old Marie from the elegant formality of a maid of honour's life in Brussels. Juliana, her daughter-in-law, and her unmarried daughters welcomed no less warmly the Princess of Orange, who did not respond; Anna was extremely angry at losing her fine houses in the Netherlands, at having to be the guest of these simple, provincial people, above all at the prospect of a life without amusement, position, or wealth. It was worse even than going back to Saxony. When, in July 1567, her husband received a letter from the King of Denmark, offering him hospitality, Anna was all for accepting. Denmark would at least be a change. But William refused, for Dillenburg had advantages which Copenhagen lacked; three days' journey from the Netherlands, it was an excellent recruiting centre for Germany, and moreover an independent State, where not only he himself but all his friends were sure of a welcome. With his brother's generous help he could make of Dillenburg the unobtrusive and unassailable centre for the rescue of the Netherlands. He had left them only to come back, and to come back as their liberator. So much was clear to him, but all else was dark. Two chief problems must first be solved: how he should go back, and when.

As for the manner in which liberation was to be achieved, his theories had undergone a sharp and painful change. All the previous winter – and from a period even more remote, from the time of his Saxon marriage – he had believed that the Lutheran princes of Germany and perhaps the

Emperor Maximilian himself would take up the cause of the Netherlands. His old friend the Emperor had failed him because he dared not and could not oppose King Philip, his cousin and the head of his house; so completely had he bowed to Philip's plans of uniting Catholic against heretic powers that he had meekly sacrificed his daughter to bind the unholy alliance between Catherine de Medici and the Habsburg dynasty, and she was even now on her way to Mezieres to become the wife of the young French king. William had been unduly optimistic in his hopes of Maximilian, but his disappointment in the Lutheran princes was bitter indeed. His appeals for their united intervention, his suggestions that they might put pressure on the Emperor, or make representations to the King of Spain, had met with apathetic refusal or frivolous excuses. Some of them had promised to act if he would first openly declare himself a Lutheran — a gesture which, in the midst of the religious troubles of the Netherlands, would have lost him his standing alike with the Regent and the Calvinists. Moreover, the German princes showed by this request a lamentable failure to understand the situation, for all these months William had doggedly striven to *prevent* the trouble in the Netherlands from becoming a religious struggle. Fundamentally, it was constitutional, and he had wanted to keep it so.

Looking upon the situation objectively from Dillenburg in the summer of 1567, he saw that he could no longer fight the inevitable; he must modify his policy in two ways, by allowing the religious element of the struggle to dominate the political, and by diverting his main efforts from the unhelpful German Lutherans to the active French Calvinists. There in France the Huguenot party, under the generous leadership of Coligny, was rapidly gaining political ascendancy. Moreover, the Huguenots were at their strongest along France's Flemish frontier, so that to have their alliance would be to place an enemy at once at Alva's elbow.

So much for William's problem of *what* to do: he had to gain the Huguenot alliance, to raise himself an army, and to invade. Next, and no less important, was the problem *when*. He must judge the right moment and be ready when it came: no easy matter, for volunteer armies are hard to raise and hard to hold together unless limitless resources are at hand, while favourable moments are quickly gone, and do not come again.

II

The first favourable moment went before William had any troops in the field. Alva had entered Brussels at the head of an army on August 22nd,

1567. Several times he saw the Regent Margaret in private, theoretically to discuss with her the best methods of billeting the army and quelling all future troubles, but in reality to tell her what he himself intended to do. On September 8th Margaret resigned the Regency. Such things as the Duke of Alva had planned should never be done under her government.

On the following day, Alva had Egmont and Horn arrested as they left the Council chamber. When the Spanish captain of the guard asked him for his sword Egmont stood dumb, then, dazed, drew out and handed to the Spaniard the blade which had served King Philip so loyally for so long. While these two were being seized in the Council chamber, Alva's officers, with a terrible efficiency, decoyed their respective secretaries from their houses and seized them too. Thus no one had time or opportunity to destroy the personal papers of the accused: anything in them which could be twisted into a hint of treason was exposed to the resourceful eyes of Alva's staff. Not that paper evidence alone was forthcoming. Egmont's terrified secretary, at his first interrogation, came all the way to meet the questioners, corroborating every insinuation against his master in obsequious terror. In vain, poor coward, the needless betrayal, for Alva, coldly scanning the report of his answers, reflected cynically, 'He talks already. When he has been put to the question he will tell us marvels'.[1] Mercy was not to be bought of Alva by turning King's evidence.

Ten days later in Madrid Horn's brother Montigny was seized. How rightly had he feared that journey to King Philip's Court! His colleague, Bergen, escaped arrest merely because he had had the good fortune to die a natural death a few weeks earlier, so it was only Montigny who had to be quietly put away, by strangling in his prison at Simancas. In vain the remnant of the Order of the Golden Fleece protested against this attack on three of its members; the Order of the Golden Fleece and all it had stood for meant nothing to Alva.

On the day of Egmont and Horn's arrest, Alva had set up an inner Council, called by him the Council of the Troubles, but given by the people of the Netherlands the name by which history knows it, the Council of Blood. Among its members were three Spaniards, Juan Vargas, Jeronimo de Roda, Luis del Rio. Indignation swept the Netherlands. Often before there had been riots and revolts, often before there had been special Councils to judge the ringleaders, but by all their charters the Netherlanders had the right to be tried only by men of their own nation. And now three foreigners were to sit in judgment on them, under the chairmanship of the fanatic Alva. Later they were to learn that they had not even the advantage of three

[1] Phillip II, I, 589.

opinions to go by, for Alva listened to none but Vargas. Juan Vargas was an able lawyer, unscrupulous and perceptive; a devil in cross-examination and obscenely cruel, he frankly enjoyed putting the accused to the torture, frequently lent a hand to the executioner and suggested several improvements in the instruments used. Even in an age when men were not squeamish, such behaviour revolted his colleagues, and Luis del Rio left the place on at least one occasion, after vain remonstrances, weeping with horror and rage.

That September of 1567, when the Netherlands were hot with anger and Alva had not yet battered and numbed the people, would have been the time for invasion. Could the Prince of Orange but have brought in an army of five or six thousand men, the whole country would have risen for him; so at least thought an English political agent in Antwerp. But how was he to bring in an army of five or six thousand? Armies cannot be raised from nothing and with nothing in four months. He had first to realize all he could on the plate and jewellery salvaged from the Netherlands; next he had to select, among that floating population of mercenary captains who drifted about Europe with swords for sale, a staff of officers to whom he could issue commissions for recruiting; finally he had to persuade as many rulers as possible to allow their subjects to volunteer. Riding hither and thither on this vital business, William himself was all but seized on the borders of Cleves by a freebooting German soldier in Spanish pay. The Spaniards regretted his escape, but were confident he would soon be taken. 'The King's arm is long,' they said.[1]

The King's arm was long, and the Prince's very short. He did not invade in that September of 1567 when the country might have risen, because he could not invade. The occasion passed and Alva, slowly increasing the terror, strangled the will to revolt. He worked with method, seizing in one rapid sweep after another every important man of whose subservience he was doubtful: the magistrates or pensionaries of the chief cities, the clerks of local courts of justice, the burgomasters and councillors, finally the wealthy merchants and landowners. Once these were taken, the smaller people lay exposed and defenceless, to be gathered in handfuls at will, wherever and whenever such a demonstration was needed. Nor did Alva disperse his effects; he had planned a mass execution and was not to be hurried. Gradually he let the evidence pile up, gradually questioned, tortured and sentenced his prisoners, the great and the small, while their families, clinging to unfounded hopes, stormed him with tears and petitions. Egmont's wife and daughters crept nightly barefoot from shrine to shrine, imploring divine

[1] Granvelle, III, 2.

intervention. Meanwhile Egmont lived, a prisoner in the citadel of Ghent, still strangely confident, after days of questioning, that the King could find no wrong in his conduct. Even on the verge of extinction, the high Burgundian nobility had their privileges; Alva himself would not have dared to put Egmont to the question.

Long before the examinations and trials were completed, Alva seized the goods of the victims, filling the coffers of his treasury with the plate and jewellery of the richest nation in Europe; the spoil of the defeated would pay for the army of occupation. Egmont's household plate alone filled sixteen great coffers. The huge estates of the Prince of Orange were sequestrated, and in that winter of 1567-68 the citizens and farmers of Breda, the labourers and foresters and rangers, the huntsmen and grooms and builders and smiths, all who had known the Prince of Orange as landlord or master, whose lives had revolved about those great estates, watched the Spanish soldiers take over the Prince's castles, watched Alva's officers with grim pleasure empty the arsenals and the armouries and ship to Ghent seven barge-loads of pikes and powder and arms and cannon which would serve now for the oppression, not the defence, of the Netherlands; saw the Spanish officials go through the books and inventories, the chests and the coffers and the cupboards. They remembered now at Breda what he had said when he left them: that they must yield and wait. At Brussels the desolate corridors echoed to the tramp of workmen's feet, as the hangings came down, and the plate was borne away; unsatisfied, however, the Spaniards seized and tortured the head porter who had tried to hide some of the pictures. They suspected, wrongly, that he had buried the best silver dinner-service, and kept him eighteen months a prisoner to find out the secrets of his master's house. He would not speak.

At Dillenburg, in the poky gothic rooms with their monstrous stoves and massive walls, to which William had sought to give the illusion of warmth with a set of tapestry brought from Breda, Anna had given birth to a son in mid-November. Like most of Anna's children, the baby was unhealthy, and there can have been little of the proud and hopeful father in William's heart when he was shown for the first time his son, Maurice. He could not know that this work of liberation to which he had pledged himself was to be an Eighty Years War, nor that this child, grown to be a man and a soldier, would turn the balance at last against the power of Spain. Born in exile of an unhappy marriage, to a woman ill in mind and body—so opened the life of the great Maurice of Nassau whose genius was to revolutionize the art of war.

The winter was bright and fine, and the child's baptism made an occasion for collecting some of those neighbouring princes for whose help William yet hoped. Anna's cousins, the Landgrave of Hesse and his brothers, came over from Cassel. They talked politics round the stoves at night and went hunting by day. They were glib with promises. As they rode away after their long week-end, they turned and waved encouragingly to their exiled host. 'Soon you will give us as good hunting at Breda', they shouted, 'as you have at Dillenburg.'[1] But their prognostications and their promises evaporated with the clatter of their horses' hoofs on the castle causeway.

With the New Year William appealed once more to the Emperor, and once more was put off with vague remonstrances of caution. Alva had celebrated his New Year in Brussels, with his first public execution. On January 4th, 1568, eighty-four leading citizens of the Netherlands died on the public scaffold. While the people were still breathless with dismay, the heralds, to the sound of trumpets, summoned William of Nassau, Prince of Orange, to appear before the Council to answer a charge of high treason. Early in February, an armed guard called for the young Count of Buren, William's eldest son, at his lodging in the town of Louvain. Taking a tottering stand on the charters of the University, his tutors appealed to the Council of Blood. 'We care nothing for your privileges', bawled Vargas in his layman's Latin, 'Non curamus vestros privilegios'.[2] It was useless to argue with a man who knew neither that Louvain had charters nor how to express himself in seemly grammatical form. The Count of Buren was taken on board ship with his faithful tutor, and set sail for Spain, while to the political troubles of the exile at Dillenburg was added the anxiety of the father. He was never to see his son again. On March 3rd, 1568, the arrest of fifteen hundred prominent citizens of the Netherlands followed. The terror had begun in earnest. 'Now the very Papists do perceive that the Duke of Alva doth go about to make them all slaves', wrote an Englishman at Antwerp.[3]

III

At Dillenburg William was setting in motion the mechanism of liberation. Among the many exiles, young and old, nobles and burghers, Catholic, Lutheran or Calvinist, few questioned his leadership and none set up rival parties to weaken and divide the common cause. If this bane of the exiled was spared to the Netherlanders, they had the Prince of Orange to thank for it, for the team he had to guide was spirited and quarrelsome; there was the vital, valuable, but uncontrollable Louis, the obstreperous Culembourg, the stubborn Hoogstraten. Later other wild elements were to be gathered under

---

[1] Granvelle, III, 615.   [2] *Apology*.   [3] Kervyn de Lettenhove, v, 90.

his guidance, as the proudly independent lesser nobles of the Netherlands revolted on the fringe of Alva's Government, with individual resistance and guerrilla fighting, and piracy on the high seas. But in double harness with these wild spirits, William had to guide respectable burghers and dour intellectuals, for Alva's heel galled alike the tyrannous baron and the devout artisan.

It was to be no easy task, and at the beginning he had to break down the mistrust of those who had seen the Calvinist rising fail and had believed that with the Prince of Orange's help it would have succeeded. The young Philip Marnix, Count of Sainte Aldegonde, whose brother John had perished outside Antwerp while William held back the frenzied people from joining in the battle, kept coldly aloof from these new preparations for attack. A man of sensitive feeling and profound convictions, he could not yet forget the apparent betrayal. He had withdrawn to Heidelberg, to the Court of the Calvinist Elector Palatine, brother-in-law to Egmont; this devout and strong-minded prince (the best then reigning in all Germany) had thrown open his Court to exiles from the Netherlands. Here, for refuge, came Brederode's handsome widow, for her husband had died during that winter of 1567-68, making an end so pious and edifying as to astonish all beholders. He was no loss; neither his opinions nor his talents would have given much help to the cause.

In the early spring of 1568 William's old friend the Pensionary of Antwerp, Jacob Wesembeeck, at length reached Dillenburg. He was the man whom William wanted perhaps most of all. Public opinion both in the Netherlands and Europe had to be properly prepared for the coming invasion; with his practical understanding of politics William fully appreciated the importance of propaganda, but his own talent did not lie that way. The most persuasive diplomatist in speech, he relied far more on manner and on the quick interchange of the spoken word than on rhetoric or well-knit argument. The line of his thought was lucid but he had the conversationalist's, not the writer's, art. What he needed now was a competent and eloquent lawyer to marshal and arrange the debating points and to put on record the rights which he defended and the wrongs he, and the Netherlands, had suffered. This Wesembeeck could do. Together they composed the first of the great manifestoes with which William was to fight Alva.

The *Justification* was printed at Dillenburg '*au moys d'Apuril Anno 1568*'. Before the end of that month so many copies had been shipped down the Rhine and into the Netherlands, and there distributed by William's agents, that Alva was fulminating from Brussels fearful threats against all who sold or read or possessed it.

The *Justification* bears as its heading a quotation from the Psalms: *The wicked watcheth the righteous and seeketh to slay him. The Lord will not leave him in his hand, nor condemn him when he is judged.* By implication it revealed William's secession from the Catholic Church, since he spoke of the victims of the Inquisition as having suffered for the *true* commandments of God. But it was in the main a political document, the religious quarrel being still treated merely as Philip's excuse for an attack on the rights of his people. Chiefly William was concerned to show that he had committed no act of disloyalty to the King, and that indeed he was still the King's loyal servant, regarding all the wrongs which had been done in the Netherlands as the work of Philip's ministers and evil councillors. 'May His Majesty being instructed by knowledge and light from heaven, turn aside and prevent further disasters; may he learn rightly to understand the actions of his good and faithful servants and subjects, at this present wrongly slandered, persecuted and oppressed. So that the world may know that all which has come to pass proceeds not from the King's own nature, but from the rumours, lies and calumnies of those who, until this time, have kept and disguised the truth from him.' To the modern ear this reads strangely, but William understood the public for whom he wrote. So long a pillar of good administration, he knew that revolt was a crime against public order needing justification indeed, and that, to the educated men of the sixteenth century, disloyalty to the legal sovereign was, however frequent, still the inexcusable crime. It was essential to have not only extremists and rebels for his cause, but the body of moderate opinion within the Netherlands and without. Above all he wanted recognition from other sovereigns – England, Denmark, the Emperor – which as a rebel he could not have.

While the *Justification* was in the press, William had gone to Cologne, the headquarters of his growing army. In spite of Alva's police, contributions were flowing in secretly from the Netherlands, to swell the hundred thousand florins which William himself had put down. The French Huguenots had promised collaboration and, when in the spring of 1568 the second religious war in France ended, they had troops to spare for the Netherlands. Under the direction of the resourceful Louis a triple scheme of invasion took shape: he himself taking with him Culembourg, and another volunteer from the Nassau family, his next brother Adolf, would cross the Ems into Friesland while Hoogstraten entered the southern provinces between the Rhine and the Meuse, and the Huguenots invaded Artois. Meanwhile William was to assemble the main army at Duisburg in Cleves, where he would be near enough to direct operations and to intervene decisively when he had seen the effect of the three preliminary moves.

Just before the armies marched, Hoogstraten fell ill and his place was taken by Jean de Villers, the treasurer and quartermaster-general. Villers crossed the Meuse at Maestricht on April 20th, 1568; Louis, with the largest body of troops, entered Friesland from Emden four days later. He had a great welcome; the gentry and peasants gladly joined his standards, while only the town of Groningen, afraid of his rough troops and even more afraid of Alva, refused to let him in. 'We have come', Louis informed them by a herald, 'with the help of the mighty and eternal God, for the welfare and protection of the entire Netherlands, to drive out the intruding, foreign and shameful tyranny of these cruel ravishers and persecutors of Christian blood, to bring back your old privileges and to maintain them; to give comfort, help, safety and support to the scattered and fearful Christians and patriots.'[1]

But almost before Louis had entered the Netherlands, both his allies were lost. The Huguenots were headed off and cut to pieces at St. Valéry by French royal troops before they could invade the Netherlands, and the little band under Villers was surrounded and taken forty-eight hours after it crossed the Meuse. Jean de Villers was no hero; he disclosed at his first examination, not merely the entire plan of campaign, but the sources of the war-treasury. From him Alva learnt of the network of William's friends still in the Netherlands and the secret contributions of the cities; half the expenses of the invasion were being met in money raised under the very noses of the Spaniards.

Remaining in Brussels to keep watch on the south, Alva despatched Aremberg and Megen, who, with Aerschot, had accepted his domination, to drive Louis out of Friesland. They had orders to give no quarter and hang all prisoners, for Alva would not accord the decencies of war to rebels and traitors. It was a dangerous and distasteful task. In Friesland, the people were hostile, ready to mislead and harass the government troops at every turn. Moreover, Louis was being re-victualled from the sea by a fleet of pirate ships which, from a base at Delfzijl, were holding up Spanish transports in the Narrow Seas. Led by other rebels against the Spanish government, they called themselves 'les Gueux de Mer', the Sea Beggars.

Time, nevertheless, was not on Louis' side. His troops were few and ill-equipped, money was running out, and mutiny seemed imminent, when he learnt, at his headquarters in the small town of Dam, that Aremberg and Megen had split their forces for a pincer movement on his position. Louis withdrew hastily and the afternoon of Sunday, May 23rd, 1568 found him at the convent of Heiligerlee, with advance guards strategically placed in

[1] Alva, 22.

the scattered copses, through which, he calculated, Aremberg's forces would approach. His calculation proved right. Aremberg was surprised as he came up through the woods and Louis, profiting by his disorder, made one of his famous cavalry charges, showing once again the reckless skill and perfect timing which had won him his reputation at the battle of St. Quentin ten years before. It was bloody but successful; his brother Adolf fell dead at his side, but Aremberg's line broke and abandoned their guns. Aremberg himself, doggedly striving to redeem his mistake, was killed. His men fled; his nine cannon and nine tons of powder, his baggage and equipment fell into Louis' hands, together with a wagonload of silver plate, the sort of personal luggage with which sixteenth-century noblemen so often and so inexplicably burdened themselves on campaign. Louis divided it among his men in lieu of wages.

In Brussels Alva took action to counteract the effect of so immediate and startling a victory. The scaffolds went up in the Grande Place and sixty more victims were brought out to die. Some protested their innocence, but others, who were Calvinists, refused the consolations of the Church and died, as the Spaniards reported, with 'a diabolical obstinacy'.[1] On Whit-Sunday, June 5th, 1568, Alva achieved his ghastly climax, for all this time he had held Egmont and Horn against such an occasion. Let the Prince of Orange issue manifestos, let his brother win skirmishes; the Spanish government was not afraid. As it did to Egmont and Horn, so in time it would do to William of Nassau.

With a bare twelve hours' warning, with no time for leave-taking, Egmont and Horn were brought from Ghent to Brussels, and through the streets of Brussels, to the scaffold and the block. Amazed innocence not yet faded from his handsome face, Egmont resigned himself to death. Never was man more innocent caught up with more inexorable cruelty in the gigantic cogs of history. He died, as he had lived, grandly, bravely, with the high dignity of his race and breeding, but without understanding what it was all about. And Horn, who ten minutes later stood on the same scaffold, saw the rich black velvet pall they had laid over Egmont to hide the blood, and, gazing at the covered body with bewildered unbelief, said 'Liest thou there, my friend?' — and had no more to say, for things, too, had passed beyond his comprehension.

All this while William was at Strasbourg, trying by every means to increase his small resources. So much depended on this campaign that it would be folly to launch it without adequate preparation. Unhappily all those to whom he appealed for help thought it was folly in any case; the

[1] Analectes, V-VII, 74.

best of them made sympathetic excuses for doing nothing, but most of them dissuaded him altogether. His wife's narrow-hearted relations, the Landgrave of Hesse and the Elector of Saxony, refused assistance, the Emperor Maximilian querulously urged him to hold back, even the Protestant cities of Switzerland regretted that they could not raise a loan. This was the situation when William had news of his first victory, and his young brother's death, and received in his hands, surely with mixed feelings, the Order of the Golden Fleece taken from the body of Aremberg. They had been brothers in knighthood, Aremberg and he; but what now was left of the ancient brotherhood and chivalry, the grandeur and the power of the Golden Fleece? Egmont and Horn had been of that brotherhood, and they too were dead.

Their execution emphasized tragically the need to strike effectively and soon, to save the Netherlands. But the triple plan, save only the invasion of Friesland, had failed. William had to reconsider his strategy, for everything now depended on the force of his own single blow. Although he valued the victory of Heiligerlee for its effect on his prestige, he was disappointed in its influence on the merchants of Strasbourg, who still regarded his cause as a poor investment. Moreover, as things stood, he did not believe that Louis alone in Friesland could help much even should he be able to hold out there, until invasion could be launched in the south. His choice lay between invading before he was ready, to retrieve the defeat of Villers and the Huguenots, and take advantage of Louis' victory; or waiting until he had gathered a larger army from the recruits now steadily coming in, until his artillery and other equipment were in order, and he might be able to challenge Alva on an equal footing. In the circumstances, he wanted Louis to evacuate Friesland, where inevitably Alva would again attack, with a large enough force to rule out the hope of a second Heiligerlee. It would be better therefore if Louis withdrew, holding only Delfzijl, from which he could retire by sea if necessary.

But Louis, an incorrigible optimist, was sure that William could cut short his preparations and invade at once while he himself would fortify Groningen and withstand attack. Unhappily, the people of Groningen refused to take him in. He remained therefore in the open country, living as best he could. Aremberg's plate and the contents of his treasury, which had kept his men paid for a few weeks, began to give out in July; he was forced to requisition food and lodging, sometimes horses and clothes, until requisitioning began to look very like plunder. The people of Friesland cooled in their friendship, and by the time Alva set out from Brussels, they were sick of the disorder. Exposed in open country to an army larger and better equipped than his own, Louis fell back towards Jemmingen on the Ems, set up his sixteen cannon to check Alva's attack, and stationed his advance posts on a series of narrow bridges spanning the trickling, divided streams of the river. But Alva's cannon were more and better than Louis' and he could dispose of more troops. In unrelenting assault, for three blazing hours about the middle of a summer day, Alva's army drove Louis and his volunteers back over the three bridges, back relentlessly through the gravelly shallows and the sparse willows, the marigolds and the waterweed, to the wide main stream of the river, where, under the raking fire of the Spanish guns, they broke and swam for safety. Many went down in the wide river weighted under heavy equipment, caught in the swirling chaos of men and guns and horses. Louis himself stripped on the bank, and, leaving his clothes and armour where Alva's people found them for trophies, swam naked to the further shore. He had saved literally nothing except his life.

Whatever disaster had overwhelmed Louis, his brother went steadily on. He had named August 8th, 1568, and Duisburg in Cleves as the time and place of the general muster. Here he reviewed a mixed force of volunteers, refugees from the Netherlands and professional mercenaries from the German states, about twenty-five thousand in all. His chief difficulty was the finding of money, for his remaining funds would not serve to keep his men much above a month, a handicap of which Alva was not ignorant. Everything thus turned for William on forcing an issue before his resources gave out; for Alva on preventing the issue being forced. The advantage lay with Alva, all the more so because William had nothing of the gambler in his temperament.

He prepared the way for his invasion with the distribution of yet another pamphlet. Once again, under the significant heading 'For Law, King and People', he assured the Netherlands that he came to restore their lawful rights and drive out the Duke of Alva. Early in September, he crossed the frontier into the district of Liége. But the moment had already passed, and Liége was the wrong part of the country. The people, among whom he was not personally known, were cowed and distrustful, and, so far from rising for him, treated him as a mere invader, a misunderstanding which was confirmed by the behaviour of his German mercenaries, who, taking the view that the inhabitants were fair game, began to loot the villages. When William forced them to abandon their plunder, some of them refused; the split between the obedient and the mutinous grew into a riot between the French-speaking and the German-speaking troops, in which swords were drawn and shots fired. A chance bullet struck and rebounded from William's sword-hilt as he forced his way into the middle of the fight, and one of his principal officers was killed.

Order was temporarily restored, but the incident made it clear that the temper of the troops would be dangerous as soon as money ran out. And meanwhile Alva refused to move from a strong entrenchment at Maestricht, whence he watched his opportunity as William, advancing quickly by night as well as by day, for there were clear nights and a full moon in the early days of October, marched up the line of the Meuse. On October 6th, he boldly crossed the river and seized Tongres, thinking that this must draw Alva out. But Alva fell back. William advanced to Loos, hoping to overtake and challenge him — money was running perilously near the limit; Alva slipped round behind him and reoccupied Tongres. With his retreat partly blocked, William hesitated to face Alva, but continued westward past St. Trond, in the hope of joining with French troops promised him by the Huguenots. On the night of October 19th–20th, under cover of darkness he tried to cross the small stream of the Jaulche, but Alva fell on his forces as they struggled through the ford, and although William managed to save most of the artillery and baggage, he lost two thousand men. Among the dead was Hoogstraten, an irreparable loss.

Yet Alva had stopped neither his penetration into the country nor his junction with the French reinforcement, which met him three days later. It was Alva's turn to be anxious, for he had not reckoned on this persistent refusal to accept defeat. Incapable of carrying a spectacular and sudden victory, like Louis, William was nevertheless undismayed by disaster. In spite of the riots among his own men, in spite of the slaughter in the darkness on the night of October 19th, he had penetrated far into Brabant and made the junction with the French which both he and Alva thought would give him decisive superiority.

Both William and Alva proved wrong. The French reinforcement consisted of a handful of ill-armed volunteers, too few to make up for the losses in the passage of the Jaulche, and encumbered by a crowd of women and children. By this time, money and provisions had both given out — the country could supply none of the first and too little of the second — and winter was at hand. To turn and fight would mean almost certain defeat, for William dared not pit his discontented troops against Alva's well-controlled force. He had paid out now all that remained in the treasury, one month's wages for more than two months' service. The men fell back to the French border, mutinous and taking such movables as they could steal by the way. The peasants of the French border, that distracted strip of land fought over generation after generation, made no distinction between one kind of army and another. All were soldiers and all were their enemies. They harassed William's dispirited stragglers with cudgels and pitchforks, hid their stores, refused them shelter, while Alva's advance-guards delivered a hail of hit-and-run attacks along the whole line of the march. And so at last, 'tired and worn out and half dead with hunger' they reached France, William himself having tasted neither bread nor wine for nine days. But his troubles were not over; indeed barely begun, for the French government indignantly ordered him to take his troops away and he struggled back at length in the New Year of 1569 to an inhospitable Strasbourg. He was so ill by this time that he could no longer ride, and his haggard and desperate condition provoked pity in all who met him, except his mercenary captains who stormed his lodging at Strasbourg threatening to make an end of him if he would not meet their wages. Abandoning all hope of retaining his troops, he sold what remained of the artillery to pay the men, left his plate, tapestries and household stuffs in pawn to the merchants of Strasbourg and escaped one dark night down the Rhine, travelling in a covered barge, almost alone.

The disaster was total. He had thrown in all the resources he had, his entire fortune, the gifts and loans of a trusting and faithful people, and he had lost everything, money, men, credit, and reputation. 'We may regard the Prince of Orange as a dead man', wrote Alva with satisfaction.[1] But he was wrong, for William, out of the trough of disaster, had written to his brother John, assessing the damage, counting his starveling hopes. 'With God's help', he wrote, 'I shall go on'. Strength lay in that lonely 'I'.

IV

Painfully he was learning. A moderate man, a far-sighted man, he had sought a middle path, had believed that men would stand out for toleration, or rise for the common weal. Gradually he was beginning to understand that only the narrow, intolerant and fanatical can fight the narrow, intolerant and fanatical. He had made his half turn towards the Calvinists a year before, but he had still clung to the hope that the nation would rise for him as a nation. Now he abandoned that hope. He made his full turn towards the Calvinists because they alone could save the nation.

The early spring of 1569 found him at Mannheim for the celebration of a betrothal. The patriarchal Elector Palatine, father of a great brood of sons, had taken Brederode's widow to his heart. He, too, was a widower. The sober rejoicings over this autumnal marriage marked a new departure in William's policy. He used the occasion to canvass the opinions of this

[1] *Documentos Ineditos*, XXXVII, 572.

Calvinist prince and his younger son the knight-errant John Casimir, who was even then on the point of taking an army to help the Huguenots in France where, after eighteen months' interval, the third religious war was about to break. More important still, Philip Marnix of Sainte Aldegonde now came back to him.

Without independent resources, without a plan, William's last hope lay in the victory of the Huguenot party and their charity to his cause, and joining John Casimir's ill-controlled forces, he and Louis offered their services to their co-religionists in France. This was the terrible summer of 1569, of Jarnac and Moncontour, of that third religious war which Coligny's diplomacy, not his military success, saved from catastrophe. But the Huguenot party maintained itself in France, and William and Louis maintained themselves with the party. Their time was not wasted, for at the Peace of St. Germain the principality of Orange, seized by the King's partisans, was returned to William, who appointed Louis its governor, thus giving him an incontrovertible position in French politics, of which he could make diplomatic use. Moreover, Louis had so charmed the Huguenot Queen of Navarre that she bought the remaining Nassau jewels to finance the liberation of the Netherlands.

Since the previous year those piratical Sea Beggars, who had come so timely to the help of Louis in Friesland, had greatly increased in numbers, and it was Coligny who urged William to exploit them to the utmost, using the Huguenot port of La Rochelle for a base. The sovereign principality of Orange gave its prince the right to his own flag on the high seas, and he now issued commissions to the captains of the Sea Beggars, giving them authority to fly the lion of Nassau on a flag of three longitudinal stripes, orange, white and blue, at the masthead. So strangely did these legitimized pirates, carrying the name and orders of the sovereign of a minute inland principality, found the Dutch navy which in the next century was to be the finest in the world.

But William's heart was not in the French campaign. He had not Louis' power of giving himself up with enthusiasm to the military problem of the moment. That summer when the Huguenot leaders lodged for a few nights in the castle of Pierre de Brantôme, their garrulous host noted with interest the difference between the Nassau brothers — Louis was alert and lively as a cricket, but William looked tired and anxious, as if 'accablé de la fortune'. He changed, however, in conversation, and when Brantôme found occasion for private talk with him, walking up and down in an alley of his garden, he found him 'a person entirely to my taste, who could talk well on every subject'; he was impressed, too, by his height and carriage and his whole manner.[1] Defeat had not embittered the sweetness of his nature, nor disaster ruffled the surface of his courtesy.

His mind was not with Brantôme's spicy prattle, nor yet with the complex fortunes of the Huguenots. His friends in the Netherlands, few and scattered though they might be, still worked for him, and France was too far away from them. Leaving Louis, therefore, and bidding a friendly farewell to Coligny, he slipped away from the Huguenot camp, taking with him only five companions, and, disguised sometimes as a merchant, sometimes as a peasant, made his way back secretly to the Rhineland.

Secret he had to be, not only to deceive the Duke of Alva and protect those brave messengers who, under cover of trade or private business, came and went between him and the Netherlands, but to escape his creditors. He owed more than two million florins; almost the whole of his salvaged possessions were in pawn at Strasbourg, while his begging letters went out to the Protestant princes of Germany — humiliating requests for loans to the Dukes of Wurthemberg and Baden, and the Elector Palatine. Such of his scattered household goods as he had not pawned at Strasbourg he was huckstering piece by piece to meet immediate necessities and to retain in his service at least a skeleton staff for the nucleus of a new army. At last even the altar furnishings of his private chapel at Dillenburg had gone.

His enemies made merry over his forlorn condition. 'Ladies will not gladly receive those who come to them penniless and ruined', mocked Granvelle.[2] He meant Anna, whose disgraceful conduct was the talk of all the Rhineland. She had sulked and raged a year away at Dillenburg, shocking her hosts by her intemperance. 'They refuse me so much as a glass of wine', she scrawled furiously to William, but she was pregnant and her excess had frightened them. At last, she fled the intolerable boredom of their society and went off with a suite of her own choosing to Cologne. Here she lived with grotesque extravagance, getting credit from unsuspecting or optimistic tradespeople. Here, when a messenger from William found her, she received him among a crowd of noisy companions, snatched the letter from him, read it impatiently, tore it in pieces, and jumped on it, shouting hysterically that, as for rejoining her husband, she would see him dead first; yes, and bury him with her own hands, the treacherous coward. But she had readily agreed to meet him when there was amusement afoot and had been present in all the glory she could muster at the Elector Palatine's betrothal. The reconciliation was brief and stormy, for she was of the same mind as her pusillanimous family who were urging him to make his peace with the King of Spain. If he would not do so, she argued, he might at least take her

[1] Brantôme, *Vie des Grands Capitaines*, II, 166.   [2] Granvelle, III, 493.

somewhere more amusing: England or France. She repeated her arguments by letter after they had parted again, she to her pleasure in Cologne, he to the French campaign. In vain he remonstrated with her — 'It is not a question of where we shall go, but of who will receive us.' In vain he implored her help, her companionship, at least not her hindrance. 'You yourself know in what perplexity I am', he wrote, 'nor is there anything in the world which can bring greater solace to a man than to have his wife with him for comfort.' A little later, reproachfully, 'If you have any love or kindness for me, these great affairs of mine should be nearer to your heart, than the frivolities with which you fill your heart and head.'[1]

Anna was unmoved. She would not even see him again; vainly he suggested meeting-places, convenient for her and not too dangerous for him. 'Ma femme, ma mie', he implored her, but she would have none of it, countering all his suggestions by total refusal or by rival suggestions which she knew to be useless to him. She even wrote to Alva, to find out on what terms she would be allowed to enjoy some of her husband's forfeited wealth.

Her last neglected baby, Emilie, was born in Cologne early in 1569, and conveyed to the care of its grandmother at Dillenburg, for Anna never showed the slightest interest in any of her children. Since the time of this child's conception at Dillenburg in the summer of 1568, William had not lived with his wife. The fault was hardly his, but Anna, who refused him her presence, felt herself deeply wronged. She had always hinted that her husband as a husband was useless. Now, with no restraining influence to control her, she remedied the lack. 'If the Princess of Orange is doing what people say she is doing', wrote a gossip-monger, 'she is only doing as any woman would who wishes to use what God has given her.'[2]

The Princess of Orange was undoubtedly doing what people said she was doing. At last debts, complaints, and censorious onlookers compelled her to escape to a country house near the small town of Siegen, in the charming wooded country of the Rhineland. Here — poor, deranged, deluded and unhappy creature — she thought she would find happiness with a refugee lawyer from Antwerp, a stout middle-aged man, with a wife and child in Cologne.

At this point John of Nassau decided, without consulting William, that things had gone too far. Foolish Anna had chosen a place within his own territory for her deplorable romance; she was surprised with her lover and both were brought back captive to Dillenburg. Anna furiously proclaimed her innocence, but her lover confessed at once. He could hardly have done otherwise, for Anna was undeniably pregnant, though he need not have been

---

[1] *Archives*, III, 327-8, 331.   [2] Granvelle, IV, 565.

so ungallant as to excuse himself on the grounds that plenty of others had done no more than he. Utterly broken by his betrayal, Anna confessed and immediately wrote to William, asking him to kill them both. Her lover, thinking of the wife and child in Cologne, was less enthusiastic for the holocaust, though at first he dared not do more than plead tentatively that he was a gentleman and ought to be beheaded, not hanged.

William had not the least intention of killing either of them. As a sovereign prince, he had precedent enough among his contemporaries for making an end of an adulterous wife, though, politically, the execution of a Saxon princess would have created an uproar. The custom of his period and his own rank, on the other hand, demanded that he should kill the man, but vengeance was something he neither cared for nor understood; he knew enough about Anna to recognize that her lover had been more sinned against than sinning, nor would his death have wiped away the years of his own unhappiness and humiliation.

The divorce was heard privately at Dillenburg, to spare Anna's family, and the marriage dissolved. Anna remained in seclusion in Nassau, because her own relatives would not have her back. William played as small a part in the whole business as he could. Only by extraordinary persistence did the wife of Anna's lover force admission to his presence, to plead for her husband's life. Like everyone else she had assumed that a prince must of necessity wipe out the insult in blood. A strange interview this, between the wronged wife and the wronged husband, an interview the undertones of which cannot have been lost on William. Abandoned by his own wife in the midst of his troubles, he could not but respect this woman, herself the injured party, who stood by her guilty husband unquestioning. He reassured her. She was Flemish and an exile; he could hardly have been unkind. Her husband was released to honourable detention in the town of Siegen, where he settled down comfortably enough for the next ten years. He was a person of no apparent importance, this John Rubens, to whom the Prince of Orange granted life, nor would history have heard more of him had he not become six years later, and by his devoted wife, father of a son named Peter Paul.

As for Anna, William never saw her again. That chapter of his life was closed and when, later, it became necessary for him to reopen it, he showed an inexpressible distaste for the very mention of her name. 'Celle de Saxe', he was to call her, and 'jadis ma femme', and 'celle que vous savez'; but never again Anna.

The most profound changes in the character of a man come from private causes and from within. The tragedy of William's marriage had been long drawn out. For six years before he left the Netherlands, he had striven to hide his wife's shortcomings from society, borne with her ill-humours, digested her insults, made allowances for her caprices and her pride: all to no purpose. The loyalty of his family, the devotion of Louis, the affection of friends could not make up for his failure with Anna, and their veiled sympathy would inflame rather than heal the hurt. To a man used to popularity as William was, easily beloved and easily loving, a man to whom personal conflict was as hateful as personal affection was necessary, this private defeat must influence his whole attitude to life. He had learnt from Anna that there are moods no man can explain, minds no argument can move, and nothing this side the grave more cruel than sheer unreason.

V

Sporadically the stifled people of the Netherlands were stirring. The Council of Blood had sent more than six thousand to the block or the gallows; the pyres smoked in every town for the men and women — but chiefly women — who would not abandon the new religion. The town councils, the learned professions, the ranks of the wealthy and distinguished were systematically decimated; the prisons were full, shiploads of emigrants left for England and caravans for the Rhineland, while estates changed hands and businesses were sold and plate and household goods came under the hammer. These were bare, hard, grinding times for the Netherlands, while apathy changed to anger, and anger to hope. Here and there about the countryside, gangs of guerrilla fighters lived in the woods, harassing the Spaniards when and where they could. Their actions could hardly be dignified by the name of 'resistance'. Alva would not even consider it as guerrilla fighting; the Wild Beggars, or the *Gueux des Bois*, as these armed bands called themselves, were in his opinion nothing but ordinary robbers and vagabonds masquerading under a political name. As robbers, and not as fighters, he dealt with them when he caught them.

Up and down the Narrow Seas sailed the armed vessels of their brothers the *Gueux de Mer*, weather-beaten ex-merchantmen, with second-hand cannon nailed to splitting decks, and patched sails bellying in the wind, manned by ruffians and patriots, Dutchmen and Flemings and French and English, the riffraff of twenty ports and three nations, and fluttering at their mast-heads the Orange tricolour with the lion of Nassau. They were a desperate gang whose disorders when in port made them unwelcome guests, who lost their ships through 'nonchalance, ivrognerie, et grand desordre',[1] and whose raids on the coasts of the Netherlands left a trail of death and damage among friends and foes. Once or twice William changed the chief command in the hope of establishing better order, but when a torch is all but extinguished it is poor policy to complain because its flame is smoky and smells of pitch. Their piratical gains at sea gradually filled again William's empty treasury against a new invasion, and in spite of the damage they did the sight of the Sea Beggars cruising off the coast kept hope alive in the hearts of those determined few who had lost neither their faith in their country nor in the Prince of Orange.

In any country at any time the heroic are a minority, but in the Netherlands they were a growing minority. Already they had their songs, their secret signs, their centres for collecting arms and money. As early as 1569 the slow throbbing notes of the *Wilhelmus van Nassouwe*, the song of William of Nassau, were heard in the Netherlands, and its verses were being hummed not without hope. Attributed to Sainte Aldegonde, they were not of great poetic inspiration, being no more than a rhymed catalogue of his deeds and projects spoken by William in the first person. Their significance lies in their emphatic association of the Netherlands' cause with him alone. There were other songs too, vengeful and sinister:

> O Netherlands, behold your choice
> For death or life now give your voice,
> Or serve the tyrant King of Spain
> Or follow now to break your chain
>   The Prince of Orange . . .
>   *We recognize no neutrals . . .*

And here and there odd straws floated in the political wind. In Antwerp Peter Breughel painted his *Massacre of the Innocents*: in the grey winter landscape Dutch peasant women clutched their murdered babies, and between the closed doors and shuttered windows of Dutch Bethlehem Herod's Spanish soldiery advanced in a serried, apprehensive group, afraid and cruel, at their head a lean grey-bearded man . . . surely Alva?[2]

So three full years passed, while, for all Alva's watch, the very brave held secret communication with the Prince of Orange, collected their offerings and slipped over the border with them and home again; while the Sea Beggars ran ammunition into the coastal villages, and on the Antwerp docks arms were brought ashore from England in bales of cloth; while fantastic rumours tautened and plucked the nerves of the exiles and their secret friends, and some men spoke under torture and some did not. Three

---

[1] *Archives*, III, 384.   [2] Bor, I, 208.

full years while apocryphal merchants called Georges Certain and Marten Willems corresponded with other merchants equally apocryphal, chiefly about the sale of classical pictures — for who would recognize the Prince of Orange under these plebeian names or guess that the cities of the Netherlands had become the gods of Greece, that Zutphen was Ariadne and Utrecht Proserpine?[1] Three full years, while the Prince of Orange grew grey and threadbare, and hid his identity under many a strange pseudonym, and gradually built up reserves to open a new campaign by land.

With no power in Europe to support the cause of the Netherlands, surely King Philip had long enough to consolidate his position. Granvelle in Rome, and his supporters in the Netherlands, advised him to go to Brussels immediately the rebels were defeated, to make a gracious, forgiving gesture, issue a general amnesty, flatter the vanity of the loyalists, and show the whole country that to be the beloved subjects of a great king was worth more than their outworn separate liberties, thus by pouring the sunshine of benevolence on the innocent to make them forget his treatment of the guilty. Philip did nothing of the kind; he promised to come, and broke his promise, but sent a belated pardon, which for six interminable months Alva failed to publish. When he did so it proved an ungenerous document, giving no reward to the loyal and crammed with exceptional clauses to trap the partly guilty. Spanish troops remained in the country, Spanish officials filled the high offices, Spanish was spoken at Alva's Court. Intense, vindictive hatred of the Spaniards, *national* hatred such as had not been known before, grew with the months. Now the whole country felt and knew the meaning of foreign domination, which before had been but a faint cloud on the political horizon. In the south, the heretical sects were stifled into silence; those who did not die or recant went underground. Only in the North, where the hand of the government was but partially effective, the stubborn sectaries hung together, an organized, disciplined group, waiting for the dawn.

Alva was a man of no imagination: because he saw no spark of organized revolt, he thought he had the country in control. But he knew nothing of the country. Deaf, or ignorant of the language, he would walk through the market place at Brussels, oblivious of the loud offensive asides of the stall-holders. The common people of the capital hated him because his house-keeping was mean, but his councillors despised him because his government was spendthrift. They were prepared for him to sign fifty death-warrants in a morning, but they were not prepared for him to draw orders for six million florins as casually as Margaret might have done for a thousand, or to sign bills on the treasury without reading them.[2]

[1] Bor, I, 223.　　[2] Granvelle, IV, 156.

Very soon the Spanish army ran out of pay. Things were made no easier by the behaviour of the Queen of England who, when galleons bearing money for the troops were storm-driven into Plymouth, blandly impounded them all. Still Alva failed to understand the danger for which he was heading. Calling the Council of State, he proclaimed his intention of raising a capital levy of one per cent, a levy on goods of five per cent, and a purchase tax of ten per cent, or as the three taxes came to be known, the hundredth penny, the twentieth penny, and the tenth penny. Nothing in these taxes seemed exaggerated to the Spanish eye, for they were based on common Spanish practice, but the outlook of the commercialized, industrialized Netherlands was very different. Moreover, in the sixteenth century the theory of taxation was still in its infancy; kings and governments were expected to live on their private revenues with only emergency help in the form of a special subsidy, or perhaps an import duty on foreign goods. The idea of State responsibility for public services, paid for out of the taxes of the people, lay almost wholly in the future. Nor indeed was this quite what Alva was asking for, for the hundredth, the twentieth, and the tenth penny taxes would not come back to the people as education and social services, as a civil police force or even a well-equipped army of their own. They were to pay for a foreign army, for courts of justice staffed by foreigners and time-servers, for the incidental expenses of torture and execution, and only in the last resort for the questionable benefit of Alva's law and order.

Very closely are noble issues bound up with material ones. Nothing could be more grossly material than the refusal to pay taxes, and the honest historian who comes to examine those occasional epic refusals will find often enough that the tax was reasonable and the refusal, on material grounds, absurd. Yet the refusal to pay taxes is one of the sacraments of history, the outward and visible sign of the inward and spiritual grace, the symbol of a resurgent spirit among an oppressed people, the assertion of the rights of man, the voice of liberty defying the dictate of authority.

Already there had been stirrings of protest against Alva's projected taxation and it was not until Queen Elizabeth seized his supplies that he decided to disregard these futile demonstrations, and proclaimed his intentions to his Council. Almost with one voice his councillors protested; Berlaymont and Aerschot and Viglius, all the loyalist Flemings who had stood quietly by, if sometimes with sick and doubtful hearts, while Alva strangled their country – now even they spoke. But Alva, with an ingenuous cunning, thought he could see through their protest, for, when he had put the financial arrangements of the country in order, the King would be able to dispense even with their advice, and naturally, he thought, they clung to what remained of their power ... It was half true, and like all half truths, extremely dangerous. Barricaded behind this conviction, Alva stood the siege of his advisers with contemptuous calm. They could not even draw his fire.

Wonderfully ignorant, for all his spies and his soldiers, of the rising spirit of the people, he did not know that even among the highest officials – those whom he had so ruthlessly combed out – the Prince of Orange had adherents. Despising the remote and watery North, he had been less vigilant in Holland than elsewhere. He did not know that the Pensionary of Leyden, Paul Buys, had secretly visited the Prince of Orange and had secretly planned with him a general rising in Holland. For lack of money it had not come to pass; but the organization stood. He did not know that a young nobleman, Dirk Sonoy, came and went between Dillenburg and Holland with money and letters and plans, nor that Arend van Dorp, a merchant of Zevenbergen, was raising loans privately in the name of the Prince of Orange. In fact, he knew nothing, and knowing nothing, imposed his taxes.

But it was too much, for the South as for the North. The Estates of Brabant, against his orders, sent a protest direct to Madrid. Alva, trying to head them off with a troop of horse, absurdly missed them by the way. Meanwhile the towns refused to pay the levies. Alva called up the magistrates of Brussels to explain their conduct; 'villacos', he shouted at them, 'low-born scoundrels'. But they were not impressed; the Duchess of Parma, they said afterwards, had been a lady.[1] Every province, day by day, added to the tale of refusal and defiance. Alva set the army in motion: any more refusals, he threatened, and he would occupy every town and village in the country, and by 'occupy' he meant 'terrorize'. Still the bloodless revolt gathered momentum.

Alva would not be warned. From the beginning of March 1572 he proclaimed that a purchase tax of ten per cent would be charged on every sale. The exchange at Antwerp closed. Every shop in Antwerp and Brussels followed suit. The women of Namur loosed the dogs on the tax-gatherers. People bartered food in the streets. Manufacture stopped. The looms of Valenciennes and the foundries of Liége were still. The hungry and unemployed gathered in vast and threatening crowds. Something deeper than economic unrest moved underneath it all, the huge inarticulate answer to three years of oppression and contempt. And Alva, at Brussels, had locked himself in his room, raging, but determined to have his will.

On March 24th, a shrewd little Catholic priest was scribbling his fortnightly bulletin of news to Cardinal Granvelle in Italy. 'If the Prince of Orange had kept his army in reserve until this time', he wrote, 'he would have succeeded in what he undertook.'[2]

[1] Granvelle, IV, 137.   [2] Granvelle, IV, 148.

Certainly, whatever Alva anticipated, he was not prepared for any serious trouble from that quarter. The Beggars' wretched fleet had recently sustained two heavy blows. Eight of the best ships had been frostbound early in the year, off Friesland, and there battered to pieces by the Spaniards. Worse than this, the Queen of England, under pressure from the Spanish ambassador, had been forced to prohibit them from using her ports. The Lord Warden of the Cinque Ports had declared it so, specifically: 'No manner of victual from henceforth shall pass to be carried to the sea for the victualling or relief of the fleet now serving the Prince of Orange.'[1] As for the land force, it did not yet exist. William was at Dillenburg, sending out invitations to the German princes for a meeting in May. If he could get the promise of help from them and permission to recruit in their countries, he hoped that he might perhaps have an army ready for invasion by the early autumn.

But events which had lagged so far behind his tenacious hopes now overtook and forced him on. The spring gales battered a squadron of the Beggars' fleet, unharboured, in the Narrow Seas. The English ports, officially closed, offered little shelter; storm-driven, they made the haven of Brill on the estuary of the Meuse. They were five-and-twenty sail, with seven or eight hundred fighting men, under the command of Guillaume de la Marck, a genial ruffian descended from a famous line of robber barons. The Spanish garrison had been momentarily called away and the inhabitants received them with enthusiasm; a good deal of booty had already been collected, when it occurred to La Marck that he was in undisputed possession of the harbour and the town, that the defences were in good order, with nobody to man them, and that the Spaniards, when they came back, would be taken wholly by surprise. With the jubilant support of the inhabitants, he planted the orange tricolour on the walls of Brill: the Prince of Orange's own flag, flying for the first time on dry land, and in the Netherlands.[2]

VI

But when he heard the news at Dillenburg William was not pleased. He had had too many disappointments; La Marck and the Beggars had been in too many scrapes; he had seen too much lost by rashness, and he was not ready. This was Heiligerlee all over again, and he could not afford the ill-

---

[1] *Historical MSS. Commission* Report xiii. Rye MSS., 3.
[2] The evidence brought forward to contradict Motley's assumption of the fortuitous nature of the capture of Brill seems to me inconclusive and out of character with the actions of the Beggars.

considered gains which brought expensive losses. Louis, at La Rochelle, with the rest of the Beggars' fleet, had no such second thoughts; he lifted the anchors, spread sail up the Channel, and seized Flushing. Whether William was ready or not, Louis knew that the moment had come which would not come again. He was right.

Flushing raised the orange tricolour on April 6th, 1572, Rotterdam on the 8th, Schiedam and Gouda on the 10th. The native garrisons were in uproar, turning from Alva to the Prince of Orange; the people, hungry, unemployed and ripe for revolt, were rising everywhere. Men were flocking to enlist at Brill. Zealand, Friesland, the district of Holland called Waterland — all declared for the Prince of Orange. In Antwerp the people openly jested, punning on the Flemish meaning of the word Brill: 'the Duke of Alva has lost his *spectacles* on All Fools Day'.[1] In Brussels, Alva made light of these remote disturbances — the secession of a few marshes and a fishing village to the Prince of Orange. But a wail went up from some at least of the Spanish party when 'Edam where the good Dutch cheese is made' flew the flag of revolt.[2] Even Alva realized what he was facing when the herald he sent to Flushing was received neither with violence nor with submission, but with jeers of confident laughter, and sent back to him with nothing but the spoken defiance, 'Let the Duke come himself. We'll eat him alive!'[3]

William's hand had been forced; he held back no longer. The hour was his. He sent his orders at once to Louis and La Marck: all Spanish taxes were to be remitted, all privileges restored, liberty of conscience was to be given to all, no victimization, no plunder. (The Sea Beggar Captains did not take the last prohibition seriously; they were the more mistaken.) The Estates of the revolted districts were to assemble as soon as possible; William was, after all, the old Stadholder of Holland and Zealand, and was merely resuming his interrupted duties. Somehow he must have an army in the field by the summer. The German princes, gathered at Dillenburg, although impressed by the revolt in the Netherlands, were still unwilling to make a rash decision. Their hesitation was cut short when Arend van Dorp arrived at Dillenburg, bringing with him a loan of ten thousand florins raised in Holland for the war expenses of the Prince of Orange. The assembled princes stared, for could it be supposed that the Dutch were investing in an unsound speculation? Without more ado they granted William leave to recruit his troops in their lands. The army sprang into being.

Louis did not wait for any army from Germany. His own diplomacy had given him a lien on the troops of the Huguenot party in France. They were now at peace and had gained the ascendancy for which they had fought,

[1] Bor, I, 266.   [2] Granvelle, IV, 180.   [3] *Ibid.*, 181.

their young leader, Henry of Navarre, was to marry the King's sister. Huguenot domination in France and the overthrow of the Guise meant the loss of Spain's great Catholic ally, and gained a friendly neighbour to the resurgent Netherlands. Knowing the value of the alliance, Louis had played vigorously for it; he had made the Queen of Navarre, Jeanne d'Albret, his especial friend and had been with her this spring of 1572 helping in the plans for her son's marriage; he was even to stand proxy for the bridegroom. But events in the Netherlands altered these plans and Jeanne d'Albret was the first to release him from his offers and speed him on his way. When on May 15th, 1572 he came to take his leave of her, she kissed him on both cheeks and gave him her watch for luck.[1]

Storming across the frontier, Louis carried Mons to cries of 'Orange! Liberté!' Strategically it was perfect. With an army mutinous and unpaid, Alva was held between two enemies — Louis in the south, La Marck in the north. He could have crushed either alone, or indeed together, but with one on each side of him he dared not turn against either for fear of what damage the other might do in his rear. They could hold him like this until William came.

All June William was in Frankfort raising money from every banker who would lend, were it never so little. This time he would have enough to keep his army in the field at least for the coming winter. On June 29th he rode out of Dillenburg with a thousand horse, at Siegen four thousand more had mustered; at Essen he made rendezvous with his recruiting officers. They counted twenty thousand men.

Evading Alva's watch, his messengers crossed and recrossed to the rebel provinces. His manifestos went before him into the Netherlands, promising justice and the restoration of their ancient rights. Zutphen, Dordrecht, Gorcum, Enkhuysen and Alkmaar, Oudewater and Haarlem, Leyden and Delft declared for him, and in the South Valenciennes, Malines and Mons. Over all the country now, north and south, his friends were singing the Wilhelmus song with its menacing, insistent, triumphant rhythm:

But it was in the north that revolt first assumed legal form. In July the deputies of the revolted cities met at Dordrecht under the presidency of Sainte Aldegonde and recognized their Stadholder the Prince of Orange as

[1] La Huguerye, I, 101.

commander-in-chief of their army, in Holland, Zealand, West Friesland and Utrecht, voting him a hundred thousand crowns in ready money with a promise of more to come. The tenth, the twentieth and the hundredth penny would not have cost them half that sum. What matter? Their rights, not their purses, were at stake.

From Essen, poised between the clouded past and the uncertain future, William was writing his farewell letter to his brother John before crossing the frontier into the Netherlands. 'My humble duty to the good grace of my lady my mother', he wrote, 'to my sister and all the good company at Dillenburg.'[1]

On July 8th, 1572, three years and ten months after his disastrous retreat, he crossed the Rhine at Duisburg, entered the province of Gelderland, and turned his face towards Brussels. This time he would either retrieve his former failure or die in the Netherlands: 'I have come,' he wrote, 'to make my grave in this land.' Nor, in fact, once across that frontier, did he retrace his steps.

[1] *Archives*, III, 462.

CHAPTER V

WATERS OF SALVATION

1572—1574

I

HOLLAND and Zealand were a fortress, with the sea behind them, where the Beggars' fleet for the time being could hold its own against the Spaniards. This northern tip of the Netherlands could be organized and consolidated as a base; with the help of Paul Buys, Arend van Dorp and Dirk Sonoy, William had laid the foundation of such organization during the eighteen months before his invasion in this August of 1572. The South was a different proposition. In the first impetus of advance, William might even have rushed Brussels, where the people were defiantly refusing to work on the fortifications under the command of Spanish soldiers, but he dared not seize what he could not hold lest by extending his line too far he should lose all. The advantage in the long run lay with Alva, who had the resources of the whole Spanish Empire behind him, reserves of men, wealth, and political prestige, with which William could not compete. It was useless to attempt in Flanders and Brabant what was being done in Holland and Zealand. The invasion in the South was intended primarily to keep Alva occupied while the rebels consolidated their position in the North. The final liberation of the entire Netherlands must of necessity come later. So much he had learnt from his failure in 1568.

But this whole southern campaign depended on the promised help of the Huguenots, and on August 24th, 1572, when William was at the little town of Roermond, his first important capture, Coligny was murdered in Paris by the Guise faction and the massacre of St. Bartholomew followed. It was, as William said, a '*coup de massue*',[1] cutting off at one blow his hopes of succour and tipping the scales of the European balance drastically in the King of Spain's favour. The Guise gangsters had done their work well and it would be years before the Huguenots in France lifted their heads again. The fruit of all Louis's diplomacy withered in that one night. Yet William may have had one private moment of shivering relief, for the occasion of the massacre had been the marriage of the King's sister to young Henry of

---

[1] *Archives*, III, 503-10; IV, cxi.

Navarre, and had Louis fulfilled his original promise to act as proxy for the bridegroom he too must have died.

At Segovia King Philip jubilated, in Rome the Pope struck a triumphant medal in honour of the occasion; Alva's spirits alone were not much elated by the news from Paris. William, hardened by years of defeat and mischance, recovered quickly from the blow, though it meant the drastic reorganization of his plans. Alva, after so many years of success, was baffled by the revolt, and the massacre in Paris was not enough to set him on his feet again. Something dangerously like panic reigned in the Spanish army, when they took the field; they found the people hostile, unwilling to answer their questions, running away at their sight, so that the villages through which they passed were empty and they could not find out where William's outposts were. Alva showed his jangled nerves in arrogance and cruelty, striving to belie his fears by a pose of contemptuous confidence. When he was informed that William with his whole army were on his heels he laughed rudely at his scouts, declaring that the Prince of Orange was still far away.

On the following day he found out his mistake. William, concentrating now on relieving Louis at Mons, tried to fight his way through at Jémappes, failed, but would surely try again. Not Alva, but Romero, the ablest of his officers, and one-time adjutant to William himself in the far-off time of Charles V, retrieved the Spanish situation when, in a bold night raid, he penetrated to the heart of the rebel camp with a band of picked men. Some were detailed to find out William's own tent, and make an end of him, but his white pug dog, Kuntze, asleep on his bed, woke, snuffed unfamiliar smells, scratched at his master's bed, yapped indignantly and finally jumped on his face. Thus suddenly roused William managed to escape, though two of his secretaries and an equerry were killed, and his camp was scattered. On the next day he drew off, regretfully leaving Louis to make his own terms at Mons; he thought better to save his army for the North, where it was badly needed. Alva, unable to pursue while Louis threatened his rear, bought the surrender of Mons on good terms, and on September 19th Louis marched out with the honours of war. The southern campaign, apparently so unsuccessful, had served its purpose and the North was ready to resist.

In common with most of the Spaniards, Alva thought nothing of the Hollanders, 'a pacific people with no courage'.[1] Give them one or two horrific lessons and they would crumple. Sending the army north under his son Don Fadrique and the gifted Romero, he gave orders to spare neither man nor woman nor city of the rebellious party. Under the first onrush of the Spanish army Naerden and Zutphen fell. They fired the town of Naerden

[1] *Bijdragen*, VI, ix 120.

at its four corners and slaughtered every living soul in it. They killed the men of Zutphen with the sword, sacked the city, and hung the soldiers of the garrison by their feet over the smoking ruins. This was war as Alva understood it. His apologists, not he, later averred that the inhabitants had been sniping after the surrender. But Alva needed no better excuse than that of giving an object lesson to the people of Holland.

It was. But not in the way which Alva had anticipated. When winter stiffened the lines of both armies into snowbound rigidity, the Prince of Orange was holding a third part of Holland, with the coastline of Zealand and parts of Friesland, and was presiding as Stadholder over a meeting of the local Estates which he himself had called. He was no longer an exile, no longer a rebel with an army of invasion, but the head of a renascent State, judge, general, and first minister of the liberated Netherlands.

William had crossed his Rubicon. He had been for five years an exile, and for four years a despised exile. After his defeat by Alva, the murder of Egmont and Horn, and the mass executions by the Council of Blood, his reputation had been so heavily compromised that his return seemed a thing impossible. In March 1572 he was generally thought of as a man who had played a double game and lost, escaping to safety himself, while others paid the price. The only justification for his refusal to rebel with the extremists before Alva came and his subsequent flight would have been the successful return which he had failed to make. The longer this was postponed, the lower must be his reputation, not only in the Netherlands but in all Protestant Europe. How many of the betrayals recorded in the history of the world have been nothing worse than faulty prognostication and inept action: miscalculation, in politics, is the unforgivable sin. Had William died in March 1572, what a wounded name had been left, faintly scored, on the history of Europe.

But eight months later, in November, when he presided as Stadholder over the meeting of the Estates at Haarlem, everything was altered.

II

There were reasons other than strategic for the consolidation of resistance in the North. The Reformation had come late to the North. Open to every breath of religious fashion, the populous, commercial South had received the earliest fruits of the new thought. The greater number of its Protestants had been Lutherans and Lutheranism is the moderate man's, not the martyr's, religion; it had been moribund in the South before Alva came. A hardier growth of Protestant thought was the dour plant of Calvinism, latest of the sects, harsh as the persecution against which it had to fight, relentless, repressive, ascetic and tyrannical, but a fighting creed, organized for survival. Beating back the Lutheran sect, Calvinism had gained strong, but only local, foothold in the South. It was powerful where it existed, at Antwerp and Bruges, Valenciennes and Ghent for instance, and vehemently practised among the working class. But its animosity to Lutheranism, and the economic rivalries between classes and cities had made it a disruptive — not a consolidating — force. Beneath Alva's persecution the Calvinists had withdrawn to their catacombs, and when they came out again it would be to plunge the South in bitter quarrels and destroy the unity of the Netherlands.

It was different in the North. Here, remote from the larger centres of commerce, in the waterlogged flats, among the tough agricultural population, the Reformation had flowered late; here, of the Protestant sects, Calvinism reigned almost unchallenged; here Government persecution had reached out a stiff, incompetent hand, too far from the nerve and brain centre at Brussels to act with precision or effect. Here the religious fervour of the Calvinists sanctified and strengthened national feeling. It was true that they were not a majority even in the North, but, since the open policy of the Catholic Church in Europe was one of persecution, and, since the Spaniards were the self-appointed executors of that policy, the Calvinists were bound to be the thrusting force of the revolt.

Sainte Aldegonde accepted this situation at once, which was not sur-prising for he was himself a Calvinist. William, to his honour, refused alto-gether to accept it up to the day of his death. His goal remained, through all discouragement: freedom from foreign control and liberty of conscience for all the people of the Netherlands of whatever creed. Even before he had crossed the border, he had written to his lieutenants: 'There is to be no alteration in religion, lest the common cause perish.'[1] The common cause to him meant the national cause, and Calvinism was to be its servant, not its master.

He was, however, too experienced a politician to think that he could defy his strongest supporters and impose a civilized moderation on a people struggling for existence. While he strove to impose religious toleration, he recognized the necessity of first establishing his political strength on the Calvinist rock. Soon he would himself take the sacraments after the fashion of the Calvinists, but he never intended that theirs should be the official faith of the Netherlands; still less did he foresee the growth of two countries, one Catholic, one Calvinist. Holland was his fortress and the Calvinists his

[1] *Archives*, III, 421-2.

advance-guard, but from this base he sought to bring once more into being the free, united Netherlands.

During the enforced peace of the first winter he made his position clear. The Estates of Holland had elected him Stadholder; his power derived therefore from the consent of the Estates, but he exercised it, nominally, as the minister and servant of the King. The legal basis of his revolt was the theory that he, the rightful Stadholder of Holland—his old office under Philip of Spain — had been recalled to his post. For many years yet his proclamations went out with the King's name upon them. This fiction, that the beneficent Philip had been misled by Alva into unconstitutional action, while the Prince of Orange represented his real will, was a necessary convention of the time. The disordered, enthusiastic, libertarian revolts of the nineteenth century were politically inconceivable in the sixteenth. If William was to gain support outside the Netherlands from reasonable men, he must have *legal*, not merely *moral*, justification. Thus he not only adopted the fiction that he was Philip's servant, but *believed* it; believed, that is, that he was acting more in accordance with a King's true obligations to his people than was the King himself, and proclaimed himself willing, when Philip gave his people the terms they wanted, to return to actual as well as formal allegiance. The terms which he wanted in the opening weeks of 1573 were the withdrawal of the Spaniards from the Netherlands, freedom of conscience for all, the removal of the Council of Blood and the restoration of all ancient charters and privileges. It was not, he admitted, in the least likely that Philip would agree to such terms, or if he did, that he would keep them; 'the great problem lies in this question of *security*', he wrote, 'for they have so often sworn they will keep no treaties of this kind and persuade themselves that they may be absolved of all promises by the Pope.'[1]

Whatever the legal fiction, the real basis of William's power was the consent of the Estates of Holland and Zealand. All final decisions rested with them: they had made and could unmake him, but in the meantime he was chairman of their debates and general adviser, commander-in-chief, minister of defence, and ultimately chief justice, with powers of life and death. In their extremity and with a leader at once so gifted and so popular, a military dictatorship might have grown up, if only to wage the war more effectively. Not for one hour did William waver in this dangerous direction; not once did he play the country's extremity or his own popularity to override the representatives of the nation. Consider the position: these people, the delegates assembled under the name of Estates, were ordinary burghers, mostly inexperienced except in the government of their small townships with a few

[1] *Archives*, IV, 50.

local nobility and landowners, some clergy, some lawyers: men of average intelligence and strong prejudices, knowing little of European diplomacy or military problems, and, except in a narrowly personal sense, even less of finance. They were divided by the usual local and personal jealousies which make up the pattern of petty political life; they were inspired by feelings of acute and often impolitic vindictiveness; they were very ready to suspect everyone of treachery on the least hint of disagreement; they were narrow, prejudiced, and fresh from embittering years of foreign rule. With all their shortcomings, they were as near to a representative body of the people as could then be found in Europe, and indeed their failings, both of temperament and of knowledge, fairly accurately reproduced the feelings of the country. Conceding to this body, persuading it, educating it – William had to fight a war for sheer existence against the greatest power in the known world. It is one of the most extraordinary achievements in the history of Europe.

III

His personality had at last found the profitable and constructive outlet for which, all these years, it had been forming. Exile and defeat, personal tragedy and public disaster, poverty, disappointment, deferred hope had made him a deeper, graver, wiser man, but not embittered him. He had lost none of his social gifts, but had gained experience, humanity and understanding enough to use them wisely. Now, at forty, he had reached the maturity which his immaturity had promised. The spare outline of his face had sagged with time; the high forehead from which the auburn hair, now fast greying, had receded, overhung deep-set eyes; the cheeks had grown haggard, the mouth more grim; the cool, calculating confidence of youth had been succeeded by a hint of wariness in eyes and lips. But the expression is more open and gentler. So much a portrait can tell; the rest must come from report. The Prince 'is a rare man, of great authority, universally beloved, very wise in resolution in all things and void of pretences, and that which is worthy of special praise in him, he is not dismayed with any loss or adversity';[1] in such words an English agent was to describe him. 'A rare man' – rare indeed the man who, by personal persuasion alone, could steer this capricious people through the shallow waters ahead.

He had always thought it wise to have as many friends as possible. 'Il faut tenir les gens pour amis', he had argued in defence of his excessive

[1] Kervyn de Lettenhove, IX, 62.

generosity, when he was twenty-two years old.[1] He could no longer dispense princely gifts, but he had the same open and friendly manner to all men: 'that man is cheap bought, who costs but a salutation,' as he used to say. 'His popular nature was of such receipt, that he had room to lodge all comers. In people's eyes his light shined bright, yet dazzled none, all having free access unto him: everyone was as well pleased as if he had been a prince himself, because he might be so familiar with the Prince.'[2] So he went about the streets of Delft, the white pug dog trotting at his heels, talked to the people he met, and in the old convent of St. Agatha, where he lived, gave entrance and audience to all. Delft is not large, and for its inhabitants the Prince of Orange was to become a local as well as a national institution. It was said that they even called him in to settle domestic quarrels. In some tile-floored living-room he would patiently reconcile angry husband and strident wife, and afterwards to seal the concord drink a draft of beer from the same blue earthenware mug as the disputants.[3] So at least the legend ran within a few years of his death, and legend is often a symbolic rendering of a whole atmosphere.

A few noblemen might sneer at this playing to the mob, but they misunderstood the spontaneous friendliness of William's character, that rightness and naturalness of his every action which enabled him to pass in one moment from a genuine simplicity to a dignity as genuine. It was so observant a critic as Fulk Greville who noted this quality of his most eloquently, describing how he came upon the Prince, unannounced, seated informally among the burghers of Delft, 'so fellow-like encompassed with them as — had I not known his face — no exterior sign of degree, or reservedness, could have discovered the inequality of his worth or estate from that multitude. Notwithstanding I no sooner came to his presence, but it pleased him to take knowledge of me. And even upon that — as if it had been a signal to make a change — his respect of a stranger instantly begot respect to himself in all about him: an outward passage of inward greatness which, in a popular estate [i.e. a democratic country] I thought worth the observing. Because there, no pedigree but worth could possibly make a man prince, and no prince, in a moment, at his own pleasure.'[4]

If he inspired both friendship and respect, he also inspired confidence which, at this time of crisis, was more important than either. At times, naturally enough, this confidence might ebb away, but always he managed to re-establish it, partly by his own serenity in face of disaster, partly by the evident sense of justice and the forethought which appeared in all his

[1] *Archives*, I, 22.   [2] Fuller, *The Profane State*, v, 19.
[3] Aubéry du Maurier, 124-5.   [4] Greville, *Works*, ed. Grosart, IV, 24-5.

actions. With no technical brilliance and none of his brother's fire, he yet gained and held the respect of his army officers and — except in occasional moments of disaster and panic — of the troops as a whole. One of the most distinguished soldiers of the age, François de la Noue, gave him a brief but significant testimonial: 'I have always taken his advice', he said, 'and those who will continue to do so will never go far wrong.'[1] La Noue appreciated that there is more in commanding an army than military talent alone; what he admired in William was his grasp of the interlocking complexity of politics and war, his Grand Strategy.

An odder tribute comes in George Gascoigne's *Fruits of War* in which the English soldier-poet tells in an ingenuous doggerel of William's consideration and good sense.

> 'Where good Guyllam of Nassau bad me be
> There needed I none other guide but he,'

he announces, and later his hopping lines almost achieve a flight:

> 'O noble Prince, there are too few like thee!
> If Vertue wake, she watcheth in thy will,
> If Justice live, then surely thou are he,
> If Grace do grow, it groweth with thee still.'

When Gascoigne quarrelled with his colonel, William assumed his usual office of arbiter:

> 'He like a gracious Prince his brains did beat
> To set accord between us, if he might,
> Such pains he took to bring the wrong to right.'

But William drew his friends and admirers from all nations and all classes, not merely soldiers and burghers, but men of such diverse intellectual attainments and individual qualities as the Huguenot philosopher-statesman Duplessis-Mornay, the frivolous chatterbox Brantôme, the chivalrous young Philip Sidney, or the grave Sainte Aldegonde, now and to the day of his death, his entire friend.

Experience had strengthened his will and drawn from his soft, social qualities of compassion and good nature positive actions for the betterment of his countrymen. At twenty, he had had little ambition save to be popular and successful with as small a sacrifice of honesty as politeness would allow; at forty, by the curious interaction of the times and his character, he had become the acknowledged leader of fanatic revolt. How right

[1] La Noue, 159.

in theory those had been who said that the easy-going Prince of Orange, the man who liked to be liked, would never be a leader of revolt. A man apt to the stilling of strife, not the raising of it, the times and that deep, ineradicable integrity which came to him from the schoolroom of Dillenburg, had forced him into the course he had taken: the rebel in the history of modern Europe, because nature had never intended him for a rebel. He kept, throughout the stormy years of alternate victory and defeat, of hatred and suspicion, the unimpassioned judgment of his early years. Later, he adopted for a device the words, *Saevis tranquillus in undis*: Calm in the raging of the tempest.

IV

The tempest did indeed rage, and there were as yet few to give William reliable or extensive help. He had gathered around him in exile all who were willing to help, all of whatever religion, or background, or character who wanted the Spaniards out of the Netherlands. Now he had to weed out the unfit. His first problem were those very *Gueux de Mer* who had gained him his foothold. He needed a man who could make that gang of pirates into a reliable fleet; La Marck, who defied his repeated commands, turned Brill into a centre of pirates and robbers, plundered civilians and assisted his men in the murder of monks and priests, was not the man. When he continued to disregard orders, he was thrown into prison with the worst of his lieutenants, and his place filled by Dirk Sonoy, one of the staunchest of William's agents in the Netherlands during the long exile, and Louis Boisot, under whose direction the Beggars became a disciplined force. In the field, and in diplomacy, Louis remained his brother's right hand. He travelled restlessly between camp and Court. Always a success with middle-aged ladies, he wheedled the French Queen-mother to do something for the Netherlands; what a chance, he argued enthusiastically, to undermine her rival, the King of Spain. It began to look as though the collapse of the Huguenots would not matter: the French crown itself might prove an ally. William needed an ally, for Dutch resources in men and money were small. The Estates had voted generous supplies, agreeing to impose taxes which made Alva's tenth penny seem a trifle, but the North was poor compared to the South, and its richest town, Amsterdam, held aloof from the revolt, not so much loyal to the King of Spain as merely indifferent. Alva had little doubt but that the spring would see the Prince of Orange dislodged and the summer suffice to break and subdue the rebels.

All that cruel winter of 1572-73 Spanish troops had blockaded Haarlem, tempted thither by an offer of surrender, officially made by the pusillanimous town council. While the messengers were on their way to Alva, the more determined minority ousted the defeatists, and the luckless councillors who had carried the offer to Alva were seized on their return and sent, as prisoners, to William at Delft. All the winter the people of Holland were fed on cheerfully exaggerated reports that the Spaniards at Haarlem were dying and deserting in thousands daily. Spring proved the rumours false. Thaw now cut off the beleaguered city from William's canal-skating messengers and the trickle of sleigh-borne supplies. Messages went by carrier pigeon to Delft and back, and often went astray. In vain William hoped that Louis would make a diversion: 'The whole country awaits your coming like the angel Gabriel,'[1] he wrote. But Louis, even if he could have abandoned his important mission to France, had not the troops. No one had. In the face of fearful odds and with little hope of relief, the governor and the garrison had continued to hold on, while William desperately collected what men he could spare. But on July 9th, 1573, the relieving force was annihilated, and three days later Haarlem fell.

The savage treatment of other cities had created resentment, even in the South. Alva, although he had just publicly burnt another thirteen religious victims in Antwerp, had clumsily swerved to the idea that generous treatment might pacify the rebels, and gave instructions to his son, the conqueror of Haarlem, to act with leniency. Straining the quality of mercy through the hair-sieve of his own judgment, the young man slaughtered the entire garrison and a selection of the citizens, just over two thousand in all, and imposed a fine of a hundred thousand écus on the town. Alva approved, and was later both indignant and astonished to find his kindly treatment misunderstood; instead of throwing themselves at the feet of so merciful a conqueror, the rebel Hollanders, with inexplicable determination, fought on.

The disaster of Haarlem, if it embittered yet more the Dutch against the Spaniards, did not increase William's reputation. Continual dangers and the fearful ruthlessness of Alva had raised a frenzy of bitterness among the people and the soldiers. Ghastly incidents had marked the long resistance of Haarlem: Spanish prisoners had been hanged on the walls in view of their comrades, and a barrel-load of grisly heads rolled out by night into the besiegers' lines, with the grim note that this was the tenth penny in kind. This ugly and intemperate humour began to gain the upper hand throughout Holland on the fall of Haarlem. The Prince of Orange was too weak, too mealy-mouthed; what had he to show but a year's catalogue of massacre and loss — Naerden, Zutphen, Mons, and now Haarlem? Was he fighting Alva

[1] *Archives*, IV, 74.

in mittens? News of Haarlem's fall came to him at Leyden and he knew it first by the mob which surged menacingly outside the house, and the rattle of stones against the windows. They blamed him entirely. He had sent too little and too late and now they were all lost. . . .

Neither for the first nor the last time, William played his personality to support his judgment. He toured the loyal cities of Holland, reassuring the people by his presence and his steady confidence, winning over the city councils by careful exposition and convincing argument. The loss of Haarlem was too cruel a blow for anyone to believe that he had let it happen through carelessness. With so few troops, with so much to hold and to strengthen, its loss had been inevitable, but it must be the last of the losses.

Meanwhile, with Haarlem lost, William's other plans had borne belated fruit. Louis, with a force newly recruited in France and northern Germany, made a diversion in the South, once again invaded the district of Liége, seized Ramillies and the fortress town of St. Trond. More immediately effective in relieving the situation was the mutiny of the Spanish army, within a few days of the surrender of Haarlem. This was indirectly the Sea Beggars' doing; for they had waylaid the Spanish silver fleet, and the army had not been paid.

The breathing space was short, for Alva had the mutiny quelled by mid-August, and his son moved against Alkmaar in September. It is a little town with a fine Gothic church, backed against the sea in the dyke-protected plain of Holland and built, metaphorically speaking, of cheese. Poorly defended within their puny walls, with only a small garrison, what hope had its people of making a stand? But the lessons of Zutphen and Naerden were not forgotten, and the lesson of Haarlem was but two months old; Spanish mercy seemed to the people of Alkmaar indistinguishable from Spanish fury. Since slaughtered they would be, best die fighting.

Thus when Alva's son, Don Fadrique, gave the order for attack, the citizens of Alkmaar, armed with sledgehammers and poleaxes, fought on their walls side by side with their garrison. Before their stubborn rage the Spaniards fell back, a thousand men the fewer — too high a price for one day's unsuccessful assault against an overgrown village. But time, number and artillery would tell, and Don Fadrique dared not give up for fear of his terrible father. Was yet another valiant city to go as Haarlem had gone? Dirk Sonoy saw a solution. Alkmaar lies a bare five miles from the overhanging sea and the Spaniards had not blockaded it on that side: let the dyke be cut and the Spaniards flooded out. Put into immediate action, the scheme worked. On October 12th, 1573, Don Fadrique withdrew, baffled from a camp knee-deep in salt water. Alkmaar was saved. It was the first emphatic check to the Spanish onslaught on the North; the tide of defeat was on the turn.

In the same week, the Sea Beggars out-manœuvred the Spanish fleet off Enckhuysen, scattered and sank the greater part of it, and towed in triumph into their own ports three capital ships and four smaller vessels, including the admiral's flagship with its thirty-two bronze cannon, 25-pounders all of them, and Admiral Bossu himself a prisoner. The capture of the loyalist Admiral was good luck for, while he was in Dutch hands, he was a hostage for the life and good treatment of their own prisoners of war, and, three weeks later, in a minor skirmish, Sainte Aldegonde was taken. It was lucky, as William wrote to Louis, that he had had no codes on him at the time, otherwise all William's correspondence with his brothers and allies would have had to be checked and reorganized, for Sainte Aldegonde held the keys to everything.

The northern autumn froze into a second paralysing winter. Both sides drew off to lick their wounds. Honours were even. Haarlem was lost, Amsterdam coldly disregarded the Prince of Orange, money was so short that Sainte Aldegonde had recently put off one creditor with the embittered words that even if he were reduced to gnawing his nails, he could not raise the half of what was needed — but the Spanish fleet had virtually ceased to exist and the Beggars were masters of the sea.

More significant was a change of government in the South. Philip had written off the Duke of Alva as a failure, and in November 1573 Don Luis de Requesens arrived in Brussels to replace him. He was a reserved, undemonstrative Castilian, without a word of French or Flemish in his vocabulary, and why Philip imagined that he would be able to rally the loyal Netherlanders more effectively than Alva was Philip's secret. But the change proved at least the deep disquiet of the King. On December 18th, 1573 the Duke of Alva took ship for Spain, a bewildered and defeated man. The Prince of Orange had won the second round.

While King Philip at Segovia, half frightened at what had happened, half unbelieving, wrestled stiffly with the idea of modifying his policy, another Philip at Madrid, the boy Count of Buren, scribbled a letter on a scrap of paper to give to a washerwoman, with a son in the Spanish army of the Netherlands, who, for a consideration, would slip it to his father the Prince of Orange. Faint, elusive hopes sprang up again for this boy of nineteen, who had been nearly five years in honourable captivity in Spain. He needed hope; while his father had been despised and forgotten, he had been well-treated; but now that the King feared his father, he was hurried from one fortress to another, deprived of the servants he trusted, cut off from his few friends, menaced by a thousand shadowy anxieties: remembering perhaps Montigny, strangled at Simancas, or the sinister rumours about the death of the King's mad son, Don Carlos.

William had his son's letter by the spring. We do not know what was in it: probably nothing very illuminating, to judge by other letters of young Philip's which went this same secret journey. What had he to say? They brought his dutiful good wishes, or an odd flash of schoolboyish jesting at the expense of the Spaniards. Heartrending, telling too little, like all letters from prisoners of war. But his father had not, and would never, forget him. He was, and was to remain for a long time, the only son who counted. Maurice was still a sickly child at Dillenburg, and Anna's child; Justin the bastard, a docile adolescent, now with his father at Delft, did not count beside the others. So when everyone expected William to exchange Admiral Bossu against Sainte Aldegonde, he would not; he held out for his own son.

The captor of Sainte Aldegonde was Colonel Julian Romero, who, under orders, had wiped out the town of Naerden. Romero was an old, efficient soldier, who had served twelve years before under William himself, when William was commander of the Spanish troops in the Netherlands. He took Sainte Aldegonde to the Hague, then still in Spanish hands, and thence to Utrecht. It cannot, at first, have been a pleasant journey. Sainte Aldegonde was a Calvinist, and Alva had already burnt one Calvinist prisoner alive; he was younger brother to a man who had led the revolt five years before, he had signed and even drafted the *Compromis des Nobles*. Indeed he was marked for destruction. His wife, to whom William wrote words of reassurance, regarded him already as a dead man.

But Alva was already on the point of leaving and the new policy of Requesens cast its shadow before it. Instead of proceeding against Sainte Aldegonde as a traitor, his captors discussed the prospect of a settlement with him and even persuaded him to write to William putting their suggestions forward. William received these advances with misgiving, remembering that the King's past changes of policy had not been reassuring. He feared a trap into which Sainte Aldegonde himself might be falling, either under pressure, or out of sheer amazement at the treatment he was receiving.

It was nevertheless his duty to put the proposition for a compromise settlement before the Estates of Holland. To his undisguised relief, they did not care for it. As several delegates pointed out, it was not a year since the French Huguenot leaders, lured on by promises of peace, had been treacherously massacred in Paris. Everyone knew the fatal dictum of the Council of Constance, *cum haereticis fidem non servandum*: no Catholic need keep his word to a heretic.

William did not, however, lose the occasion of negotiating with Romero himself for a proper undertaking about the treatment of prisoners. This the old soldier was thankful to give; Alva had indeed broken the first rule of military good sense, as well as good form, in treating William's men as traitors or outlaws, not as soldiers with accepted rights. Ill-treatment of prisoners recoils on its perpetrators, and that barrel-load of heads rolled into the Spanish lines at Haarlem had been bad for morale. In future, both sides agreed to accord each other the decencies of warfare, and on the whole they stood by the agreement.

So the old year went out, and the New Year and the new governor came in. The first and harshest phase of the war had ended. As the end of 1572 saw William established in his corner of the Netherlands, so the end of 1573 saw him and his people accorded a tacit recognition: in name still rebels, but in fact an articulate nation, no longer doomed without trial to the edge of the sword, but offered terms and formally asked to appoint commissioners for peace.

v

It was better; but it was still not safe. There was very little money to spare, for William, whose lands were almost all in Spanish-occupied Brabant, had none of his own, and Amsterdam, the richest of the northern cities, remained outside the revolt. Taxation, voted in the Estates, increased formidably, the people willingly accepting burdens which far exceeded any Alva had imposed. Even so the rebels had to resort to the doubtful procedure of selling Church lands – another wedge driven sharply between Catholic and Protestant which it would be hard to draw out again. In the New Year 1574 William was writing to Louis imploring further help. Louis had not relaxed his efforts. He had been at Heidelberg and at home, as well as in France, and now with an army in which the Elector Palatine's son Christopher, and the youngest Nassau brother, Henry, were both serving, he was planning a fresh invasion in the spring.

William meanwhile was gradually rounding up the last outposts of resistance in Zealand. Middelburg, with a garrison of Spaniards and Walloons, held out against him, and this time it was the Spaniards' turn to send relief which failed. The Sea Beggars broke up a squadron coming to revictual the town and, on February 18th, 1574, it capitulated. This was William's chance to show his enemies how to behave to surrendered cities. After escorting the defeated garrison to their embarkation point, to protect them against the hostile peasantry, his troops took possession in perfect order. The only casualties were some Spanish soldiers who, in their famished condition, devoured too quickly the rations given them by their victors. A heavy cash indemnity had originally been demanded from the citizens according to the usual custom of war, but William, courageously pursuing the policy he felt to be right in spite of his own necessity, remitted almost the whole of it. The war was to be paid for by taxes freely voted by the Estates, or by loans freely negotiated, not by punishing the defeated. He wanted the citizens of Middelburg for his friends, and fully understood that a city occupied by a loyalist garrison would find revolt difficult. His war was against the foreigner alone, and he regarded every inhabitant of the Netherlands as a potential friend, thus tempting the waverers to his side and lifting as far as he could those roots of bitterness which soured the soil.

Meanwhile Louis stood ready to make a diversion in the South. The need had never been greater, for the Spanish armies, refreshed and reinforced by Requesens, were blockading Leyden, and little would be the value of capturing Middelburg, if this great city were lost. The town, with a mixed garrison of Dutch and English volunteers, was ill-provisioned and, if once the blockade formed, could not hold for long. In the early spring Louis with his youngest brother Henry, and his cousin Christopher of the Palatinate, at the head of fifteen thousand men, crossed the Meuse above Maestricht, marching as if to join William in Holland. On April 14th, 1574, a Spanish force outmanœuvred him at Mook Heide and surprised him into giving battle. Leading the charge which was to break the encircling force, Louis was shot in the arm. He pretended for a few moments that all was well with him but he was losing blood too fast and two of his friends got him out of the mêlée and into a charcoal burner's hut. By this time it was evident that the day was lost. Henry and Christopher had both gone down in that first bloody charge, and Louis implored and finally ordered his two companions to save their own lives. They left him unwillingly to an unknown fate; neither living nor dead was he ever seen again.

'My brothers are assuredly dead,' wrote William to his brother John, on the first mangled report of the battle. But he could not believe it, and since no recognizable trace of either Louis or Henry had been found on the battlefield he had the long torment of uncertainty yet to go through. His immediate personal anxiety was for his mother, lest the blow be too much for her to bear; Louis was her favourite son, and Henry — little Heinz — born shortly before his father died, her youngest. The Elector Palatine, hearing of his son Christopher's death, might stoutly declare his pride in so honourable a bereavement, but it was harder for Juliana, widowed and growing old, to bear at one hearing the loss of her two dearest children. 'I pray you give me good counsel', wrote William to John, 'what I am to tell my lady my mother, knowing not whether to condole with her on the loss of my brothers, being still ignorant whether they be dead or living; I would not distress her without cause.'[1] But as the weeks lengthened into months and nothing was heard of Louis, William could cheat himself no longer. Hardly again after that anguished summer of 1574 did he mention Louis's name and his first letter to John after he had the news of the battle turned the key, as it were, on his admission of personal grief. 'Not to return to this sad event . . .' he wrote after a brief account of the disaster, and devoted the three more pages of his letter to political and strategic analysis of his coming plans, with requests for advice and help.[2] Once only, much later, when he was composing his *Apology*, his official defence against Philip of Spain, did he break his silence in a phrase whose note of personal grief rings out from the measured arguments of a political document – 'mine own brethren, whom I loved more than mine own life'. The love between him and Louis, born in the happy companionship of their young manhood, strengthened by the disaster of Anna, tried and tested during years of shared exile and a shared cause, went too deep for words. Silence enclosed it, like a tomb.

Louis of Nassau had not been a good general, but he had that touch of chivalry and daring, that hint of the picturesque, which is otherwise so sadly lacking in the drab heroes of the Protestant cause. He has been described as the 'chevalier sans peur et sans reproche' of the Reformation. And when he died it was as if a torch had been extinguished.

Meanwhile in the South, Requesens made a disturbing move; he lifted the tenth penny and issued a pardon to all who would yield to the King. William was not in the least impressed, for not only were many persons excepted by name from the indemnity – himself the chief – but no provision was made for restoring confiscated property, while the heart of the problem remained untouched: there was no suggestion that Spanish troops were to be withdrawn, religious toleration granted or the ancient privileges restored. Without these concessions, fair-seeming promises were valueless. He himself had been secretly approached by an emissary from Requesens with offers of a private peace between himself and the King of Spain. He answered courteously but clearly that he could consider no private peace, for he was no longer a private person, but 'serviteur et élu defendeur' of the Estates of Holland.[3] But would the Estates themselves, tired with a long winter, despondent at the catastrophe of Mook Heide, see the iron hand under the velvet glove? 'There is no people in the world', William wrote, 'which rejoices more at good news, nor any more easily cast down by some unhappy accident.'[1] He feared for their constancy, and clearly, with Louis dead and no foreign ally openly in support of his cause, he needed to strengthen his position against the insidious attack. That majority of the Estates of Holland which had recognized in the autumn that the Spanish menace was still the Spanish menace, though it cooed like any sucking dove, was growing perceptibly smaller. For the sake of weakening members, he would have been glad to produce emphatic foreign support.

Negotiations with France languished now that Louis was dead. Elizabeth of England wavered, not wishing to be embroiled with Spain. That left the Emperor Maximilian, an ally to whom William had had, all along, a strong personal leaning. He therefore suggested, as a solution of the Netherlands problem, that Holland should join the Hanseatic League and proclaim Maximilian its protector. The plan came to nothing; perhaps it was never intended to do more than gain time and increase confidence.

The dangerous situation was eased for William, not by diplomacy but by an outbreak of mutiny in the Spanish army. Lack of pay was the perennial reason, and Requesens in desperation commandeered the drapers' stocks in Brussels and paid the men in bales of cloth. William's mastery of the seas and his careful control of his own resources had gradually reversed the positions of the two armies; his was now the disciplined force which did not need to live by plunder. He was gradually getting rid of all officers whose standards were lower than his own, and when a certain lady and her daughters had been molested he smoothed matters over with a personal apology of which one phrase – 'Je ne fais pas la guerre aux dames' – acquired popular currency. All this was not lost on the country still occupied by Spanish troops. Moreover, the loyal nobles and gentry of the South liked their masters less and less, complained loudly of the disorders among the troops and openly resented Philip's appointment of yet another Spaniard as their governor, in succession to Alva. He should have sent a Prince of the Blood, at the very least. In their cups the nobles were lewdly abusive of Requesens; 'it is not to be believed what these gentlemen say, openly at dinner, and in front of pages and lackeys, as is their wont after drink taken',[2] Granvelle's informant wrote to his patron. Requesens could not be positive that some of them, the haughty Aerschot for instance, were not in communication with William, while the loyalty of the native, and even of the Spanish, troops was doubtful, and Antwerp had been all but yielded by treachery to

[1] Philip II, III, 499–523; *Archives*, IV, 388.
[2] Granvelle, V, 90.

William's fleet. At Whitsuntide the Beggars won yet another naval victory, sinking or taking fourteen ships.

Yet William and the Dutch had to face the fact that Spanish resources were in the long run inexhaustible, and meanwhile Leyden was in danger. Louis's last campaign had effectively drawn off the besiegers, but only for eight weeks; at the end of May, with the Spanish army restored to order, the blockade was formed again. William, who had foreseen this but had too few troops to prevent it, had vainly advised the improvident citizens to lay in stores of grain and ammunition. But Leyden, like most Dutch cities, was divided by faction, a small determined party only standing for strong action, while the timorous or lethargic made up their minds to nothing. In time of crisis alone did the determined group take charge and then it was often too late to repair past negligence. Indeed, in the false security of their temporary relief in April, the people had not only abandoned all defensive works and done nothing to lay in stores but had even expelled their garrison. Thus, at the end of May 1574, when the Spaniards once more formed the blockade, Leyden, ill-defended and ill-provisioned, found itself cut off not only from supplies and support but even from communication with the outside world. Pigeon post, or occasional signalling by rockets from the church tower, was for weeks at a time to be their only contact with the rest of the country. Sure of his prey, the Spanish commander Valdes did not hurry himself to waste men and powder on an assault. Give Leyden but a few weeks and hunger and plague would breach her walls for him.

VI

This was the situation when on June 5th, 1574, William opened the Estates of Holland at Rotterdam. His first task, which proved easier than he had feared, was to dissuade them from swallowing the bait of the general pardon offered by Requesens. His second was to urge on them the only possible measure to save Leyden: the measure which had saved Alkmaar. Outnumbered on land, William's forces were masters of the water: the dykes must be broken, and their own element once again called in to their rescue. Leyden lies in the triangle between the Ysel and the Meuse, below the water-level, so that by opening the sluices of these two rivers just above Rotterdam the country could be flooded and the city relieved by a fleet of canal barges. William saw no other way and the military experts, with some of the engineers, agreed with him. Others, less hopeful, pointed out the great distance which the waters would have to flow — twenty-two miles from Rotterdam to Leyden — and the unlucky formation of the terrain, for the land rises just short of Leyden itself, so that, although this district, called Rynland, lies below the sea, it is perceptibly higher than the stretch between itself and Rotterdam, and it was doubtful whether the waters would effectively cover it. The flattest barges which could be found would still draw from two to three feet of water.

His plan for the relief of Leyden depended upon a combination of favourable circumstances extremely improbable at that time of year, for the waters would not flood that last vital stretch of country without the joint help of a strong wind and a high tide to force a torrent through the broken dykes and such a combination at the height of summer was improbable. Had there been any other way of saving Leyden, William could hardly have advocated a plan which would make thousands homeless and lay waste a fertile land, with at best but a slender chance of success. But there was no other way of saving Leyden.

Why did William insist so strongly? Why did he wear himself out during that parched summer of 1574, in the foetid damp of Rotterdam, arguing with these delegates who had so much to lose by the flooding of their farms and fields, until at last, on July 30th, the Estates of Holland passed their heroic resolution, until he himself could stand, on that significant third of August, haggard and feverish, watching the pioneers breach the Meuse dyke at Capelle, until, from Gouda to Yselmonde, from sixteen great gashes, the dykes bled over the green land they had so long defended? Why all this for Leyden, when Haarlem had been so lightly lost?

Haarlem itself was the answer; William's cause could not have sustained one more defeat. After Haarlem, it had taken weeks to steady the faltering nerves of the burghers, and after Leyden it might well be impossible. Even if this colossal sacrifice did not save Leyden, it would surely bring all Holland together in common heroism and common suffering. When the burghers and landowners of the Estates freely voted their own loss, when the homeless people gathered, mute, determined, carrying on their backs and in piled wagons all that they could save, to watch the greedy waters slowly devour their fields and their homes; when the burgomaster of Delft, seeing the grey salt flood creep up through his orchards and his farms beyond the city wall, said stoutly to the citizens watching with him, that all he had lost was a cheap price for driving the Spaniards out of Holland: then Holland was already saved.

Gone now was William's fear that his people would swallow the deceptive bait of a Spanish pardon, or be deluded by the overtures of peace which

Requesens made all that summer. Philip held aloof from the negotiations, a fact which should have revealed their hollowness to everyone, yet had the despondent mood prevailed in Holland, the Estates might have fallen into the disastrous trap. As it was, William received delegations from Requesens with equanimity and the Estates eschewed temptation, standing firm on the two cardinal points which Requesens could not offer: the recall of the Spanish army and toleration for the Protestant sects.

All this while Requesens sought by tempting personal overtures to separate William from his people and buy him off. In vain: with a touch of his old gallantry, William answered that the fair maid of Holland had many suitors, but he was the man she had honoured with her choice. He would not desert her.[1]

In one last effort to shake his resolution, Requesens released Sainte Aldegonde on parole and sent him to argue the case for a compromise settlement. For the past nine months Sainte Aldegonde had had no news save what his captors gave him, and naturally enough he believed William's position to be more perilous than it was. Moreover, he was a native of Brabant and may already have feared that the northern revolt, if carried to extremes, would jeopardize the unity of the country. Be that as it may, he had already written to William more than once from his prison urging him to negotiate for a settlement on the basis of toleration and to lay down arms.

He returned to his captors after his brief visit to Rotterdam a changed man. So far from bringing William to his point of view, he had been brought to William's, perhaps by apt reminders of the fate of Coligny when he made peace with Catherine de Medici, and the non-obligation of Catholics to keep faith with heretics; more probably by his own observation of conditions in the North. He must have noticed in that short visit what even the most casual traveller noticed in Holland that summer. A nation had been born.

Leyden was in travail for the birth of Holland. After two and a half months of siege, plague was raging and famine, not at the gates but in the city. Soon they would be distributing the hoofs and skins of animals to the gaunt housewives; fats and grain were already exhausted. But through the fanaticism of some few among the citizens the city held on. The burgomaster, Adriaen van der Werff, toughest of the resisters, withstood all demand for surrender, and stilled a hungry mob with the fierce words that they might eat his flesh, but surrender never. Meanwhile with all their lines cut off, they could not tell what plans there were for their relief, and

[1] Gachard, III, 382-8.

heard only doubtful and uncertain rumours. Not until August did a deputation manage to get through to Rotterdam.

William received them in his bare room, at the deserted convent which
was his headquarters. Dumbfounded they saw him in bed, unattended,
worn out with fever, weak and very thin, so that the leader of the deputation,
startled into forgetting his own troubles, exclaimed in horror. Answering
their questions in a voice painfully weak, he admitted that he was very ill,
so ill that he preferred to send his servants away for fear of infection.
Anxiously he went on to ask how long their city would and could hold
out. Help would come, he assured them, for already the dykes were broken
and a fleet of barges, loaded with stores, was ready to sail. When they assured
him that they could hold out yet for some few more weeks he seemed to
regain strength, and sent them back with letters of comfort and congratulation to their heroic city. The Estates added their praises: 'Leyden saved is
Holland saved', they wrote to the defenders. Later, across the far, flat plain
the rockets flashed from Leyden steeple, telling that the messengers had
come back and that Leyden would hold out to the uttermost.

But William was indeed very ill. His doctors put it down to melancholy
and may not have been far wrong; for he had still to bear the terrible uncertainty about his brother's death with its burden of cruel and futile speculation.
The irretrievable breaking of this, the only strong emotional attachment
left in his ravaged private life, had induced a melancholy and a lack of
resistance to the malarious fevers hovering about the swamps of Rotterdam.
Mentally and physically he felt worn out: 'My head is so dazed with the
great multitude of my affairs that I scarcely know what I am doing,'[1] he
wrote to John. For nearly two years he had been carrying every responsibility of State and army, of diplomacy and finance, without respite, without
relief, and with few even of the amenities of life. He did not live in luxury
now as he had done in Brussels, but had few servants, slept hard and little,
ate as and when he could, and lodged in whatever quarters he could find.
Ever since his youth he had been subject to fits of nervous exhaustion; he
had always taxed his nerves and his energies to the limit, and restored them
with occasional days of total prostration in bed. Such occasional relief had
long been impossible for him, and in the last months he had been ill on his
feet, until at last recurrent attacks of fever overcame him completely.

Conditions at his quarters in Rotterdam were uncomfortable. He
occupied a noisy room on the first floor, whose walls of varnished wood
reflected the scorching heat. Whether anyone thought of opening the
windows we are not told, but, in the still heat of summer, it would not have

[1] *Archives*, IV, 390.

made much difference. To cool the atmosphere they laid green branches on the floor and sprinkled them with fresh water. Once or twice while his servants were re-making his bed he fainted clean away at the mere effort of sitting up. The fever heightened, the intervals grew shorter, the attacks more exhausting, while anxious doctors vainly trying to reduce it by bleeding, drained off what strength he had. For days and nights he could not sleep, but dozed fitfully for a few minutes at a time. Thirst was the crowning torment. In that sultry heat they could provide nothing cool, and since water was never safe they plied him unwisely with wine. He could eat nothing, or at least nothing that was offered to him.

At this point Peter Forest, of Alkmaar, was brought to Rotterdam. He was a dietician and an experimentalist of some distinction;[1] more important, he had the knack of managing William, a difficult patient. Forest began by forbidding the wine; in future William was to drink nothing but barley water and fruit squashes, while at frequent intervals he was to take such nourishment as spoonfuls of red-currant jelly, and bilberry jam, or junket and white of egg. On this delightful diet he began to mend at once, the fever grew less, he slept more easily, while as his condition improved Forest built up his strength with a tonic of his own invention, consisting of beer, wine and sugar. A fortnight later he was on his feet again.[2]

It was high time. Although Paul Buys had acted during his illness as the efficient chairman of the Estates, and Louis Boisot, the Admiral of the Sea Beggars, had been organizing the fleet for the relief of Leyden, his own invigorating presence was needed, for in that September of 1574 it looked as if, in spite of every sacrifice, Leyden would not be saved. All the sultry summer, wind and tide had fought against the Dutch. The water trickled with appalling slowness over the doomed pastures of Schieland and Delfland, making an island of Delft, crammed with homeless refugees, crept to the borders of Rynland and slowly, slowly to the first great barrier which, built to prevent flooding, opposed its strongly engineered flank to the rescuing waters. The *Landscheiding*, as it was called, ran clean across the country to protect Leyden from the accidental danger of high tides and burst dykes.

Meanwhile the citizens of Leyden faced dire starvation; they fell dead in the streets, or stumbled to bed at night never to rise again. Things had reached a pitch where human flesh and blood would stand no more; perforce the burgomaster doubled the miserable daily ration, and at one stroke halved the allotted time which the city would hold out.

---

[1] His published works are in Latin, though the curious may care to investigate his treatise translated into English in 1623, *The Arraignment of Urines*.
[2] *Archives*, v, 51; *Bijdragen*, III, iii, 18-22.

It was on September 11th, 1574, that the citizens heard distant gunfire and their hearts bounded with hope. Then silence for five days, then gunfire again louder and nearer; then silence again, then firing from another direction, flashes by night, the tang of powder in the air and fragments of charred straw carried on the wind. Still they waited. Meanwhile desperately and, as it seemed, with all the powers of nature and the Spaniards linked against them, the relieving force struggled to break through. Boisot's great fleet of barges had left Rotterdam on September 10th, pushed and poled forward in the shallow waters, a monstrous ungainly formation. They found the great *Landscheiding* barely defended; landing some expert pioneers they breached it effectively on the night of September 11th, with a mere exchange of shots with the Spaniards. The water poured through the gap; the barges did not follow for, as the Dutch well knew, a little way beyond the *Landscheiding* ran a great raised road, the *Voorweg*, as strong a barrier as the *Landscheiding*. And here Valdes had concentrated his defences, his batteries trained on the gap through which the Dutch must come. Boisot saw that it would be impossible to dislodge him without guns, and how was he to use heavy artillery from the quaking barges? All the same it must be tried. Within five days he was ready, with cannon swiftly brought from Rotterdam made uncertainly fast on the largest of his barges. Overloaded, they stuck in the mud. The crews shoved them clear, Boisot often helping. From their eminence on the *Voorweg* the Spaniards pounded them; Boisot's guns gave spasmodic answer, but the planks shivered and split with the recoil of the cannon, which from their rocking emplacements aimed at random. Night fell on September 16th on the soaked and sweating Dutch among their foundering fleet, and the Spaniards still on the *Voorweg*.

Boisot pored over maps, talked with engineers and those who knew the country. He did not again try a frontal attack on the impregnable enemy. Six days later, by a bold move and under cover of darkness and driving rain, he breached the *Voorweg* at an unguarded spot far below the Spanish position. Once again the waters poured in, creeping up now on both sides of the *Voorweg*, cutting off the Spanish outposts. But Valdes was a commander worthy of Boisot; besides he was not afraid of the water. His men could fight knee-deep as well as the Dutch. He drew in his outposts and waited, and the relieving fleet waited too. At first the waters had rushed in, flooding Rynland to a depth of three feet, then when all seemed well, the wind changed, the uncertain waters trickled away from the steeper fields of Rynland. The plumb-line showed six inches – a plumb-line indeed was hardly necessary. The barges settled in the mud. The least of them needed eighteen inches to float.

In this fearful anxiety, on September 28th, William arrived on the scene of action. He could do nothing save assume a calm and confident air that he was far from feeling and send by pigeon-post one last message of re-assurance to the citizens of Leyden. It was a growing terror that the besieged, not realizing how near their rescuers were, might capitulate even now.

Their fate lay in God's hands. On the following day William reached Delft where, among the crowded refugees, he waited for news, waited and prayed. The churches were never empty.

And at last on October 1st a steady wind from the north-west coincided with a high tide. The miracle had happened. Steadily the waters rose, twelve inches, two feet, three feet. The barges stirred, lifted, were afloat.

Even so, Boisot thought they would have a struggle yet. The water was not so deep but that a man might wade and fight in it. The Dutch knew the power and the limitations of the element they had themselves called in, but the Spaniards did not; the whole thing was mad to them, laughable when the water was beyond the barriers and the grotesque barges foundering in the shallows, but horrible, incomprehensible, and frightening when the barriers broke, and the water crept up and slowly up, and the fantastic fleet came menacingly on, shoved through the shallows by swimming and wading devils, men who seemed like some unknown amphibian race, a nightmare from a traveller's tale, while behind them whistled the cold and rainy wind, whipping the waters into a flurry of greedy waves. Valdes had reasoned sanely that the fields would barely be navigable to Leyden gates and his men could fight knee-deep as well as the Dutch, but his men did not think so; panic spread like a storm among them. At daybreak on October 3rd the Dutch found that the Spaniards had gone, marching knee-deep, waist-deep, fleeing before the encroaching element, their belongings on their shoulders, their cannon abandoned in the swirl of waters, their wagons all awash.

The desperate gamble had succeeded; Leyden gates swung open as the creeping waters reached them, and the people came out of their houses, men and women and children, pale as ghosts, leaning on each other for strength, with haggard cheeks and bloodless lips, and eyes bright with hunger, laughing and crying helplessly as the heavy barges moored at their gates with corn and meat, butter and loaves and eggs and sausages and cheese. Leyden was saved, and with Leyden, Holland.[1]

October 3rd, 1574 fell on a Sunday. At Delft in the little chapel of the

[1] The best account of the siege is in Fruin. An English translation by Elizabeth Trevelyan exists: *The Siege and Relief of Leyden*. Amsterdam & London, 1929.

deserted convent which was now his home, William, with all his household and many of the townsfolk, was at prayer, when the sentry on duty at the gate slipped suddenly into the church and handed him a despatch that moment come from Leyden. He read it under the inquiring eyes of a congregation no longer attentive to exhortations to repent, and presently passed the major part of it towards the pulpit. So it was that when the service was over the people of Delft learnt that Leyden had been saved.

The sign had come for which they had waited. At the eleventh hour God had spoken, and the wind had changed.

William was at the heroic city within twenty-four hours of its relief. Not fifteen months before, these same people, who received him now with tears and cheers of welcome, had stoned his windows when Haarlem fell. Now both he and they were vindicated, the fearful disaster wiped out and the future of a whole people foreshadowed in this first national act of supreme devotion.

It was a moment for joy-bells, for speeches and congratulations, and the striking of commemorative medals. The relief of Leyden was something which must be remembered through all the ages, and by what monument could this be achieved? In his choice William revealed the constructive greatness of his mind. The erection of a column, or the striking of a coin, means little enough ten years later. He sought instead a living monument which would grow with the reborn nation, and enlarge and refresh its national life. To commemorate the liberation of Leyden he founded her great University, offering thus in the midst of war and destruction, of change and violence, a salute to the things which are true and enduring, the freedom of mind and the intellectual liberty for which he was fighting.[1]

---

[1] Significantly one of the first acts of the Nazis on occupying Holland in May 1940 was to close the University of Leyden.

CHAPTER VI

LEAGUES AND CONFLICTS
1574-1577

I

WILLIAM had seen at the relief of Leyden both the great possibilities of the Dutch people and their limitations. The whole population had joined in sacrifice, from the wealthy burgher to the poorest labourer's wife salvaging her only saucepan from her one-room cottage deep in water. Fisher-folk and dock-hands, bargees and stevedores had manned the relieving fleet; illiterate, brutal, smeared with tar or clothed in rags, caricatures from Breughel, these men, under the vigorous command of Boisot, had carried out the stupendous relief of Leyden. If William had feared that the courage of the people might bend under the enormous strain placed upon it, he knew now that the Dutch were of such mettle as toughened under pressure. But they lacked education, vision, political experience. He did not naturally expect such gifts of the whole populace, for what sane politician does? But he could have wished for more of them among the middle and upper classes, on whose consent his authority was based. If the Estates were capable of heroic measures they were also capable of haggling and arguing and referring matters back to their town councils, and raising lawyers' points over phrases for weeks, even for months. They had voted the cutting of the dykes to save Leyden; but they had first disputed for several weeks. Relief had come by four days' margin only. . . .

The councils of the cities, too, displayed stubborn improvidence. What might not Leyden have been spared had those in authority paid attention to Willian's suggestion in the previous April and laid in stores against a siege? Using the intoxicating moment of their rescue to override local privilege, William insisted that the Leyden granaries be stocked with a two years' supply of corn, and removed from the town council those of its members whose loyalty he doubted. It was, as the burgomaster Adriaen van der Werff indignantly complained, unconstitutional interference. But William by this time knew the temper and needs of his people well enough to make, in a case of evident necessity, an occasional exception to his principles. He had to solve the problem of fighting a war in defence of government by consent without sacrificing the principle or losing the war. At no time in history has this been an easy task.

Apart from the perennial difficulty of preserving a form of government which inevitably slowed down its own defence, there was the more immediate need for outside help. The Dutch, inordinately encouraged by the relief of Leyden, were in danger of falling victims to that common delusion of the peoples of small nations — namely, that it is possible to hold out indefinitely against a far stronger opponent. William knew that it was not, and intensely as his people disliked mortgaging their newly-gained independence, contemptuous as they were of the potential protectors suggested to them, some foreign ally was essential. William saw a choice of three: Catherine de Medici, Elizabeth of England, and the Emperor Maximilian. In fact Maximilian as an ally was an illusion of William's, a legacy perhaps from the time long ago when he had known and liked him. Baffled and browbeaten, Maximilian had long ceased to pursue any policy not sanctioned by the head of his family — the King of Spain. That left Catherine and Elizabeth.

When William invaded the Netherlands in 1572, the plan had been to act with the help of the French Huguenots; the Massacre of St. Bartholomew had not merely wrecked this plan but had inconveniently confused the issue, for, whether Protestants or Catholics, the Huguenots or the Guises controlled the French crown, the French monarchy remained the chief potential enemy to the King of Spain in Europe. William, who had grown to manhood when Europe was dominated by the antipathy of the two great monarchies — an antipathy now once again emerging from the temporary veil of a religious alliance — could hardly fail to recognize this ancient enmity as the structural background of European diplomacy. The religious issue, the fact that the Kings of France and Spain were both Catholics, was misleading: a fanatic King might put the Church first. But France was not at present ruled by fanatics, but by a harassed, elderly woman, struggling to keep some kind of order among headstrong factions and to do the best she could for her unhappy brood of sons. Catherine de Medici was perfectly amenable to overtures from the rebels in the Netherlands. The fact that they were Calvinists did not disturb her in the least; indeed she saw in their war a useful outlet for the militant activity of what remained of her own Huguenot party. She rather encouraged volunteers for the Prince of Orange. William for his part was not affected by recollection of her previous policy, for whatever she had done in the past, her help in the future would be invaluable. This coolly political view was not shared by the Estates of Holland: there was much persuading to be done if they were ever to regard the Jezebel who had planned the Massacre of St. Bartholomew as a suitable ally. This was one of the occasions when William found it convenient to be sovereign Prince of Orange, since the existence of this little enclave of his in France gave him a wholly legitimate excuse for maintaining friendly relations with Catherine on his own, and when her third son ascended the throne, his congratulations and good wishes were prompt and cordial.

Certainly he was acting like a wise politician, for he had hitherto received only the most grudging help from Protestant allies. Among the German princes the Elector Palatine and his own brother had been the only effective allies; outside Germany, the King of Denmark made friendly but insubstantial gestures, and no one else moved. Elizabeth of England, on the face of it the most obvious ally, had conceded to Philip's insistence and given Requesens permission to use her ports. The Dutch had a staunch friend in her Secretary of State Walsingham, but the majority of her Council still feared above anything an *imbroglio* with Spain. In these circumstances William had to weigh his immediate needs against Elizabeth's dubious friendship; his fleet had been hampering the war-preparations and finances of Requesens by a moderately adequate blockade of the southern ports, which hit English trade probably harder than that of any other nation. In the circumstances he disregarded Elizabeth's increasingly acid remonstrances and impounded such English ships as had the misfortune to be caught while running the blockade.

William celebrated the New Year of 1575 at Middelburg. Here on the last day of the old year he was sought out by an old acquaintance from Brussels, the lawyer Albert Léonin, more habitually known after the fashion of men-of-law by his latinized name of Leoninus. In earlier times, he had done some legal work for William and been a fairly frequent visitor at his house when the Estates General, of which he was a member, had met in Brussels. Things had changed since then, and now he came from Requesens to discuss the possibility of peace. Whether William resented this exploitation of an old friendship, or suspected yet another attempt to separate him by bribery from his people, or whether — more simply — Christmas fare was lying a little heavy on his stomach, he received Leoninus with reserve, and although he entertained him to dinner, the chilly atmosphere did not recall the pleasant evenings which Leoninus had once spent in the Palais de Nassau.

By New Year's Day, however, William's charm of manner had returned and he devoted the morning to a full and private discussion of the papers Leoninus had brought. Requesens offered no more than he had done already: the lifting of unpopular taxes and permission to Protestants to emigrate. Nothing was said either of toleration or of the withdrawal of the Spanish army. William was courteous but not optimistic, explaining that everything depended on the will of the Estates without whom he had no power to act. When Leoninus pressed him for a personal opinion he would say nothing, for the Estates alone had the right to express an opinion in this matter. He added, smiling, that he could not congratulate Requesens on his tact, nor anticipate much applause for an offer addressed 'to those *who call themselves* the Estates of Holland'.[1]

His prediction was vindicated when, three weeks later, Leoninus met him again, this time in council with the delegates of the Estates, whose answer to the offer was brief and negative. William, knowing that an appearance of total intransigeance is never wise in politics, managed to keep the discussion on fairly friendly terms, and even persuaded the delegate to soften the wording though not the purport of their answer, thus ingeniously shifting the onus of breaking off negotiations back to Requesens.

He had the situation well in hand and was in high good humour, turning the edge of the discussion time and again with a laugh or a joke. Misled by this, Leoninus made a false move. He could not believe that the Prince of Orange, who in the old days in Brussels had never been what anyone would have called a religious man, could stand so firm on this question of freedom of conscience; would he but abandon that, he indicated, the government would make their peace with him *personally* on any other term he cared to ask. Mistaking silence for encouragement, he scattered a few hints about William's lost possessions in Brabant, and the high offices he might expect for himself and his family. By this time the silence had become ominous and surely Leoninus should have known that the celebrated silences of the Prince of Orange never betokened his agreement. The slip was not an easy one to retrieve, and the meeting broke up with a somewhat crestfallen emissary taking an embarrassed farewell of his quietly triumphant adversaries.

11

William's good humour may have had a personal cause, for he had come to an important private decision during the winter. He was about to marry for the third time — and for love. What lay behind the formal proposal which Sainte Aldegonde carried in the spring of 1575 to the Princess Charlotte de Bourbon is conjecture, but pleasing conjecture.

Charlotte was one of the five daughters of the Duke of Montpensier who,

[1] Philip II, III, 259.

wishing to save their dowries for his only son, had looked about for suitable cloisters in which to settle his girls. Charlotte had been packed off to Jouarre, where her aunt was abbess, when she was still a baby; in course of time the little girl was expected to sign a paper renouncing her inheritance in favour of her brother, and content herself with the prospect of succeeding her aunt as abbess. So planned the tyrannical father, but the aunt died inconveniently, when Charlotte was twelve, below the age of consent. Faced with the alternative of losing the appointment for his daughter, or flying in the face of the Church, the Duke chose the latter. The Church and its representatives made no protest: the nuns meekly agreed and a priest was found willing to give Charlotte the veil and place the ring of office on her finger. They reckoned without Charlotte, who protested with considerable vehemence that she. did not want to give up her dowry, still less to be a nun or an abbess. In vain, for both her parents descended simultaneously upon Jouarre in a storm of rage and threats, and Charlotte, mute and in tears, was driven to the altar. 'La pauvre enfant', as her nuns called their new abbess, proved when she grew up an efficient and orderly administrator. She was an intelligent, conscientious girl, seriously educated and with time for much thought; inevitably the scandal of her own reception into religion made her critical of the Church, and once criticism was aroused it was simple enough for her to get into contact with those underground movements of Protestantism which flowed within the Church itself. One of the priests who ministered to the nuns of Jouarre instructed her in the doctrines of Calvinism, and at last, when all efforts to obtain her dispensation had failed, she took her momentous and dangerous step, discarding the vows she had not verbally taken and slipping away one winter morning to Protestantism, poverty, and freedom. Denounced by her family, exiled from France, she had found a refuge at Heidelberg, where she had lived as the guest of the Elector Palatine, year by year selling her few personal jewels, piecing and turning her shabby dresses.

One or two marriages had been suggested for her. Louis of Nassau, John Casimir of the Palatinate — but she was dowerless, and perhaps she was too serious to attract the average suitor, or her heart was already given. When William was at Heidelberg in the early spring of 1572 just before the rising began in the Netherlands, Charlotte had been out of her convent only a few weeks; her interesting story, and the fact that she had been suggested as a wife for Louis, must have drawn his eyes to her. What passed between them can only be guessed; both were outcasts of fortune, exiles and poor; each inevitably was interesting to the other, he for the cause he stood for, she for what she had done. Some understanding there must have been, for when, three years later, he sent Sainte Aldegonde to ask her in marriage, she came back with his emissary with only such delay as was needed to ask the Elector Palatine's blessing and pack her few belongings.

Every political argument was against this new marriage, just as every political argument had been in favour of his previous one. Charlotte had no dowry, at a time when William urgently needed money for his cause; she had no friends, when he needed allies; she was a renegade nun, when renegade nuns were fair game for every lewd speculation. Nor was a new marriage politically advisable, for Anna was still living and William could not take another wife without first publishing his divorce, hitherto a secret, and thus proclaiming the guilt of his repudiated wife, and offending her family. Offended they certainly were, and showed it by petty unkindness and public attack. They demanded Anna's dowry back, they said that William ought not to marry again when his family already had to keep his children, they quarrelled with the Elector Palatine, and launched a persecution of the Calvinists in their own territory. But for Anna herself they would do nothing. Sent back to Dresden, she died two years later in an obscurity from which the veil has never been lifted. For William, however, the important question was whether he could afford to offend the Elector of Saxony and the Landgrave of Hesse. In view of the fact that neither of them had so much as raised a finger for the Netherlands, and that Anna's indiscretions had made her conduct notorious for months before he divorced her, William thought he could.

Not so his family, who protested forcibly. His brother John, in whose jurisdiction the divorce case had been heard against Anna, positively refused to let him have the relevant documents; even her own relations suggested that it would be more politic merely to give out that Anna was dead. William, typically, abandoned the effort to win over his obstructive brother, and instead had the evidence re-examined by a theological commission in Holland. As for his new marriage, he defended it with engaging frankness, for, as he wrote to John, he was tired 'of this state of widowhood in which, to my great regret, I have had to remain for so long'; after all, he was not old. John, comfortably provided with a wife, retorted with a smug lecture on the efficacy of prayer, to which William replied that he saw no reason to importune God in such a matter when God — in contradistinction to the Saxons — had no objection to his marrying again.[1]

Probably for the first time in his life, he was deeply in love. The romantic explanation is, for once, the only explanation which fits, since nothing but a genuine attachment could have dictated a choice so lacking in political

[1] *Archives*, v, 250.

advantage. He had only one serious anxiety, lest the Queen-mother of France should be offended, for Charlotte's father was cousin to the King, and moreover had recently married again, a sister of the Duke of Guise; both her father and stepmother sternly disavowed the runaway nun. William therefore took steps to ask Catherine de Medici for her approval and presently Catherine, flattered at the attention, and not much caring for Montpensier and his vixenish new wife, sent to say that, while she could express no official approval, she privately considered the Prince of Orange a happy man and Mademoiselle de Bourbon a very lucky young woman.

They certainly thought themselves so, when, on June 11th, 1575, they met after three years' separation at the city of Brill. William, over-anxious to forestall disappointment and knowing that three years and his illness had altered him, had specifically instructed Sainte Aldegonde to tell the bride that he 'was beginning to grow old, being about forty-two years of age.'[1] Charlotte, who was about thirty years of age herself, was not likely to be deterred; she wanted William of Nassau, not Adonis.

Meanwhile, the Dutch Calvinist divines pronounced that the divorce of Anna was in accordance with God's law, and on Sunday, June 12th, 1575, in the church at Brill, the ex-abbess of Jouarre became the third Princess of Orange. It was a quiet wedding in the Calvinist fashion, and was followed by a quiet little supper, with not more than three or four tables of guests. Dancing was definitely ruled out. But the welcome given to the bride by people, cities and Estates was genuine, and the simple, solid presentation cups and goblets which they bestowed as wedding gifts were the spontaneous expression of their goodwill to her and gratitude to him.

Thirteen years and ten months had passed since, with stupendous pomp at Leipzig, with wagon-loads of gifts for the bride, William had received the bitter prize of Anna. She had come to him with a great dowry, stiff with jewels, and had been decked by him as lavishly. There was nothing of all this for Charlotte. The bridegroom's gorgeous household goods, pawned in Strasbourg, had come under the hammer and been finally dispersed not long before. He was extremely poor, could no more make her a jointure than she could bring him a dowry; he promised to build her a house in Middelburg, and that was all. The broadsheet, crudely engraved with their pictures, for sale at the time of the wedding, varies Dutch doggerel in praise of bride and bridegroom with a text in Hebrew, and shows Charlotte dressed in what might be the Sunday-best of a burgher's wife, and William in armour. Can he really have been married in armour in the middle of June? It does not seem likely, yet it may well be that a suit of armour was

[1] *Archives*, v, 191.

the only still elegant attire which his scanty wardrobe provided. We do not know what presents they exchanged, though from the will which Charlotte made a year or two later something may be guessed. She had not very many beautiful things — a dressing-table set of four silver boxes which she left between her maids, Cecile and Jaqueline, a crystal looking-glass, the thoughtful gift of Catherine de Medici. Her treasures she prized greatly and allotted with anxious care, particularly the pendant of nine diamonds given by 'Monseigneur' her husband, to whom also she left personally an opal set in rubies: his betrothal and his wedding gifts, perhaps?

No rumour of William's marriage was heard in the South until the bride reached Brill. Then what a howl of execration went up from his enemies! The Prince of Orange takes a new wife, they sneered, as if everyone did not know that his last had been too much for him. But then this one was a nun — more laughter. What a nun, too! She had been the mistress of his brother Louis, they whispered, and John Casimir's and Admiral Coligny's for full measure. Within two months of the wedding, they were confidently saying that 'la nonnain' was to be divorced, the deceived husband having found out her previous unchastity with his own brother.

The only dignified answer to these malicious slanders lay in Charlotte's own life. Her attraction for William must have lain at first in her unlikeness to most of the other women he had known, with their easy elegance and gaiety, their bold and witty ways. Charlotte, educated for a life of seclusion and virginity, joining the society of other men and women only in her twenties and in circumstances of singular difficulty, can have had little superficial elegance; even her clothes must have been shabby. Contemporaries described her as beautiful, a claim hardly sustained by the scrappy and incompetent line engravings which are all we possess of her: it is possible only to guess at strong, regular features and fine eyes. But she had a singular sweetness of manner, an unaffected naturalness which appealed immediately to the Dutch. We catch glimpses of her nursing her husband through a heavy cold, worrying about his diet, writing the family letters for which he had no time, and little by little gathering together and making a home for the scattered children of her predecessors, Marie and Anne and Maurice: later even seeing deputations or presiding on those festive occasions for which her husband had not the leisure. Gradually she lifted from his shoulders the personal and private and social burdens, releasing all his energies for his public duties. The disapproval of her husband's family melted before her unassertive goodness; immediately after her marriage, she had written to Juliana; presenting her humble duty to her mother-in-law, she claimed no place for herself in the eyes of the Nassau family or of the world, except such as might be allowed

er on his account 'for whose love I hope you may grant me some little
part in your good graces'.[1] The appeal went straight to Juliana's heart, and,
until her death, they corresponded affectionately, Juliana in German,
Charlotte in French, each having to have the other's letters interpreted, but
each content, Charlotte that she had been approved by the formidable
matriarch, Juliana that her incomparable son had found at length a wife
worthy of him. They never met, but later Charlotte was bold enough to send
her mother-in-law a present, a bracelet of which Juliana made special mention
in her will, not without pride. But it was the hostile John who accorded her
in the end the highest praise, saying that his brother had found in her 'a wife
so distinguished by her virtue, her piety, her great intelligence, in sum as
perfect as he could desire her'.[2]

III

Reconstructing a home for her husband was to be no easy matter, as
Charlotte must have realized in that first summer. He had arranged for her
to stay for the time being at Dordrecht, where the Estates were in session,
and whither he would be returning at intervals to attend to the political
affairs of the provinces and to snatch occasional moments of quiet with his
wife; but five days after the wedding he had been at Zierickzee inspecting
the fortifications, then to Rotterdam to the fleet, and so on all that summer.
Little by little his broad and tolerant policy was bearing fruit. His own
people, looking to the South, saw a disorderly foreign army, a harassed
and divided people, a Spanish governor surrounded by Spanish councillors,
the native lords mutinous and the native Estates disregarded. But the people
of the South, looking towards Holland, saw an efficient Stadholder keeping
the Spaniards at bay, a council of native advisers, the Estates in frequent
session, and the provinces exceptionally prosperous. From present observation and past experience they knew, too, the merciful and tolerant character
of the Prince of Orange, and his gift for practical administration. It was not
very remarkable that the song of William of Nassau was being sung and
whistled defiantly over all Brabant.

Brabant was the province which had known the Prince of Orange best
as landowner and social leader. Here he had spent his youth, and from Breda
to Brussels, from Antwerp to Louvain the South knew him by hearsay and
recollection. In the old days his relations with Holland had been those of
the Stadholder to his province only: administrative, practical and impersonal.

---

[1] *Archives*, v, 130-1.   [2] *Ibid.*, vii, 327.

Since his return, therefore, he had been able to build up in Holland a picture of himself wholly unlike the memory which he had left in the South. The gay, brilliant, frivolous nobleman was nothing but a legend to the Dutch; his real face to them was the homely face of 'Vader Willem', as the people spontaneously called him. 'Monseigneur' and 'Your Excellency' remained the formal direct address, but 'father' would be slipping in now and again when the country folk talked to him. The confidence felt by the ordinary people was fairly reflected in the conduct of the Estates whose growing trust in him would have been a temptation to a more ambitious man, but although more than once in his career he might have used his personal popularity to concentrate in his hands something like dictatorial power, no crisis, however serious, did in fact tempt him to overstep the bounds of that authority which the Estates had conferred on him, nor when they voted the increase of his power did he exploit his position or forget the ultimate source of his greatness. By this means he was able in the midst of war to create a state organically sound.

It needed something more than that persuasive personality which his contemporaries noticed to achieve so much within so limited a framework. Thoroughness, patience, personal courage, a balanced judgment and a cool head: of all these things we have sufficient evidence, but all these things would not have been enough. There was still his obstinacy, the family quality and the family joke — the 'opiniâtreté de Nassau' — to be reckoned with. He could stick to a point with a persistent good humoured determination which tired out opponents. But sometimes in a crisis there would be the sudden flash of indignation, the angry word, the acid comment, which, because so unusual, was so effective. With this mental strength went too, in this last decade of his life, his enormous physical energy — tribute perhaps to Charlotte's unobtrusive vigilance over his health. His mind and body in ceaseless activity, he was everywhere and saw to everything. Finance or fortifications, trade difficulties, constitutional problems, the rights of the cities, the administration of justice, foreign policy or the strategy of the next campaign, he had investigated it all, taken counsel, stored his memory with the facts, and was ready with his answers. 'His Excellency is, thanks be to God, well', a friend reported of him to his family in Dillenburg, 'but so charged with affairs of state, with labours and toils and troubles of all kinds from morning to night, that he has no time even to breathe.'[1]

William's moral and political strength grew with every month that passed, but his military strength was still inferior to that of his enemies. On the failure of his negotiations, Requesens determined to redeem this year in the field what he had lost the year before. He had attacked Leyden

---

[1] *Archives*, v, 360.

in 1574 thinking to break Holland in two; in 1575 he planned a more elaborate campaign, tending to the same goal. Strengthened by the ships which had
at last come from Spain in sufficient numbers to oppose a strong force to
the Sea Beggars, Requesens decided to beat William's troops out of his
sea bases on the islands of Zealand, force him on to the mainland, and there,
cut off from help, batter him down. All that summer, on Tholen, opposite
William's island of Duiveland, he collected his ships and his men, unhurried,
with patient immovable thoroughness. He, too, like William, had learnt
the lesson of Leyden; he no longer underestimated his enemies, and his
soldiers no longer feared the water. On the night of September 29th, 1575,
his advance-guard attacked. The rest of his troops were to follow in the
ships but, since the ships could only cross by daylight and were vulnerable
to the Beggars' fleet and the guns on Duiveland, the advance-guard went over
the strait by night, at low tide and on foot, neck-deep in salt water, knee-
deep in muddy ooze, four abreast. They made the strand of Duiveland at
daybreak, their powder soaking and their firearms clogged, but carried the
Dutch fortress by assault with naked pikes and swords. The next day they
waded the second strait and took the larger island of Schouwen, driving
back the Dutch into the fishing port of Zierickzee.

It was a serious reverse and nothing immediate could be done to redeem
it, although Boisot hoped to relieve Zierickzee from the sea in the spring.
For William the problem was principally that of maintaining the confidence
of the people and more especially of the Estates, in their own cause, with no
miracle and no victory this year to show for so much labour, life and money
expended. He hastily moved his wife from Dordrecht, now dangerously
exposed, and set up his own headquarters once more at Rotterdam. A
winter of painful anxiety set in, while he reorganized the defences and
redoubled his efforts to gain allies abroad.

His own chief object was to secure help from France, and indeed he had
already half formed a plan for placing the Netherlands under the protection
of Catherine de Medici's youngest son, the Duke of Anjou. It would mean
taking the drastic step of throwing off that theoretical allegiance to the King
of Spain to which he had hitherto clung, but it would not be, dynastically,
an outrageous move. A younger branch of the Valois family had originally
ruled in the Netherlands, until the line ended with that Duchess Mary who
had given her hand and her inheritance to a Habsburg prince: to bring in a
new Valois Duke just a century later would merely be a reversion to the
ancient dynasty. All this sounds academic in modern ears, but it meant
something concrete and comprehensible in the sixteenth century, when
legality, inheritance, dynastic and divine right were real.

Meanwhile in France the Queen-mother was gradually abandoning her influence to a King with a stronger character than his predecessors. Henry III, a fanatical and superstitious Catholic, with a taste for the more stimulating forms of corporal mortification, sexually inverted, intermittently self-indulgent, had come to the throne in 1574, the third of the four neurotic sons of Catherine de Medici, with whom the house of Valois was to end. He had been his mother's favourite, not without reason, for he was intelligent, sensitive, and with his pale, spinsterish, old-young face, more attractive than his vacuous elder brothers. His religion was a purely personal matter, and for reasons of policy he was ready discreetly to support any rebel against the King of Spain, and glad enough at one blow to remove at the same time the danger of William's alliance with the Huguenot party, to give his Protestant subjects a safe outlet for their militant activities, and possibly to get rid of a singularly undisciplined younger brother.

Relations with the Queen of England on the other hand continued to be unsatisfactory. Playing for time, she had graciously offered to mediate between the King of Spain and his rebellious subjects; without very much relishing the offer, William in the winter of 1575-76, after the fearful reverse in Zealand, thought better at least to entertain it, and accordingly despatched Sainte Aldegonde and Paul Buys on an embassy to London. Encouraged by the ready sympathy of Walsingham, they nevertheless made no headway with the Queen. Indeed a crisis over the blockade of the Southern ports was fast approaching, since William totally refused to set free the ships he had impounded. The plain fact was that he preferred direct negotiations with their merchant owners to the slippery machinations of a Government which was evidently unwilling to give him any real support.

Forgetting that he had survived more fearful winters and faced more hopeless springs, William's enemies rejoiced in his imminent downfall. 'The Prince of Orange has run himself out of breath', jeered Granvelle's Belgian informant, 'he has not a farthing of money and no credit, unless the English send him help.'[1]

IV

One faint hope appeared with the anxious dawn of the year 1576. Philip of Spain, perennially unable to meet the expenses of his many governments, had once again gone bankrupt, and when naval reinforcements arrived at Antwerp so decrepit as to be useless, it began to look as though Requesens

[1] Granvelle, VI, 9.

would be unable to follow up the successes of the autumn. In fact a more irrevocable fate prevented him, for at Brussels on March 5th, 1576, he succumbed to typhus. His death left the South to the unpopular and uncertain control of a Council of State on which Aerschot and Mansfeld were already tugging a different way from the Spaniards del Rio and Roda and their satellite Berlaymont. In Holland, meanwhile, the joy-bells were ringing for the birth of a daughter to the Princess of Orange. Charlotte, dutifully striving to reconcile her still indignant father to her conduct, called the child by the nearest feminine equivalent to his name, Louise, though there was presumably another and a dearer Louis as well in the minds of both parents when they chose the name. For a second name the little princess was called Juliana.

It was the end of March, and the gardens and greenhouses of Holland were bright with daffodils. In the days of his splendour at Brussels and Breda, William and his friends had brought costly offerings to a new-delivered mother and a new-born infant; gold and silver christening mugs, necklaces, rings, robes stitched with gold, jewelled rattles. But Charlotte's room was filled with spring flowers, the offerings of her ladies and their friends, so many indeed that she was at one moment overcome by their scent, nobody having thought to open one of the windows.

While Charlotte made a slow recovery, William was presiding at important joint meetings of the Estates of Holland and Zealand. These two provinces had been hitherto separate and autonomous; in the past unity had been superimposed on them, as on all the other provinces, not always effectively, by the Estates General in Brussels. But during the whole period of the revolt, a common organization, however slack, had been entirely lacking. William, as Stadholder of both, had thus had to control two separate assemblies, while conducting one single war, a feat which was not unlike guiding two self-willed ponies, unbroken to the shafts, in double harness over a narrow road flanked by a precipice. Holland, leading the way, had given him after the relief of Leyden unchallenged authority over defence and foreign policy. During this winter of 1575-76 he had been working patiently for a federation of the two provinces, and in April 1576 the Act of Federation, or, as it was popularly known, the Union of Delft, was passed by delegates from both Estates. By this Act, the two provinces jointly granted to the Prince of Orange interim powers which at no other time in their history had they been willing to yield to any ruler on any pretext whatsoever. They made him supreme commander by land and sea, they gave him the right to make all civil and municipal appointments, they even conceded to him the extraordinary power of conferring the Protectorate of the two confederated provinces, should he think it necessary, upon a foreign prince, which meant that they would accept even the unpopular French alliance on his good faith. They did, however, stipulate for the strict preservation of the Calvinist religion in all circumstances, and wished to prohibit all other forms of worship. On this point William tactfully secured a compromise clause, guaranteeing toleration to all religions not inconsistent with the Gospel. Just and fair in Holland and Zealand, where a great part of the population still belonged to the old Church, the modification was essential if the South was ever to be regained. Calvinism, the rock on which this northern citadel of resistance was founded, could never be the broad basis of the liberated Netherlands for which William was fighting.

The death of Requesens, without a successor, furnished William with an opportunity for canvassing the South, which he immediately used, disseminating propaganda among the people, and working on his knowledge of the native nobles, their weaknesses and sympathies. The men of whom he had hopes, the Duke of Aerschot and his brother, the Marquis de Havré, the young Baron de Hèze, and some others, were noblemen of the old school, and he was careful not to offend their sense of feudal obligation. No hint of secession from the King of Spain was yet put forward: Philip should retain the sovereignty of his forefathers but he must be forced to abandon the illegal and misguided attempt to govern his Netherlands as a conquered province, and to impose, with a bloody hand, a unity of religion which did not suit its vigorous people.

Underground in the South, the seed germinated and began to work. But in the meantime the summer brought its fresh crop of anxieties. The Calvinist Elector Palatine, so long a friend and supporter, died, leaving a Lutheran heir, uninterested in the Netherlands. There was a minor personal worry, too, for William's son, Maurice, was at the Electoral Court at Heidelberg and it was important at the present political juncture that Maurice should be a Calvinist. The child was precocious, delicate, needing more care than could be given him by tutors and strangers. Too much harassed by political cares, William had had little time to think of his children: the girls were safe with their grandmother, but the eldest was already marriageable. And now this problem of Maurice's education. . . . One detects the hand of Charlotte in the arrangements made during the ensuing months to reunite all three children with their father in the Netherlands.

William, hurrying from his wife's bedside to the fleet at Rotterdam or back to the Estates at Middelburg, had his hands and his head fully occupied with the defence of the provinces. Zierickzee, valiantly defended by Arend van Dorp, had become the Leyden of 1576. Two hundred ships sent to revictual the port failed to run the Spanish blockade, suffered indeed a major defeat in which Boisot himself was drowned. At the end of June Arend van Dorp negotiated for terms, and, on July 1st, the exhausted garrison marched out with the honours of war, after a siege lasting nine months. The whole island of Schouwen was now in Spanish hands.

William received the news with a bitter heart. Was there no help to be had in all Europe? 'We had hoped that the recent peace in France might have released us a little from our cares, but it seems that everyone is interested only in his own affairs and cares nothing for those of others,' he wrote to his brother John. 'For all that we will not be downhearted, but will hope that when all the world abandons us, the Lord God will stretch out his right hand over us.'[1] His trust was not in vain. The Spanish troops had had no pay since their last mutiny nearly two years before, and the capture of Zierickzee was the last effort of an exhausted and exasperated army. Moreover, their old privilege of plunder had been drastically curtailed, since the Spaniards could not afford to appear worse controlled than William's troops. The fall of Zierickzee was the last straw, for their general gave the city honourable terms and defrauded them of the pillage on which they had been reckoning. Mutiny was the answer.

The professional armies of the period, it must be remembered, recognized no authority save that of the paymaster; they had a corporate feeling as an army, but none, or little, as a nation. Mutiny in the ranks might be quelled, but when — as sometimes happened — officers and all turned on the Government, the army resolved itself into an independent power, fighting for its own hand. The Spanish army, owning no further master, was thus loosed upon Flanders. In vain the people of Brussels wailed indignant protests to the Council; in vain the Council called the troops to order. Entrenched in all the strong places and key points of the land, the army made a mock of their threats.

V

This was William's opportunity. Flanders and Brabant were in uproar; the King of Spain, to whom they had remained loyal, had proved himself unable to defend them even against his own troops who, after living on the country for the last eight years, had turned on their hosts with more virulence than an invader. Shouts of 'Mort aux Espagnols' echoed ominously

[1] *Archives*, v, 380.

in the streets of Brussels. Violence followed: Jeronimo de Roda's secretary, who had once incautiously announced that he would wash his hands in Flemish blood, was lynched by the mob, and Mansfeld, Roda and Berlaymont themselves shivered within their barricaded houses while the people threatened to pull them out. In this electric atmosphere, on September 1st, 1576, the Estates General met. In the North, the Estates of Holland and Zealand were in session at Middelburg and immediately, on William's advice, they sent to their brothers in the South offering to negotiate the reunion of the Netherlands.

The bewildered South, lacking any guiding genius, inspired by varying and negative ideals, by resentment, injured vanity, and a growing envy of the North, could find no real unity of purpose. Different groups and classes eyed each other with unconcealed hatred; the irresponsible nobility who reeled in to the sessions after dinner and interrupted debates by blowing candle-grease in each others' faces,[1] represented the most reactionary and useless elements in the State, but through sheer hatred of Spain were ready to accept overtures from the North. For entirely different reasons the representatives of the cities were willing to consider an accommodation: already they saw the northern towns usurping their trade and hoped to end both this competition and the vexatious blockade of their ports. Popular feeling was rising strongly everywhere for the Prince of Orange. Only ten years before, when the troubles began in Antwerp, the mob had shouted vociferously 'We want the Prince of Orange!' Now the same cry arose. The years of defeat and disaster seemed forgotten, and the people, remembering how they had once believed in him, were beginning so to believe again.

William was already in touch with many of the nobility, exploiting their vanity and egoism, not because he saw much hope for the Netherlands in this unstable group, but because he knew very well that in the South their influence was a factor of outstanding importance. The problem of how to encourage their support without alienating the townspeople was not, to one of his diplomatic gifts, insurmountable. It was easy for him to get into touch with men whom he had been familiar with only ten years before, and he was corresponding with the haughty Aerschot by the end of September. More immediately important was the shifty and ambitious Baron de Hèze, the commander of the native volunteers hastily recruited for the defence of Brussels. Hèze was fertile ground; how far William knew his man and guessed that he was as stupid as he was time-serving it is hard to say, but he was a practised hand by now at using any instrument, however feeble, and

[1] *Bijdragen*, v, iii, 34.

Hèze soon imagined that power and authority for him (which was all he cared for) lay in supporting the Prince of Orange. Meanwhile he was borne forward on the tide of popular enthusiasm, the hero of the moment. Early in September 1576, using his office as Captain of the town guards of Brussels, Hèze invaded the Council of State and seized all its Spanish members together with the fiercely protesting Mansfeld and the whimpering Berlaymont. Aerschot, on whom he had undoubtedly had his eye, had by luck, or foreknowledge, been 'ill' and absent at the time. One Spaniard only escaped, Jeronimo de Roda, an original member of the Council of Blood, who fled to Mons, and in a useless effort to stem the revolt, proclaimed himself Governor-General in the King's name. There were now four powers in the Netherlands: William in the North, Roda and his shadow council at Mons, Hèze and the Estates in Brussels, and the Spanish army at large.

William alone had the power to do anything effective against the Spanish army, a consideration which finally decided the Estates General and what remained of the Council of State in Brussels to appoint commissioners to discuss terms with the North. What remained of the Council of State was chiefly the Duke of Aerschot; as acting president of the Council he saw no better way out of the existing chaos than to ratify the decision of the Estates. He did not like, never had liked, the Prince of Orange; a jealous, avaricious, difficult man, without the ability to hold his own in the politically troubled age to which he had been born, he had always resented William's greater influence with the people, and the respect which his intelligence had commanded in the old days when they had sat at the same Council table. It was therefore with personal reservations, and with motives unblushingly egotistical, that Aerschot lent himself to the negotiations with the Prince of Orange.

Meanwhile disorders grew, the Spanish soldiery had seized Maestricht and were terrorizing Ghent. Appealed to for help William sent picked troops from the North to restore order, and a fleet of ships with grain for Antwerp, short of food owing to the disorder. In the meantime commissioners, headed by Sainte Aldegonde, had met the delegates from the Estates General at Ghent and were debating the terms of a settlement. The expulsion of the Spanish army and general toleration were the basic articles put forward. The first hardly needed discussion. The second presented more serious difficulties. Forty years of persecution, punctuated by explosions of Protestant frenzy and concluded by a war, had left enduring scars; Catholics and Protestants throughout the land smarted at the remembrance of the outrages they had inflicted on each other. Moreover, there was the complicated question of property to be settled: confiscated Church lands in the North had been fruitfully speculated in by the Hollanders, confiscated Protestant goods in the South engrossed by the State or put up to auction. Who was to disgorge what, and to whom? William not unnaturally claimed the return at least of Breda.

Yet these were minor matters. The important thing, as William eloquently pointed out, was the reunion of a State which should never have been divided. Not William's appeal, however, but a further and unexpected disaster precipitated the decision. On November 8th, 1576, Spanish mutineers from Alost rushed Antwerp, were joined by some of their own people who had been hemmed into the citadel, and together drove out the local guards and sacked the city. 'They neither spared age nor sex; time nor place; person nor country: young nor old: rich nor poor . . . they slew great numbers of young children . . . and as great respect they had to the church and churchyard as the butcher hath to his shambles. They spared neither friend nor foe, Portingal nor Turk: the Jesuits must give their ready coin, and all other religious houses both corn and plate. Within three days Antwerp, which was one of the richest towns in Europe, had now no money nor treasure to be found therein, but only in the hands of murderers and strumpets: for every Don Diego must walk jetting up and down the streets with his harlot by him in her chain and bracelets of gold. And the notable *Bourse* which was wont to be a safe assembly for merchants, had now none other merchandise therein, but as many dicing tables as might be placed round about it.'[1] The disaster was nothing short of appalling; about seven thousand of the citizens had been killed and nearly a third of the town burnt down, in the 'Spanish Fury'.

News of the disaster cut short all argument at Ghent, for it was now evident that only William's army could restore order. Two days later the delegates met at Ghent agreed to pool their military, naval and financial resources for the expulsion of the Spanish troops. When this object had been accomplished the Estates General were to discuss religious toleration on a regional basis, while persecution for the time being was to be suspended on both sides. William's position remained undefined, but in fact as Stadholder of Holland and Zealand, and general of the only effective army in the country or navy on the seas, events had already sufficiently defined his power. For his own part the situation was very much to his liking, since this Pacification of Ghent — as the treaty was called — stood out as the work of the Estates General of the Netherlands, an Act showing at last their adult and joint responsibility for their country's future.

[1] Gascoigne, *The Spoyle of Antwerpe*.

VI

One province had taken no part in all these actions, the rural and hilly outlying district of Luxembourg, centred about its rocky fortress, a stronghold of reaction, where the peasants were still serfs. By the winter of 1576 it alone remained outside William's influence, and it was here, in Luxembourg, while the Spanish troops were sacking Antwerp, that there arrived the new Governor of the Netherlands, appointed in Madrid: Don John of Austria, half-brother of King Philip.

A bastard son of the Emperor Charles V by a German woman – who was in this year 1576 embarrassingly notorious in the night-life of Brussels – Don John was vain, unbalanced, imaginative and brave, not without charm when he cared to use it, certainly not without intelligence, but a man who had failed, all his life, through a certain egocentricity, an uncertainty of himself masked in arrogance: the common failing of the bastard. In 1571 he had virtually driven the Turks out of the western Mediterranean at the resounding victory of Lepanto, and had been insufferable ever since.

He approached the Netherlands with absurd optimism, planning to settle the northern revolt in a twinkling, then to invade England, set free and marry the imprisoned Queen of Scots, and restore the British Isles to the Catholic Church. So little did Philip approve this ambitious design that – had he been able to find any other Governor for the Netherlands – he would probably not have sent Don John.

Great therefore was the new Governor's dismay when he found himself confronted by the union of sixteen provinces at the Pacification of Ghent. He halted in Luxembourg, taking stock of the situation, considering how best to divide the provinces and undermine the Prince of Orange. New to the Netherlands, without councillors he knew or more than a handful of troops to rely on, Don John showed no mean perspicacity in his management of the situation. It would have been simple – and fatal – to denounce the action of the Estates General and threaten the new union with the distant thunders of Spain; instead Don John was all for accommodation. Peace? He desired nothing more. Had the provinces united to get rid of the unruly Spanish army? But of course he would help them in the task. His honeyed words flowed fast in letters not only to the Estates but to the great nobles of the South, for he, like William, saw the importance of this social group, and he had an advantage over William in his wooing of such men because he was not himself one of them, and they could not feel resentful of his influence as they could, and did, of William's.

From his stronghold in the North William watched with growing anxiety. For a little it seemed almost as if the Pacification of Ghent was to be torn asunder within a few weeks of its making, for in the Estates General the delegates of the Southern provinces yearned after Don John, but Holland and Zealand stood firm for the Prince of Orange. If the South came to an understanding with the newcomer, the North would break away from the ephemeral union.

Wisely William refrained from coming South in person. With his usual wariness he saw that the pacemakers for the alliance with Don John were the nobles, led by Aerschot. If he came to Brussels now he would risk being involved in a mere squabble for power and his cause and reputation would be merged with the meaner and more personal ambitions of egotists like Aerschot and Hèze. If he stayed in the North he could remain the unsmirched champion of the country's interests as a whole and his appeals to the Estates General would have all the more effect, while his point of view could be effectively expressed to the South in his absence by the delegates from Holland, Sainte Aldegonde and Paul Buys.

These two performed their task well in the Estates General, seeing to it that if a split came it would be a lateral split, between the nobility and the burgher class, not a longitudinal split between the North and the South. The leader of the southern nobility, Aerschot, made their work easy; his arrogance was offensive and, convinced of his natural right to authority, he never so much as veiled his personal ambition. The contest between them lasted until the New Year of 1577, when on January 9th the Estates General gave solid and lasting confirmation to the Pacification of Ghent by a second treaty, the Union of Brussels.

It was an effective check to the policy of Aerschot and a heavy blow to Don John after all his gracious overtures. It should have taught him (though it did not) that the nobility were less important to him than the burghers; these latter formed the majority in the Estates, who, with the lesser landowners, had carried the Union against the will of the higher nobility. In order to leave Don John in no doubt as to their feelings, the Estates next flatly told him that they would negotiate with him no further, unless he would himself subscribe to the Union of Brussels. Since they intended thus to break off relations with him, they gave him precisely four days' notice.

Desperation lent sudden brilliance even to Aerschot, who, surprisingly, advised Don John to accept the Union. With unruffled graciousness Don John declared himself only too happy to do so. It was a jarring end to William's successful struggle with Aerschot: just as he had dragged his defeated opponents over the line, they, as it were, dropped their end of the rope.

Certainly when Don John accepted the Union of Brussels, William was left with an empty victory. For what was to be done now? Here was Don John still offering to do all the things which the Estates wanted done, to quell and remove the mutinous Spanish army, to re-establish peace, order and unity; here was Don John, unsnubbed, unoffended, patiently and intelligently working himself into the position of saviour of the Netherlands or at least of the South — and all to hand them back again to the tyranny of King Philip. There lay the rub, for William had not the slightest doubt (and rightly) that this was the ultimate trend of Don John's policy. Intercepted letters to Jeronimo de Roda seemed to prove as much, and if the Spaniards, frightened of the propaganda use which William made of them, declared them forgeries, that was but the usual defence in the game. As William knew only too well, should Don John but gain his end, the Union of Brussels would go by the board; as Spanish troops were drafted out, new Spanish troops would be drafted in, and the question of religious settlement would be shelved for ever.

But momentarily William was at a loss, and Don John followed up his advantage. By the middle of February 1577 he had so far induced the delegates of the southern provinces to believe in him that terms of peace had been briefly formulated. Chiefly, he agreed to gather together and remove the disorderly remnants of the Spanish army, and on this basis, with every other political issue left vague, all the provinces, saving only Holland and Zealand, signed the so-called Perpetual Edict of Peace on February 17th. Don John was now the accepted Governor of the Netherlands and as such he entered Brussels to begin his rule.

Now it was William's turn to finesse. He had some cards left in his hand, for the Perpetual Edict did not of itself either cancel or supersede the Union of Brussels, and Don John's troubles were all to come. He had promised to remove the Spanish troops, and the Estates General, by the Union of Brussels, had agreed that a religious settlement was essential. But if Don John could make a show of removing the Spanish soldiery, on the religious question he was bound to play for time, since Philip would never agree to a compromise settlement. Moreover, William's consistent policy of building up the influence of the Estates, and the total breakdown of the central government in the South since the death of Requesens, meant that Don John was in fact dependent on the goodwill of the Estates General as no earlier Governor had been. His long months of patience and voluntary humiliation had won him only a modified victory.

It remained for William to assemble the potential and scattered opposition of the Estates General and pit it against Don John and his few supporters.

The delegates of Holland and Zealand issued, conjointly with him, a formal protest, describing the Perpetual Edict as an infringement of the Pacification of Ghent, and all that spring of 1577 letters of protest and reproach from the North rained on the assembled delegates of the South in Brussels, formally and privately, officially and secretly. In spite of the winning manner which at first conquered those who came into touch with Don John, he could not hold the ground he had so cleverly gained, for in fact he neither could nor would get rid of the Spanish soldiery and was moving, surreptitiously, to gain control of the key points in the country. Whenever Spanish troops made a movement, William was sure to draw the attention of the Estates General to it and express the gravest doubts of Don John's intentions. In April he himself quietly installed a garrison at Gertrudenberg, a counterpoise to any machinations of Don John.

The move gave Don John the occasion he had long been seeking to accuse William in his turn of breaking the Pacification of Ghent. Both sides felt that the time had come for a show-down, Don John hoping to force William into breaking off relations with the South, and William as determined to wean the South from Don John. The situation was as complicated as it was delicate: Don John was officially recognized as Governor in thirteen provinces, William was Stadholder in two; two more (Friesland and Utrecht) recognized neither fully; yet all were still technically bound by the Pacification of Ghent, and pledged thereby to drive out the Spaniards and evolve a religious settlement. The Perpetual Edict, incidentally, made no mention of a religious settlement. From Don John's point of view, the important thing was to prove that the Perpetual Edict had nullified the Pacification of Ghent; from William's, to prove that the Pacification of Ghent made the Perpetual Edict invalid.

Six delegates from each side met at Gertrudenberg on May 20th, 1577, William being the chief spokesman of his own party, seconded with wit and ability by Sainte Aldegonde. Aerschot, who opened his mouth once during the entire debate, was in theory Don John's chief delegate, but the contest was in fact chiefly waged by the wily little lawyer Albert Leoninus. His brisk cleverness, however, was no match either for William's sure and practised skill or Sainte Aldegonde's dry and learned ironies. The day had been selected at William's request to coincide with his state of health; he was suffering from a tertian ague, and had asked Aerschot to avoid if he could one of his feverish days. Aerschot could hardly refuse, though if Sainte Aldegonde's account of the meeting is entirely fair to the other side, it is evident that even with the handicap of a fever William would probably have out-argued his opponents.

He gave them the difficult task of opening the debate, thus forcing them to show their hand. The gist of their argument was that since the seizure of Gertrudenberg they misdoubted his intentions. William, instead of bursting into an exculpatory defence, asked whether he might have their views in writing. After fluttering consultation his opponents refused, afraid doubtless of committing themselves too far. It was an easy move for William to say coolly but kindly that spoken negotiations were invariably misremembered and misinterpreted. Doctor Leoninus hedged uneasily: an informal talk, at least to start with, was usually very helpful, he hazarded. But William was agreeing to no such platitudes; people who broke the written terms of the Pacification of Ghent, he said firmly, would not be very likely to stand by what they merely *said*.

Leoninus tried to make a diversion. Among the lesser terms of the Pacification of Ghent had been one providing for the release of William's eldest son from his long imprisonment in Spain. Citing this clause, in a meaning way, he pointed out that *all* the clauses of a treaty could not be fulfilled immediately; but *some* might be. Presumably he had hoped that the thought of his own son would be sufficiently powerful with William to divert his attention from the other clauses of the treaty. He may even have hoped by promising a speedy attention to this particular matter to prevent William from insisting too strongly on the salient points which Don John was so evidently not carrying out. But this of all things would not draw William; he had failed too often in attempts to set free his son, and resenting the clumsy attempt to play off his feelings as a father against his duty as a statesman, he passed the hint over without comment. The whole question of the Pacification of Ghent, he said, should be laid forthwith before the Estates General so that immediate steps could be taken to put it into force.

Again shifting his ground, Leoninus insinuated that the Estates General were ignorant and obstructive. Give them their heads and what did they do? You had only to look at France and the civil wars which they had precipitated there ... But he could not trick William into saying anything against the Estates General. Failing there, he began on a new tack, this time challenging his opponents to state in what particular points they felt the Pacification was being neglected. He hoped for something — anything — which could be twisted to show that William was pitting North against South, or the Calvinists against the Catholics, but he got nothing except the cool statement that he had better have a look at the terms of the Pacification. Blundering hopelessly by this time, Don John's delegates said flatly that they could not disband the Spanish troops, for what guarantee had they that William would keep his part of the Pacification; he might even wait until they were defenceless and then make war on them. 'War?' said William with beautiful astonishment, 'What are you afraid of? A handful of men, a worm turning against the King of Spain? You are fifteen provinces, and we are two. What have you to fear?'

Perhaps that was not such a good move after all. 'Yes,' said one of Don John's people, 'we have seen what *you* can do.' Merely hold the northern provinces, unaided, against the forces of Spain for a matter of five years; merely reduce Don John to humiliation and impotence . . . Sainte Aldegonde slid in a phrase to restore reality to the debate. 'We have never made war,' he said soberly, 'but in our own defence.'

Don John's people now quite openly shifted the whole argument to the religious question, vainly trying to force William into admitting that he was pledged exclusively to Calvinism. He would admit no such thing, claiming that the settlement as suggested in the Pacification must be laid before the united Estates General of all seventeen provinces. Leoninus saw a heckling point; the Prince of Orange, he suggested, would surely not submit to the decision of the Estates General if they were to decide unanimously and exclusively for the Catholic Church. The point was, as everyone knew, theoretical. If Holland and Zealand were represented in the Estates General, such a decision was absolutely impossible. But William was not going to argue the point. Turning the question into a joke, he said disarmingly, 'Indeed I should not . . . for we have no intention of letting ourselves be exterminated'. At this moment Aerschot, making his one contribution to the debate, chimed in suddenly. 'Ho!' he cried, 'nobody wants to be exterminated.' Though whether he was merely making a general statement, or indicating obliquely that his party were as ready to fight for existence as the Prince of Orange's, must for ever remain doubtful. It did not greatly matter, for by this time William and Sainte Aldegonde had it all their own way. By obstinately standing to the Pacification of Ghent and refusing to particularize or to be drawn, they had made it clear that in their opinion the Perpetual Edict was an infringement of the Pacification and therefore null and void, while as far as they were concerned the Pacification was still in force. Don John's people failed utterly to get from them any suggestion that the Perpetual Edict had definitely *destroyed* the Pacification of Ghent; a few angry words might have done it, a few sentences which could be twisted astutely to prove that William and Sainte Aldegonde had themselves declared that the Pacification was void. They did not say those words and Don John's six delegates returned disconsolate to Brussels.

William followed up his debating points by letter to one of them: 'We see now', he wrote sharply, 'that you on your side are not keeping faith, that not one clause of the Pacification has been carried out, nay that you infringe it daily more and more as if it had never been made and sworn. You would have difficulty in finding one single article which you of your part have frankly and freely fulfilled. For either there will be cavilling and subterfuges, or sophistical glosses, all to save you from having to do what justice demands and your own oath constrains you to; or else you prevaricate and find reasons for delaying, or refuse pure and simple. In this way you keep the provinces apart, goods in confiscation, prisoners under duress, foreign soldiers in the land, and maintain the citadels and fortresses in repair, which are so many nests of tyranny and rapine; the privileges of the country are obscured and obliterated, the religious laws still in effect, many citizens in exile, and all those of the Religion in irreconcilable antagonism to the Government. And when we of our part complain, you ask us for guarantees . . .'[1]

As long as William persisted openly in this attitude Don John's position grew daily more insecure. His initial popularity, gained by a pleasing, open and generous manner, began to wane when the Estates and the citizens of Brussels and Antwerp discovered that he could not carry out his obligations. Recognizing the hopelessness of any further attempt to gain the people from William by peaceful persuasion, he left Brussels unobtrusively during the summer, pretending that he had to make arrangements for evacuating the troops. But it was not their evacuation which he was planning.

In the meantime at Middelburg, where Charlotte had given birth to a second daughter, William had cause fully to realize the growing strength of his position. A year before he had been barely recognized by European rulers, but now that foreign political agents in the Netherlands were unanimously tipping him as the rising power, he was treated in a very different manner. The Queen of England had graciously agreed to be god-mother to the new baby. Soon she was to send over precious gifts to the Prince and Princess by the hand of the Earl of Leicester — a golden dove for Charlotte encrusted with jewels, and a golden lizard for William. The dove symbol was obvious, but Charlotte puzzled over the lizard until she remembered Pliny's story, that the watching lizard protects the sleeping lion and warns him of the serpent's approach; even so had William watched over the Belgic lion.[2] But gifts and embassies were some months preparing and meanwhile the new-born Elizabeth must be baptized, so that when the ceremony took place at Middelburg on May 30th, 1577, not the magnificent Leicester, but his young nephew, stood proxy for the godparent. Philip Sidney was

[1] Gachard, III, 304.
[2] *Archives*, VI, 190.

twenty-three years old and enthusiastic for William's cause — without a shadow of diplomatic reserve. The meeting was an unmitigated success.

Not only was the Queen of England now extending a gracious hand, but the Duke of Anjou was taking an almost embarrassing interest in the development of events — embarrassing because his interest, as William well knew, was purely selfish; he wanted a principality of his own and fancied the Netherlands, though whether to oust Don John as the candidate of the southern nobility, or to usurp William's position he was as yet undecided. On the pretext of drinking the waters at Spa, his pretty sister Margot set off on a summer progress through the southern provinces, keeping her eyes and her ears open, and her mouth shut. In July 1577 she was at Namur where Don John fêted her and saw her on her way to Spa. What he was doing at Namur, so far from Brussels, remained a mystery until Queen Margot and her ladies were safely on their way. Then, denouncing the Estates General and the Prince of Orange for treason to King Philip, he rushed the citadel with a company of Spanish troops.

VII

William had been waiting for this, though he can hardly have expected Don John to act so foolishly or so soon. Unable to carry out the terms of the Perpetual Edict and unwilling to carry out those of the Pacification, Don John had played for time until he could play for time no longer. He had hoped that the southern nobility would unanimously join him, but he had reckoned neither on their egoism nor on their genuine doubts, and had failed utterly to realize how small a group they were. He had failed also to understand how bitterly the people felt against the King of Spain, and how strong for once they were, not only in their representatives in the Estates, but in the great numbers of local volunteers which each city had raised as a defence against the Spanish mutineers.

The rash seizure of Namur precipitated a crisis fatal to Don John. His few troops were driven out of cities and villages, Antwerp as always leading in the uproar. Here as soon as the Spanish soldiers had been expelled, the entire working population fell to and demolished the citadel. Alva's statue, discovered in one of the vaults, was hacked in pieces by the delighted mob, and trundled through the main streets. From Brussels the Estates General sent immediately to William, imploring him to take over the government.

Still he hesitated. His only surviving brother, John, was on his way from

Dillenburg to visit him in the Netherlands; to him William intended to entrust the northern provinces if he had to go south. But he still hesitated, misdoubting this colossal burst of popular enthusiasm and fearing lest he should jeopardize the national cause by entering the South as a demagogue. He did not believe that a stable settlement could be born in the present uproar, and since Don John had committed political suicide, he could afford to wait until the initial storm abated and he could see his way more clearly.

In any case if Holland and Zealand, his devoted provinces, were to be left, even for a short time, he would have to gain their consent and leave their affairs in good order. All the month of August he toured the cities, settling outstanding problems. At Utrecht, but recently come into the Union, and much divided in religion, Charlotte feared trouble. With victory and increasing power, the dangers to her husband's life were also increasing. Utrecht received them joyously with a salute of cannon, but a fragment from one of the guns struck their coach as it passed, and Charlotte, throwing herself in front of her husband in sudden terror, cried 'We are betrayed!' He had soothed her all in a moment and no one took the incident amiss — indeed the unsolicited evidence of wifely devotion pleased the people — but ever afterwards William strove to prevent the firing of salutes: usually in vain.

By mid-September he bade her farewell. As far as his personal life was concerned this call to the South had come at the wrong moment, for in spite of Juliana's unwillingness to let them go his three elder children, Marie, Anna and Maurice, were on their way to join him escorted by their uncle John. Only the youngest, Emilie, eight years old, was left behind with her grandmother. The home planned by Charlotte was at last coming into existence, but the Prince of Orange had no right to a home, no right to be a father to his own children, since he had to be a father to a people. He could wait only to greet his brother John and the children at Gertrudenberg, on his way to the South, and to present the children to their stepmother and two little sisters, before he had to leave them.

Charlotte's letters followed, warm and reassuring: 'We love each other very much', she wrote, 'and are very happy together.' 'Our daughters, big and little,' she called them; hers, as well as his. It was five years since he had seen any of them. Marie was already twenty-five, fragile and sweet as her mother had been, but with more gravity. Charlotte made her at once her special friend, and soon her letters were full of the doings of 'Mademoiselle d'Orange et moi'. Anna was fourteen, round and blonde and smiling; Maurice was not quite ten, flaxen-haired like his mother, reserved, alarmingly intelligent — of a *divinum ingenium*, said his tutor — but his health was an anxiety. He suffered from boils on the neck, which Charlotte took in hand at once, and successfully.

Within a little, however, William was planning for them all to rejoin him. Breda had been given back to him: damaged, empty, changed, but still his home. How much he felt it to be his home is clear from his immediate suggestion that Charlotte with all the children should take up their residence there. What he had quietly planned with his wife we cannot know, perhaps some family reunion at Christmas like the happy days of his youth. It was not to be, for in the seven remaining years of his life he was to pass a few nights only at Breda, so intense, so unrelaxing the pace of his political duties.

But now the South would wait no longer; by ship to Oudenbosch, and thence on horseback he travelled towards Antwerp where on the morning of September 18th, 1577, he made his entry to the resounding cheers of the people. Crying with joy, they crowded round the man they had not seen for more than ten years. 'His last departure was not more doleful than his return was now joyful,' said the English agent Davison, himself deeply moved. The people accompanied him all the way to his lodging, letting off pistols and arquebuses until the air was thick with smoke. The town council implored him to stay but, as he said that night privately to Davison, if he stayed in Antwerp people would soon be saying that he was exploiting the support of one city to make himself a demagogue. He might return to Antwerp, but his first duty was to present himself to the Estates in Brussels.[1]

Two days later he travelled by the new canal to Brussels. It was a triumphal progress; the Antwerp guards brought him on his journey and the Brussels guards came out to meet him. All the way the canal was lined with the cheering populace, waving green branches, and throwing flowers in front of him. At every lock orange-red hangings and carpets met his eyes, and he had to stop and exclaim over the *tableaux vivants* representing apposite biblical scenes in his honour, while bands of musicians played the 'Wilhelmus van Nassouwe'. At the gates of Brussels the great men of the South were ready to meet him, and this was the least pleasant part of the day, for here were many who had played Don John's game and abandoned him only because they feared for their lives if they stood by him now. Aerschot was no friend to the Prince of Orange, but this, he knew, was not the moment to show it; his young son at his side, Aerschot welcomed smiling the man whom he had worked for eight months to keep out of Brussels.

The bad moment over, William was within the city walls, deafened almost by the acclamations of the people, and here, too, many were crying

[1] Kervyn de Lettenhove, IX, 524, 528.

with joy. In the market-place the colonels of the town guard offered him a ceremonial drink, but he would not have it unless all the officers would join him; so with laughter they toasted him in full view of the people, and everyone remembered that this had always been the way with the Prince of Orange. 'They could have done no more', Davison wrote home, 'had he been an angel from Heaven'; they 'received him *ut Pater Patriae*, for so they commonly call and account him.' All the way up the hill from the Grande Place to the Palais de Nassau, it was shouting and cheering and the cracking of pistols, right to the very gates; and since the Palais de Nassau had stood long neglected and unrepaired, several slates hurtled off the roof and some loose bricks came crashing down — though luckily no one was hurt — at the merciless and reiterant vibrations.[1] Of the empty rooms hastily furnished with necessities, of the overgrown garden, the neglected courtyards, we hear nothing in accounts of that glorious day, as little as we know of the doubts and anxieties, the memories and the hopes, the alternate joys and griefs which must have swelled and constricted the heart of William of Nassau. Politics and the immediate future were foremost in his mind, but what panorama of his past must not the remembered streets of Brussels have evoked — here he had grown up, here tasted the first sweets of life and manhood, here been first in pleasure and first in power, and here been proclaimed a traitor. Yet never among all the acclamations he had heard in his resplendent youth had he known such an hour as this, when the whole city from end to end shouted but the one name, wanted but the one man, and that man, himself.

[1] Kervyn de Lettenhove, IX, 538-9, 546; Blaes, II, 45-6.

CHAPTER VII

NO SURE FOUNDATION

1577–1579

I

W<small>HILE</small> the mob cheered and shouted outside his doors, William was already planning the first moves in his campaign to reconcile the distracted and divided South with itself and with the North, to re-create the free and ancient Netherlands. Ten years of revolt and repression superimposed on centuries of urban risings, of disputes over privileges and rivalries between burghers and peasants and nobles, of differences of religion, race and language, had ill prepared the country to be a nation. Two distinguishable groups had always existed: the French and the Flemish-speaking. The revolt and resistance of the northern provinces had added a third group by splitting the Flemish-speaking people in two and creating, in full and proud consciousness, the individuality of the Dutch nation. William's adoption of their language as the official usage of the North, although reasonable at the time, was bound to underline the fissure now that North and South were reunited. In the South, moreover, the old animosity between Walloons and Flemings, quiescent in the stress of general disaster, was gathering strength again by the autumn of 1579. Add to this, that Holland and Zealand, hammered into union through six years of heroic struggle, were unwilling to abandon their independence and return to the inferior position which they had held in the days of the South's greatness. They alone had vindicated the national greatness of the Netherlands when the South had crumpled, and — more practically important — they had built up a shipping trade in the last three years which would be hindered by reunion with the South. Still less did the South, with its more ancient traditions of wealth and domination, care to accept the North as its equal.

The religious problem, however, submerged the national. Politically the North was Calvinist, because the Calvinist minority had acquired control of the State machinery and had justified that control by successful management of the war. Politically the South was Catholic, and the existence of strong, isolated Calvinist minorities in Brussels and Antwerp, in Valenciennes, Bruges and Ghent, served only to accentuate a general distrust of the creed.

William, though he stood for toleration, had been a practising Calvinist for the last five years and had inevitably become identified with the Calvinist party simply because he was identified with the North. His root problem was therefore to hold the Catholic South without losing the Calvinist North; to unite both without sacrificing either.

His secondary problem was to keep the South politically united within itself. Unlike the ignorant Don John, he would not miscalculate for lack of knowledge; he knew all there was to know about the South, and what he knew was not encouraging. In the North the nobility had dropped into the background, while the burgher class, merging with the small landowners, ruled unchallenged. But in the South even this situation was quite un-resolved. Feudal die-hards like Aerschot might bitterly resent Spanish interference, yet they felt a far stronger loyalty to the King, as King, than they felt towards their countrymen of a lower social standing. They feared with a passionate prejudice the increasing influence of the burghers in the Estates, and hated and despised the committees of townsfolk who governed Brussels or Antwerp or Ghent and whose influence, in these troubled times, was growing rapidly. Those of the southern nobility who, like Sainte Aldegonde, had moved with the times and put their country or their faith before their private interests were already among William's supporters, had suffered exile with him, lost their southern lands and thereby their influence in the South. The class quarrel was therefore perfectly clear-cut and all the more dangerous. The second and probably the more serious trouble in the South was the Calvinist minority; liable as William knew to dangerous out-bursts, usually to be found in alliance with extremist popular groups in the cities, the Calvinists might easily, by too much enthusiasm, undermine the confidence of the majority in William's plan for union and toleration. They lacked entirely the political sense and solidarity of their northern brothers.

The military situation was for once much less worrying than the political. Don John, with the remnants of the Spanish army, was not at the moment dangerous. William's own fleet and troops had the situation by sea and land well under control. The local volunteers and the remains of that native army, which had loyally co-operated with the Spaniards until the mutiny of last summer made further co-operation impossible, were ready enough to act under the authority of the Estates and against the Spaniards. Their effective commander was Admiral Bossu, whom William had known of old during Margaret's regency, and had seen something of during the eight months in 1574 when he had held him prisoner.

Such then were the difficulties which he envisaged, such the groups whose egoism he would have to curb or delude, and whose animosities he would have to reconcile before the Netherlands could emerge from the long night of Spanish rule a united and living nation.

II

The first to greet him at the gates of Brussels had been Aerschot and the nobles; they were the first with whom he must reckon. Aerschot could not have been — for him — more friendly. In his letters to William he was now always 'your most cordial friend to serve you' and he offered a supper invitation for that very night. William accepted, and within an hour or two of his arrival in Brussels, walked across without further formality to Aerschot's house, where he remained half the night eating, drinking and making merry.

He was no longer as rich as he had been in the remote past, but he had been given some of his lands back and he could at least return hospitality more or less in the Brussels style. Quickly adaptable, he knew that the in-formal manner of Delft would not do in the capital of Brabant, where even the demagogues expected a certain style of a man in his position. He kept his habit of strolling through the streets on foot, but the entertainment at his table was lavish and frequent. Brussels had not changed its methods of doing political business, and William, with his usual naturalness and perspicacity, slipped easily back into the time-honoured ways.

On the following morning he took his place in the Estates General, by right of his lands at Breda, as one of the nobility of Brabant. The assembly without further ado voted him Stadholder of that province. It was tanta-mount to voting him Governor of the Netherlands, for the control of Brabant was by long tradition vested exclusively in the Central Government, and the offer seems to have taken him by surprise. Twice pressed, he twice refused, playing at least for time to consider the situation. But when the assembly asked him for the third time he could only accept. Watching this Caesar-like refusal of greatness with sour looks, Aerschot and his friends thought they recognized the sly *poseur* they had always distrusted. Mis-judging, as usual, both the man and the situation, they calculated that he had served their turn in getting them out of the dead end whither Don John's policy had led them; it remained now to get rid of him and start again.

Brussels was alive with intrigue and rumour. From Middelburg the anxious Charlotte wrote imploring her husband not so to expose his person; she had heard — truly enough — that he was supping and dining every day in the houses of Aerschot and his friends, or with the leading citizens of

Brussels, or the delegates from the Estates. That it was politically necessary for him to maintain close and persuasive contact with all these people she could not doubt, but must he dine with men like the Duke of Aerschot, who so notoriously disliked him, or go through the streets entirely without protection? She hid her personal fears under the guise of others' protests, for, she wrote to him, some of the citizens of Holland had particularly asked her to use her influence with him for his own safety. Soon, however, she was to share his dangers; early October found her on her way south with the children. They stopped a few days at Breda, opening up the great house and making it ready against the coming days of peace, and thence travelled on to Antwerp, where William received her and the children on October 23rd, 1577.

The happy reunion fell when a crisis was fast approaching in the political situation. Not to be outshone by the Prince of Orange, Aerschot had bullied the Estates of Flanders into making him Stadholder, later removing himself to Ghent to evolve his own plans without interference. All negotiations with Don John had been broken off, and except where his troops were in occupation he was no longer recognized as Governor. Abandoning him with the utmost callousness, Aerschot had recently made overtures to another Habsburg prince, the Emperor's brother Matthias, persuading this foolish young man that if he would but put himself in his hands he could become Governor and perhaps sovereign of the Netherlands. He planned to unite the jealous nobility and extreme Catholics — a party already beginning to be known as the Malcontents — under the figurehead of Matthias, thus to oust the Prince of Orange and become himself the acknowledged saviour of the Netherlands.

No secret could ever be kept for long in the spy-ridden South and William was very well acquainted with Aerschot's intentions. Once or twice in October certain citizens of Ghent had come to see him, notably two lawyers, both of land-owning stock, calling themselves gentry, but both in varying degrees involved with the Calvinist-popular party in Ghent. Ryhove and Hembyze were characters inspiring little confidence, Ryhove an impulsive demagogue, nervy and cruel, Hembyze a pusillanimous exhibitionist who liked to be cheered by the people and encouraged them to call him 'Junker Jan'. But they had, with all their faults, a genuine desire to see their city restored to its ancient glory; Ghent, perennially the scene of spectacular risings, had overreached itself in the time of the Emperor Charles V and been savagely quelled by the removal of all its charters. It had thus played a very minor part in the recent troubles, and was only now, in 1577, beginning to resume something of its old, obstreperous vigour. Ryhove and Hembyze had, if nothing else, at least a sincere desire to see the charters of their great city restored.

Sympathetic to this desire, but seeing with his usual perspicacity how it might be used to make an end of Aerschot, William listened to the two demagogues, and if he did not precisely give them his blessing he at least forebore to restrain them. Probably they did not tell him how far they intended to go, and perhaps at this stage they did not know themselves. In any case, no sooner did the two return to Ghent than they stopped Aerschot in the public street on his way from church and with every formality requested him as Stadholder to restore the privileges of their city. The Duke of Aerschot was a singular mixture of arrogance, indiscretion and dishonesty; of all the politicians in the Netherlands he seems to have known least when to prevaricate and when to be silent. On this occasion he bellowed indignantly, for all the street to hear, that he would emphatically *not* restore the privileges of Ghent to please the rascally burghers; no, not even if the Prince of Orange was behind them. 'Canaille!' he added superfluously.

Now no one except Aerschot had mentioned the Prince of Orange, and to drag in William's name with evident spite and at the top of his voice was not merely to give himself away but to put himself ludicrously in the wrong. For all that happened to Aerschot in the next twelve hours he had no one but himself to blame. The whole afternoon the city buzzed with indignation, and late that night, the town guard having closed the gates and made themselves masters of the walls, a handful of them broke into Aerschot's lodging with instructions from Ryhove and Hembyze to seize him. Speechless with rage, clad only in his dressing-gown, hatless and barefoot, Aerschot was marched through the streets and shut up in the citadel,[1] there to ponder the villainy of the populace and the iniquity of the Prince of Orange.

William immediately disclaimed all knowledge of the plot, but the nobility noted sourly that he did nothing immediate to have Aerschot released. He had his answer for them: why so much anxiety for Aerschot when not one of them had raised a finger, ten years before, to save Egmont and Horn? Nevertheless he persuaded Aerschot's captors to let him go as soon as he had agreed to resign his office of Stadholder in Flanders. His credit being for the moment exhausted, the haughty Duke withdrew fuming into Germany to satisfy his tyrannous nature during the next months by compelling his twenty-year-old son to marry a wealthy, invalid widow more than ten years his senior.

It was something to be so easily rid of Aerschot, but the powers which William had conjured up were not quickly to be stilled. Hembyze and

[1] Arend van Dorp, I, 208.

Ryhove once in the saddle knew no moderation; they threw all their enemies into prison, however honourable and respected, threatened devout Catholics, encouraged inflammatory sermons from Calvinist preachers, and shortly after initiated the usual sodomy proceedings against the local Franciscans. Very soon indeed William realized that whatever he had gained by the removal of Aerschot he would be likely to lose by the disastrous violence of the Ghent Calvinists. The gust of frenzy from Ghent blew up the storm clouds over all the South.

In an effort to calm the city, he decided to go thither in person, but although his reception was vociferously cordial, he could not feel any real satisfaction in it. A beautiful young maiden charmingly presented him with a gold lion set with jewels, its paw laid upon its heart on which was engraved the single word 'Sinceritas', and at every street corner he had to exclaim in appropriate pleasure at the usual *tableaux vivants*, while the batteries notified his passing with a thunderous salute. In the evening the wives of some of the imprisoned Catholic citizens came piteously to see him; they found him unexpectedly kind and altogether reassuring, and he promised that their husbands would be released. But later they cursed his duplicity, for Hembyze was confirmed as chief magistrate of the town and no one was released.[1] William's desire had outrun his authority, for in fact Hembyze controlled the town, and without provoking dangerous riots William could not remove him or even set free those whom he had seized. He had paid a heavy price to be rid of Aerschot.

III

All this while Aerschot's protégé, the young Archduke Matthias, little knowing that his protector had disappeared, was on his way to the Netherlands. He crossed the frontier on the very day of his patron's arrest, and finding no one to receive him, hung about in bewilderment at Maestricht. A hero to no one but himself, the Archduke Matthias was a pale youth of twenty, mouse-coloured, watery-eyed and effete; he liked to pose, his lanky person encased in Roman armour, a wreath of laurel rakishly tilted over the bulbous forehead, which, unmarked by eyebrows, looked higher than it was.

How was William to handle this now unattached puppet of Aerschot's? Evidently as Aerschot himself had intended: as a substitute for Don John. Matthias had distinct advantages; vain, good-natured and a fool, he could be led by the nose, so long as his vanity was appeased, a task which presented

[1] Halewyn, 73-5; Blaes, II, 125-6.

no difficulty to William. But above all, as a candidate for the nominal governorship of the United Netherlands he would satisfy the Catholic population, without making concessions to Spain or dismaying the Protestants. By supporting him, William believed that he might reassure those who had taken fright at the Calvinist excesses in Ghent and forestall a fresh landslide into the camp of Don John.

Deplorable indeed were to be the future instruments of William's policy, so deplorable that we are tempted to-day to ask why he did not proclaim himself what in fact he was, the leader of the Netherlands. The answer lies partly in his wise anxiety to avoid giving substance to a charge of personal ambition, partly in the legal sanctions of his time. Such an act would have been as false to the ancient charters of the provinces as to his own feudal obligations: all through his career he punctiliously preserved the outward forms, and wherever possible the spirit, of the ancient rights. Looking back four centuries, we see the Netherlands struggle in a foreshortened perspective, and recognize in it many of the characteristics of a national revolt, and, as a national revolt, a break with the past. But the men concerned in it were familiar only with present loyalties, with traditions which seemed natural to them because they had been bred in them, and which they did not much question. William's experience of the Netherlands convinced him that only a Protector universally recognized could reunite and stabilize the country. That Protector must come of the ancient dynasty of the Burgundian Dukes. William himself had no hereditary right to such a position and far too just a sense of the situation to put himself forward; his personal services to the Netherlands were, in this context, perfectly irrelevant, and if, in a misguided attempt to strengthen his position, he had grasped at sovereignty, he would have sacrificed the substance of his power, for the people trusted him only because he had never by word, or sign, or deed overstepped the authority which they had conceded to him.

As things now stood in Europe, William had a choice of two possible princes: the Archduke Matthias and the Duke of Anjou. Matthias, a descendant of Duke Charles the Bold, a Habsburg, and a cousin of King Philip, was legally the better candidate. Politically much depended on the help he could command from his brother the Emperor, or the opposition he called forth in Spain. In the winter of 1577-78, it seemed possible that King Philip, battered and defeated, would hand over his recalcitrant Netherlands to his young cousin. On the other hand, should Imperial help prove weak and Spanish opposition strong, Matthias might have to be discarded. The second choice, Francis, Duke of Anjou, was, personally, even less prepossessing than Matthias. Where Matthias was an inoffensive nonentity, Francis of

Anjou was egotistical, dishonest, self-indulgent and ambitious; but he was brother to the King of France and could, if he agreed to protect the Netherlands, give very considerable help. Dynastically, he came of the same family as the original Valois Dukes of Burgundy.

This was the prolonged tragedy of William's closing years; he had but two weapons to fight for the freedom of a nation: one brittle, and one whose cutting edge turned viciously against the hand which sustained it.

While William played Matthias against Philip's Don John, that prince from his retreat in Luxembourg was still active. The triumph of his great adversary, as the English agent put it, 'doth fret him to the guts',[1] but it fretted him also into further action. He was still, with one hand, offering peace to the Estates, though nobody now set any further store by these overtures. A political medal in common circulation showed the King of Spain holding out an olive branch, left-handed, to the Belgic lion, while concealing a collar and chain behind his back. 'If the King be *able* to make a war, there is no peace to be attended,'[2] the English spies reported; the Duke of Guise, leader of the extremist Catholic party in France, was hovering in a suggestive way not far from the Flemish frontier, about to bring help — so it was rumoured — to Don John. Anxiously watching events from Dillenburg, the aged Juliana, with maternal solicitude, wondered if her son fully understood the duplicity of his enemies, and wrote warning him to beware of delusive offers of peace made by 'Sattan in Schafsbelzkleyde' — Satan in a sheepskin coat.

But William feared Spanish duplicity less than Spanish force. In the autumn of 1577 reinforcements of nearly twenty thousand men were on their way under Alexander Farnese, Prince of Parma, the only son of the Regent Margaret. Parma had always been popular with the Netherlands mob, whether as a vivid attractive boy or as a fashionable young man, for he was spectacular, generous and friendly. William could recall him as he had known him in those days ten years before when he had been the central figure of the great wedding festivities which in November 1567 had been such convenient cover for the plotting of the Confederates, when he had come out of the bridal chamber to his wedding guests, lifting three fingers and laughing. Even then William had recognized, under the frivolous exterior, the real intelligence. Now, after ten years of error, King Philip had at last chosen the right man to win him back his Netherlands — and it was William's turn to be anxious.

The Archduke Matthias was a poor counterpoise for this new opponent, but no readier help was forthcoming. Francis of Anjou was universally

[1] Kervyn de Lettenhove, IX, 549.   [2] *Ibid.*, 547.

distrusted and at the present moment very cool in his attitude to the Netherlands. Elizabeth of England, whose intervention William had hoped for
rather than expected, still refused to take definite action. In the circumstances
there was nothing for it but to persuade the Estates General to elect Matthias
for their Governor under suitable guarantees. The vacuous boy was to be
no more than a figurehead, a position which he seems to have accepted
more or less with relief; politics were never to be much of a vocation for
this brainless and bewildered oaf whose destiny made him more than once
the pivot of a political crisis, and in whose amorphous reign as Emperor
Germany was to slither into the Thirty Years War, chiefly because he could
not imagine how to stop it.

Everything, however, in the Netherlands depended on the Prince of
Orange, to whose guidance Matthias yielded an almost touching confidence.
The governing authority was vested in a council chosen by the Estates, on
which Sainte Aldegonde should represent William's voice. He would not
have a place himself, presumably to hold himself independent in case of some
crisis. His direct authority was still, strictly speaking, the Stadholdership of
Brabant, though to this was now added, by overwhelming and irresistible
demand of the Estates, the chief command of the joint armies of North and
South.

On January 19th, 1578, he escorted Matthias from Antwerp to Brussels,
to present him to the people and the Estates. The new Governor was well
received, though the greater part of the cheering was probably not for him;
nevertheless his vaguely good-humoured expression was appreciated and
William took care to show him the most explicit and punctilious reverence.
When, as the first nobleman of Brabant, he knelt in the traditional position
to swear fealty to Matthias enthroned under a crimson canopy, it was noted
how low he bowed his head over the Archduke's hand, barely lifting it to
touch his lips.

IV

Eleven days later, Parma justified William's estimate of his abilities by
attacking the camp of the Estates' army at Gembloux while far too many of
the officers were merrymaking in the capital, scattering the troops and
heading immediately for Brussels. William hastily manned the outer defences and transferred both the Estates and the Archduke rapidly to Antwerp,
but a dispute in the Spanish command saved the situation. Don John, supported by most of his staff, thought it wiser to settle the outlying districts

first, and Brussels gained a reprieve while Parma carried his victorious arms into the southern, French-speaking provinces. Nivelles, Beaumont, Chimay, Philippeville, Limburg, Daelhem — the catalogue of disasters lengthened, while William, now in the distressed gathering of the Estates General, now with the angry town councils of Antwerp and Brussels, now among the mutinous and despondent troops, strove as he had done so often before to re-establish the confidence of the people. It was no easy task. Torn by internal division, the South needed the cement of easy victory to hold it together, and because William had been acclaimed all too vociferously as a saviour, the first setback jerked even his supporters into jangling discord. The Calvinists recalled how he had refused to help John Marnix outside Antwerp in 1567, and in the army the officers, many of them young Catholic nobles, began to ask themselves how it was they had agreed to fight for the Estates and the Prince of Orange. Things had changed since the great Spanish Mutiny, the resulting outcry against foreigners, and the decision of the native army in the South to band itself with the North against the Spanish intruders. *Then* there had been no royal Governor save the insignificant Roda, no Spanish army save a mutinous rabble. *Now* there was a fine soldierly commander, Parma, under whom any officer would be glad to serve. It was unreasonable in such circumstances, they argued, to expect them to stand by obligations undertaken so long before and to fight under the command of the Prince of Orange, a man whom they had in the past repeatedly vanquished. Only perhaps through the rigid loyalty of the more experienced officers, above all of his chief of staff, Admiral Bossu, did William manage to prevent the disintegration of his southern forces during the disastrous spring of 1578.

With a disillusioned army, with the Estates frightened, sullen, and therefore unreasonably unwilling to vote money even for their own defence, outside help had never been more desperately needed. This was where William had hoped that the Archduke Matthias would help, for his own brother, the Emperor Rudolf, would surely support him. But Rudolf dallied and, hoping to engage the princes of Germany in the undertaking, preferred to call the Imperial Diet before making a decision. William closeted himself with the indefatigable Sainte Aldegonde, drawing up an appeal at once factual, persuasive and eloquent to move the lethargic senses of the Germans. In vain. Even the convincingly clear and pointed arguments which Sainte Aldegonde manipulated so well would not move them to vote supplies to their Emperor's brother for the assistance of the Netherlands. This was their chance, had they but seen it, to destroy the Spanish menace, to break the house of Habsburg in two, pitting the Austrian against the Spanish branch; but the princes of Germany could not see beyond two preliminary facts — that they would be doing the Emperor's brother a favour and making the Prince of Orange uncommonly powerful. 'They have let the Prince of Orange move too close to the net to be willing to play ball with him,' wrote one of the Rhenish delegates.[1] The German princes — Calvinist and Lutheran and Catholic — could not bring themselves to forget that the hero and liberator of a nation, the hope of Protestant Europe, was by birth nothing but a count of Nassau, of the Dillenburg line moreover, and the younger branch, and therefore to be kept strictly in his place. So the Diet broke up with no help for the Netherlands, and all that the Emperor Rudolf could suggest was a conference at Cologne to settle the difference between Philip and his subjects over the council table, himself as mediator.

v

Perhaps in the dearth of courage and decision which afflicted the German rulers one should be grateful even for the irresponsible activity of that John Casimir, Calvinist soldier of fortune and younger brother of the reigning Elector Palatine, with whom William had served in the French campaign of 1569 and who had once thought of marrying Charlotte. He aimed at being the Protestant Don John, and was never happier than when careering about somebody's country valiantly, if erratically, defending the Protestant Cause. Save the Netherlands? Of course he would. Writing simultaneously to Elizabeth of England for financial help, he offered his sword and services to the Estates General. In their present straits they could hardly refuse, and, the Calvinist minority overriding the Catholic majority, on May 29th, 1578, they accepted John Casimir's offer.

William found no comfort in this new ally. He had never in the past thought very highly of John Casimir, but quite apart from personal misgivings, he was more than ever anxious to hold the balance fairly between Catholics and Calvinists; a notorious and irresponsible Calvinist was thus the last ally he would have chosen, when all his tact and judgment barely served to retain the loyalty of the Catholic majority. On this majority in the long run depended the reunion and solidarity of the Netherlands, and it was therefore with the very definite intention of counterbalancing John Casimir's unsought alliance that William turned to listen to overtures from France.

Meanwhile the Duke of Anjou was again spying about for an advantage,

[1] Bezold, II, 295-6.

smiling graciously on all envoys from the Netherlands at his brother's Court and much encouraged by his mother, who wanted to see him settled. Anjou cared nothing for the cause of the Netherlands, but he liked the idea of independence and a kingdom; all that spring he had kept a couple of envoys dancing attendance on the Estates, whetting their appetite with vague offers of goodwill, trying to create a party for himself in the Netherlands. That proved beyond the power of his envoys, for public opinion was so unfavourable to Anjou that he was even credited with a plot to assassinate the Prince of Orange and make himself sole ruler of the Netherlands. The negotiations hung fire from May to June 1578, when Anjou decided that his hour had struck, and trailing an enormous suite of guards, servants, ushers, pages, and his usual quota of favourites, appeared uninvited at Mons. William knew what use to make of him; that Anjou's intervention was purely selfish, he did not doubt, but it was at least apposite, for help was grievously needed, and Catholic help was especially welcome. Moreover, though Anjou was an uncertain friend, he would be a dangerous enemy. Making a mouthful of the unpalatable pill, William persuaded the Estates to accept the proffered alliance. Anjou promised ten thousand infantry and three thousand cavalry for three months; he guaranteed freedom of conscience and, on persuasion, withdrew his initial demand for certain towns as security. In return he was presented with a title which William had ingeniously invented for him: Defender of the Liberties of the Netherlands. All that he had achieved was to stake out a claim to the reversion of Matthias' position.

While the agreement with Anjou was still being debated, John Casimir's coming had already cast its shadow before it. At Bruges, Antwerp and Brussels the mob broke loose against the Catholics, and at Ghent, uneasily calmed in the previous winter, the Calvinist minority silenced the less enthusiastic members of the town council, attacked or closed the Catholic churches, drove out and imprisoned monks, priests and devout citizens. Hembyze and Ryhove, now in control of the Council, listened to no prompting save that of the mob and an irresponsible Calvinist preacher, Dathenus, who had the mob at his bidding.

The outburst could not have happened at a more distressing moment. Unwearyingly present among the troops, riding from the camp only to the councils of the Estates, dictating letters on twenty different details within a morning, receiving envoys, considering reports from North and South, from Parma's camp and his own, William strove through it all to impose his larger ideas of unity on the small separatist factions, to mould and influence daily events towards that end alone. This question of religion lay at the heart of all; if that could be fairly settled — as by the Pacification of Ghent had been laid down — then the chief threat to the re-established unity of the provinces would vanish. William had planned to deal with it at leisure, when autumn brought the war to its seasonal halt. 'If they of Ghent had not so suddenly broken forth', he said to the English ambassador, 'the matter might have been stayed till the end of September.'[1] Now the Calvinists insisted on an immediate and therefore an ill-considered settlement for which the country could not be properly prepared.

In the general haste and anxiety William had little time to receive the English embassy which Elizabeth had at last sent. Walsingham, for the past five years the persistent advocate of the Dutch cause in England, was hurt at this neglect; he had come expecting an effusive reception from a prince of whose courtesy he had heard so much, and for whom he felt he had worked devotedly. But when at last the interview took place he was disarmed and convinced by William's frankness. The disappointment, he saw now, was more justly on William's side; Elizabeth had wavered, retreated, promised and retreated again. She had said she would send Leicester and an expeditionary force, and had sent neither; she had talked of loans but done little. While William fully understood and appreciated the sympathy of individual Englishmen he was, he explained, 'loth to open his intentions to those of whose assistance he is doubtful'.[2] Walsingham was too just and too intelligent a man not to see the force of this.

On his way to Antwerp Walsingham had sagely noted the temper of the villages and townships through which he passed. They were in great part Catholic and he gathered a clear impression of the suspicion and anger of the greater number of the citizens at the new settlement and the arrogant claims now put forward by the Calvinists. The truth was that, as always when hope dawned for the Protestants of the South, the exiles were coming home. The Netherlands are small, and East Anglia or Cologne but two or three days' journey away; thus it was no great trouble for the restless, fanatical fringe of exiles who had never settled down either in the North or the Rhineland or England to come home again. These people, inevitably, were the throwouts of society, men whose passions and angularities had made them incapable of beginning a new life abroad and who were drawn back to their old haunts not by the desire for home or the hope of taking up lives which had been broken by Alva's coming, but simply by the need for change and disturbance. Most political parties attract such a fringe and it was the misfortune of the Netherlands to be so placed geographically, and so ordered economically, as to encourage the growth of this group.

[1] Kervyn de Lettenhove, X, 573.   [2] Ibid., 590.

While these people inflamed the mob, William's every movement and gesture, the slightest expressions of his countenance even, were suspiciously watched. Did he leave the Estates looking confident or depressed, merry or grave, did he smile on such a one, or speak a phrase aside to such another — all was reported, whispered and speculated on in the market-place and taverns of Antwerp and Brussels and in widening circles, day by day, throughout the Netherlands.[1] Wherever he was known to be, the populace collected, sometimes to cheer, more often now to observe and criticize. During a dinner party at the Palais de Nassau on a hot summer day he left the table and stood for a few minutes by a window, his profile to the street, talking with Leoninus: he looked tired and stern. Aha! the people whispered, the old fox Leoninus was trying to trap him in the Catholic interest.[2]

His private life had for the time being almost ceased to exist. Charlotte and the children had been for some months at Breda, she joining him when she could for brief visits, jolting over the roads in a springless sixteenth-century coach for half a day to be with him for a few hours. But she was pregnant again and after the spring this kind of journey grew impossible for her. She moved to Antwerp for her lying-in, bringing the children with her. Young Maurice had been joined for companionship by his cousin, Philip, John's son, a year older than himself and his devoted friend. John himself moved between North and South, acting as Stadholder of Gelderland officially, unofficially as his brother's confidant and adviser. In the last months they had grown much nearer to each other, though John's harsher temperament and aggressive obstinacy could never make him so valuable an ally as Louis had been. His unswerving Calvinism, too, made him sometimes an embarrassment, though sometimes, admittedly, an asset: when he went to Ghent William usually took John as his companion. Then there was the favourite sister Catherine, who with her husband the Count of Schwartzburg, was now almost permanently in William's circle. But his days were too full to relish the pleasure of their company, and even family events had to be considered in the light of their political repercussions. So far his entire household practised their Calvinist religion in absolute privacy, thus meticulously keeping to the Pacification of Ghent. Not until the religious settlement was officially discussed and confirmed by the Estates would William take advantage of his position to make an exception of his family.

It was policy, of course, directed at reassuring the Catholic majority,

[1] See Blaes, II, passim.

[2] Blaes, II, 308–10; the anonymous writer of these memoires has evidently confused occasions, for he states that William was entertaining at this party on June 13th, 1578, Aerschot, Chimay and the English ambassadors, none of whom were in the country at this time. Nevertheless the glimpse of William with Leoninus at the window, and the popular reaction to it, ring very true.

but as the months passed he realized that without concessions to the Calvinist minority he would precipitate more immediate trouble in the South than could be forestalled by propitiating the Catholics. Ghent and the mob were forcing his hand. At the end of July 1578 a truncated religious settlement was pushed through the Estates; it granted roughly what the Accord of 1566 had granted — rights of worship within the cities to the Protestant sects. This was too little for the Calvinist extremists who wanted their religion exclusively everywhere, and too much for the Catholics who saw themselves exposed to demands for the use of their churches backed as often as not by mob violence.

William's temporizing policy was failing. Here and there he was even forced to take monks and priests into protective custody — and it really was protective custody, though the Catholics represented it as plain imprisonment. Early in August John Casimir crossed the frontier with his troops — an undisciplined band of freebooters who overran the country round Ghent while he himself entered the city to the jubilant acclamations of the people. Catholic opinion was beginning to crystallize, not in support of the insignificant Matthias but in support of Parma and Don John. Already the Walloon provinces were breaking away, as Parma ingeniously played up their traditional rivalry with the Flemish group.

How far this difference of language meant anything fundamental at this time is still an undecided question: certainly William underestimated its significance, knowing in a sense too well that the joint interests of Fleming and Walloon lay in union. A fluent linguist himself, able to change from French to Flemish or German without so much as thinking about it, he made too little of the irritation and misunderstanding caused by the simultaneous currency of two languages within the small compass of the Netherlands. Officially in the South he spoke and used French, as had always been the custom of the southern Government; French, too, was the language of his household, for Charlotte knew no other. But linguistic consciousness among the people had developed sharply since William was a young man, and while the Walloon provinces thought him too Dutch, the Flemish provinces thought him too French. His relations with Anjou scarcely improved matters; among the complex and the varied issues with which he had to deal, he was gradually playing up Anjou in order to substitute him for the wan Matthias, and thus supply a new Catholic protector. Yet he did not altogether realize that such value as Anjou had for the religious question was far outweighed by the fact that he was a Frenchman. The Calvinist minority hated him for his faith, and the Catholic majority for his nation. Had but Matthias had the personality of a Parma ... But the dispassionate justice of fate having put so remarkable a personality as the Prince of Orange on one side of the board, kept the balance for the other.

The English envoys, impressed as they were by William's pose of serenity in the midst of so many troubles, did not much care for the way things were going. Frankly William had told Walsingham that he was 'no otherwise inclined to run the course of France than extreme necessity shall lead him',[1] yet Walsingham, turning things over in his mind, felt some solicitude – not unlike Juliana – lest the benevolent prince should think too well of those with whom he had to deal. Something there must have been about William's manner, mellowed by middle age, or about the way he spoke which encouraged this impression, for later one of his Huguenot friends reproached him – 'You are too ready to think well even of those who have done you most harm.'[2] In any case Walsingham pondered the matter: 'It will behove the Prince', he reported doubtingly, 'to look substantially into the matter [of Anjou's alliance], and not to forget the late accident of St. Bartholomew's day.'[3] The late accident of St. Bartholomew's day ran continuously in the minds of street corner politicians; when in mid-August a rope-ladder was found mysteriously hidden in someone's garden in Brussels the wildest speculation gained general acceptance within a few hours: either Anjou's agents were going to murder William, or (among those who disliked William) he himself was going to do the murdering, but in any case a second eve of St. Bartholomew was at hand. August 24th passed, however, without disaster, and investigation proved that the ladder's purpose, if not innocent, had at least not been political: it was 'une échelle d'amour'.[4]

Some marked concession to Calvinist opinion seemed essential if serious disorders were to be avoided. William sought to relieve the pressure by the formal, if unostentatious, resumption of his own public worship. Charlotte had been brought to bed of a third daughter; he made it the occasion for presenting his request to the Estates to be allowed to make arrangements for the devotions of his family according to the concessions granted in the newly published religious peace; at the same time he offered his newborn daughter as a godchild to the Estates General. They accepted the honour with alacrity, and certainly with the sentimental populace the annual birth of a daughter to the Princess of Orange was to be of considerable assistance to her husband's popularity. Sons would have brought up questions of inheritance and the dynasty best kept in the background; Charlotte's little girls, on the other hand, became almost an institution, the more so that their parents made each in turn the godchild of a city or a province. Louise and

---

[1] Kervyn de Lettenhove, x, 590. [2] Duplessis Mornay, II, 378.
[3] Kervyn de Lettenhove, x, 457. [4] Analectes, XIV-XVII, 218.

Elizabeth had been born in the North, now came this third daughter, Catherine Belgica, and in the ensuing years, the tactfully named Brabantina, Flandrina, Antwerpiana. Fortunately no fears of mocking playmates have to be considered in the christening of princesses.

On a Sunday afternoon in September 1578, the infant princess was austerely baptized in the Calvinist fashion in a converted guard-room at Antwerp. William thus showed significantly his disapproval of the seizure of Catholic places of worship; if he, the Prince of Orange, wanted no more than a large empty room for his devotions, surely the Calvinists need not seize Catholic churches. The hint, broad enough, was taken by no one.

In this matter of religion William was out of key with his time. Dispassionate and philosophical always, he had become genuinely religious as he grew older, but his faith remained doctrinally formless. Calvinism had become essential in the North, and Calvinism he had adopted, but Catholic, Lutheran or Calvinist he had always worshipped the same God, a God with a decent respect for human individuality and compassion for human failings. Himself unwilling to use torture when torture was an ordinary political instrument, was it likely that he would believe in a God who consigned nine-tenths of his creation to eternal torment? He kept the outward, sober forms, took the communion in both kinds, and sitting, but thought no ill of those who received it differently. 'Calvus et Calvinista' he had joked once, passing his hand regretfully over what remained of his once thick auburn hair, 'Bald and a Calvinist'; but his Calvinism, like his baldness, was not from choice. Every so often a slip of the tongue or pen would reveal his doctrinal vagueness; more than once he referred to himself as a 'heretic', and not with cynical intent.

Even among his closest friends, even in his own family, his religious position was regarded as unsound. His widely tolerant views met with no sympathy whatever from the matriarch Juliana, or his surviving brother John, or Sainte Aldegonde; even his wife may not altogether have understood them. Charlotte, who had seen in her youth only the worst of the Catholic Church, who had struggled alone through the travail of personal conversion, was a convinced and devout Calvinist, and sometimes worried about her husband's spiritual welfare; she did not like him to miss his devotions.

So, in this summer of 1578, not one of his family or friends foresaw, as he did, the impending tragedy; not one of them helped, and most of them hindered him. John, for instance, an energetic conscientious man with no imagination, had the greatest affection for his elder brother, but frequently thought him soft, undecided, over-cautious, or merely wrong. On these

occasions John followed his own judgment, as for instance at this present time
in the Stadholderate of Gelderland where he was inopportunely encouraging
the Calvinists against the Catholics. The family occasion of the baptism
made an excuse for drawing together some of William's more tendentious
supporters and quietly discussing the problem. Besides the delegates from
the Estates, his sister Catherine of Schwartzburg and John Casimir were
godparents. Typically John Casimir presented the child's mother with a
portrait of himself set in rubies and pearls.[1] The Estates, more usefully, had
voted a dowry to the little girl.

VI

Although William had by this time partly redeemed the setbacks of the
spring, the Estates were far from solid in his favour, and Parma, rather
against Don John's will, was fishing for peace in troubled waters. But Don
John was not to agitate the Netherlands much longer with his stormy
presence; on October 1st, 1578, the eve of the eighth anniversary of Lepanto,
he succumbed suddenly to typhoid fever. Dying, he had sent for Parma
and handed over to him the insignia of his office. As soon as he was dead,
without fuss, without demands on the Madrid government, competently and
smoothly, Parma took over the command; not for some months was he
confirmed as Philip's Governor of the Netherlands, but there was never much
doubt that he would be. Even Philip could not be so stupid as to withdraw
the only man he had yet found who could take the Prince of Orange on at
his own game. Parma was a decorative personality, whose persuasive charm,
his chivalry, good nature and serene loyalty to the King, inspired confidence,
but he was also an astute politician and diplomatist. He aimed first at
separating the Walloon provinces from the Union, intending to rebuild the
country round this nucleus, and do with Artois, Hainault, Douai and Lille
what William had done six years before with Holland and Zealand.

He had his agents among the 'Malcontents' all over the country and
especially in the army, doing surreptitious damage. In the neighbourhood
of Ghent, among people dismayed by the excesses of John Casimir's troops,
they made a good harvest, and some companies of the Estates army even
exchanged their allegiance in Parma's favour. Panic spread in Ghent where
Sainte Aldegonde was vainly striving to restore order against the irresponsible influence of John Casimir and the inflammatory promptings of the

[1]Delaborde, 279.

preacher Dathenus. An angry mob, headed by Ryhove himself, stormed the prison where some of the leading Catholic citizens had been lodged, dragged out one poor old gentleman who was that moment sitting down to a dish of tripe, jostled him out of the town and hanged him on a tree. It was said, with what truth cannot now be ascertained, that Ryhove marched back into the town wearing his victim's white beard as a plume in his hat.[1]

If Sainte Aldegonde, who was in the town, could do nothing to prevent such excesses, William from the distance of Antwerp could do still less. In vain he had written sternly to the town council and reproachfully to John Casimir, pointing out how irrevocably they were compromising the cause of unity, how inevitably driving the Catholics into the arms of Parma. But they would listen to nothing but the words of the Lord as vociferously interpreted by Dathenus who was now, with many thumpings and bangings on his pulpit, asserting that the Prince of Orange was an unprincipled time-server who shifted his religion as lightly as an ornament on his doublet. John Casimir indeed wrote back with the greatest assurance that not Ghent, but Antwerp with its many Catholics, was the danger spot of the Netherlands. He was in fact privately toying with the idea of setting himself up as the Calvinist champion of Flanders and overthrowing the Prince of Orange entirely. His plans came to nothing for the reason that his troops could not be paid. Queen Elizabeth's gift had failed to materialize, while neither the Estates nor the city of Ghent had anticipated any call on their funds when they accepted his assistance. Disclamatory letters were bandied between them while the indignant knight-errant waited in vain. Both at last appealed to William. The extremists of Ghent might abuse him, the Estates doubt his wisdom, but the least dispute brought them running to him to settle it.

William was not particularly enthusiastic about going to Ghent, not wishing to be served as Aerschot had been. Accordingly, he took the pre-caution of bringing a strong body of guards with him, as well as his unim-peachably Calvinist brother, John — physical and moral support. Of the two men in power at Ghent, Ryhove was wholeheartedly for William; not so Hembyze, who made a last effort to raise the town against him, and would have called in Parma and the 'Malcontents' themselves to serve his personal ambition. His *coup* failed, and on December 2nd, 1578, William made his formal entry.

Outside the town the usual crowd of idle citizens, headed by John Casimir and the rivals Hembyze and Ryhove, had gathered to welcome him. Getting out of his coach, followed by his brother John, he walked over to greet them, gave his right hand to Hembyze, a courtesy which took

[1] Halewyn, 92-5.

he councillor aback, and offered John Casimir a lift in his coach, whereat Hembyze, bustling forward, would but for an adroit movement of William's have scrambled in beside them. Riding disconsolately alongside he strove, by leaning and poking his head down, to join in the conversation, but William, with a skill born of years of practice, avoided his eye during the whole of the journey, and, in spite of several false starts both from John Casimir and Hembyze himself, discussed the weather in considerable meteorological detail. All the way, the people, in a manner wholly gratifying to William and disturbing to Hembyze, shouted 'Vive le Prince d'Orange!'

Nevertheless William thought it wisest to guard against possible treachery, and posted soldiers round Hembyze's house that night. It was evident that Hembyze would never again be appointed to a position of trust, and a crestfallen demagogue waited obsequiously on the Prince at eight o'clock on the following morning, with the rest of the town council. William summed up the situation briskly, explaining the dangers which threatened the united country and pointing out the folly of irresponsible conduct at such a moment. Gradually he turned the edge of his speech towards Hembyze, thus cleverly exonerating the other councillors and isolating his chief opponent. Building up from advice to reproach and from reproach to accusation, he demanded to know what precisely Hembyze imagined he was doing in encouraging the 'Malcontent' troops. Hembyze, conscious of a general coldness and the Prince's eyes relentlessly fixed upon him, became engrossed in tickling the ears of the white pug dog, the famous Kuntze, which had trotted in at William's heels and was now curled up under the table. He made no answer.

So far, so good. 'As always happens in places where popular feeling runs high', William wrote, 'some few, relying on the natural ardour of the people, will thrust them into doing things which infringe the common duties we owe to each other . . . but experience has taught me that this number is very small.'[1] So in Ghent his intention was to isolate this minority and thus bring the rest to a cooler state of mind. That very night he continued his campaign when at dinner with John Casimir and the leading citizens. This time it was John Casimir he intended to expose, deliberately choosing a time when the heating effect of wine could be drawn into account to cover any unusual violence of expression. As John Casimir grew unsteady, William gave the conversation an uncomfortable twist, quite suddenly telling him that his behaviour had been abominable. John Casimir opened his mouth to reply, but was no longer master of his tongue, and William immediately asked him

[1] Gachard, IV, 124.

whether he regarded it as consonant with honour and friendship to accuse him of atheism and pagan self-indulgence? Shamed by this evidence of his past indiscretion John Casimir was silent, but one of his people imprudently intervened, with obsequious denials. To the amazement of everyone, William, the suave, the diplomatic, the silent, swung round on him — 'Lick-spittle!' he said, with finality, 'Canaille!' the only words of frank abuse ever recorded from those judicious lips.[1]

John of Nassau, who believed in decisive action rather than finesse, was impressed; he had not credited his brother with such capacity for anger. On Sunday, the Prince's party went ostentatiously to a church in which Dathenus did not preach, and he was heard to say — still in a rage — that he would have the slandering rogue whipped out of town. The threat was never imple-mented, but Dathenus, the once valiant spokesman of the Lord, was now explaining to everyone likely to repeat it that he had never intended the least disrespect to his Excellency.

The chief troublemakers were now divided and scattered, but there were still 'so many different humours', as William wrote to Charlotte, that 'it needs time to bring all to reason'.[2] He worked at it patiently for nearly six weeks, until John Casimir had made the best of his way to England to see if he could raise funds and his troops had deserted to Parma — to be rid of him even at this price was cheap. Meanwhile the Catholics of Ghent had to be given reasonable assurance of safety and as many of their places of worship as William could persuade the Calvinists to give up. In securing release of those who had been arrested he was far less successful.

It all took time, and time was what William could least afford. Early in January 1579 Charlotte rejoined him, and it is probable that he would have prolonged his stay in Ghent some little time longer to have a thoroughly secure settlement, but on the 9th he was vehemently recalled to Antwerp: the strategic situation had grown suddenly worse when Parma, with careful forethought, cut the trade route between Antwerp and Cologne, thus delivering yet another disastrous onslaught on the crumbling fabric of Antwerp's commercial greatness. There had been rioting and William's soothing presence was urgently needed.

Altogether the year had opened badly. All the winter Parma had been conducting negotiations with the delegates of the Walloon provinces, and in the New Year faced William and the Estates with the so-called Treaty of Arras by which Lille, Douai, Orchies, Hainault and Artois proclaimed their union under his protection in the common interest of good government and good order. William was only a fortnight behind; he had sent

[1] Bezold, II, 330-2.   [2] Delaborde, 180.

his brother John to Utrecht to prepare an equivalent alliance as a counter-poise to Parma's plans. The Union of Utrecht, signed in February 1579, joined the provinces of Holland, Zealand, Friesland, Utrecht and Gelderland for the same purpose, but under the Prince of Orange.

History was to give these rival Unions a significance far different from their original purpose. Because of certain military accidents and political complications, that union of the entire Netherlands for which William had hoped was never to be achieved. Arras and Utrecht were to become each the starting-point of a separate State. But the fatal division between North and South did not occur in this year 1579 and neither the treaty at Arras nor that at Utrecht was meant to precipitate it. William on his side, as Parma on his, each intended his Union as a magnet ultimately to attract all the provinces of the Netherlands. But the basis of each separate Union was religion: Arras was in essence the Catholic protest, as Utrecht was the Calvinist, against the policy of toleration. Theoretically either might have served for the nucleus of a reunited Netherlands; in practice neither would do so, for uncontrollable forces, already fatally gathered together, were to prevent for ever the closing of that fissure which had developed so fast during the last decade and which was to become a chasm during the next.

The struggle was changing its character: the Netherlands against Spain was becoming the Calvinists against the Catholics. Once the religious issue submerged the political, William's ideal of the restored and reunited Netherlands was irretrievably lost. The winter of 1578-79 marked the turning of the current; so much is clear in the perspective of time, but it was not clear to William, still in the midst of events, still fighting for a cause the relinquishment of which would have meant the betrayal of all he valued. While accepting in principle and thankfully the work his brother John had done in bringing about the Union at Utrecht, he protested against the strongly Calvinist aspect of some of its clauses. It was a point on which, more and more strongly, he did not agree with his brother: history was to prove John right. But it might not have done so; for as long as William lived, re-union was the object of his policy and re-union was never wholly impossible. Anxious but never hopeless, he died in the belief that the Nether-lands would rise again, as they once had been, for strong as is the pressure of events, nothing in the history of mankind is truly inevitable.

VII

Back at Antwerp William found a despondent and angry city, not in the least comforted by the insignificant presence of their nominal Governor, the foolish Matthias, and indignant at the rising prices of provisions which had followed the encampment of its own defending army in the neighbourhood. The Estates and the towns had continued the whole of the previous year extremely recalcitrant in voting money. As Charlotte had despairingly written to her husband, they could so well have spared the personal tributes, the banquets, the *tableaux vivants*, the presentation goblets and bales of rich materials proudly offered by smiling burgomasters, if they would but have voted that money's worth to the army.

By the spring of 1579 the troops were already mutinous; in the previous autumn Admiral Bossu had died, a loss which William felt very keenly, for not only was he an old and personal friend, but the most experienced soldier in the service of the Estates, and one who held the army as no one else could. Some of the foreign volunteers, too, were giving trouble. A Hungarian captain left precipitately after a stormy scene with the Prince of Orange and the English volunteers became exceptionally difficult, setting an example of insubordination which was likely to infect the whole army. It was an ugly situation, with Parma's front line now within reach of Antwerp and the peasants of Flanders taking arms to defend themselves against the excesses not of the Spaniards but of the native troops, and William needed something different from his usual good nature to maintain his authority as general. He had given John Casimir and the demagogues of Ghent the rough side of his tongue with salutary effect, and he gave some of his English troops as sharply to understand that his approachability was not to be exploited, when three or four of them came lurching up to him as he was making one of his frequent tours of the camp, demanding their pay with menaces. William, with unexpected adroitness, seized the foremost by the collar, smacked his face vigorously, and with the words 'Allez, mutins', walked immediately on.[1] Whatever the strict justice of the action, it was evidently in the circumstance the only possible line of conduct to restore some kind of order and respect.

In a crisis, however, the foreign volunteers were still reliable. In February 1579, to the dismay of Antwerp, Parma's advance-guard appeared within sight of the walls, and for a few hours it looked as though the assault would be given to the city. William was ceaselessly on the walls, too busy and too anxious to care that the fickle mob screeched and hissed at him as

[1] Blaes, IV, 54.

he passed, though he took the elementary precaution of having his guards with him. Trenches were hastily thrown up across Parma's advance, and when on March 1st, before daybreak, the Spaniards opened the attack they were met by resistance of startling ferocity, directed by the Prince of Orange from the city walls. The brunt of the fighting fell on the English and French auxiliaries, Parma having been almost right in his belief that the native army and the citizens were altogether divided and mutinous. But their failing morale was negative only; it did not lead them to betray their own city as he had undoubtedly hoped, and within a little he drew off, unable any longer to keep up an attack so far from his base.

Spring brought presage of disaster, summer brought fulfilment, both in strategy and in politics. In March more Calvinist rioting occurred in Ghent and Haarlem, and on Ascension Sunday, William came out of his guard-room chapel to hear that while he and his family had been at prayers the town guard, in an access of Calvinist zeal, had forcibly prevented the cathedral clergy and congregation from performing their usual procession, and hunted them back into the cathedral, where they were holding them prisoners. The Archduke Matthias and his entire suite, who were among the congregation, had been for the last two hours shivering with apprehension in the choir. Taking his own lifeguard, William rode immediately to the cathedral, pushed himself a passage through the besiegers, and rescued the prisoners, escorting them home well ringed-about by his own lifeguard. No harm was done to him, not a stone was thrown, but there were menacing shouts of 'Who killed John Marnix?'[1] Whether the incident of Marnix's death in 1567 was remembered or forgotten was always the best index to William's popularity in Antwerp, and certainly he had never been less loved than in this summer of 1579.

Money was the vicious circle wherein his troubles ran, for the Estates and the cities refused to grant the subsidies which alone would keep their army strong, contented and well-armed; then when the first advance of the enemy destroyed the shaken morale of the troops, when rioting and mutiny broke out, when the country began to wail at the indiscipline of the soldiery, and the peasants to take arms against them, *then* the Estates and the cities self-righteously declared that it was no use subsidizing so disreputable a force, accused and abused the officers and the Prince, but still held back supplies. With the French auxiliaries in the previous year had come the famous La Noue, already a soldier of high reputation and soon to be the author of his classic *Discours Militaires*; as chief of staff in succession to Bossu, La Noue strove to check the rot in the half-defeated army which was all the defence

[1] Blaes, IV, 279.

remaining to Flanders and Brabant. A stern Huguenot, known to his contemporaries as 'Bras de Fer', La Noue was calm, just and a disciplinarian. Though without money he could do little to stop the incessant pillaging of the peasants, he could at least tighten the control of the troops, get rid of that 'mass of whores' he had complained of to William when he first reached the army, and see to it that the roads were no longer 'choked with drunkards and the air echoing with blasphemy'.[1] But money was the vital question; and no money came.

In June 1579 William called the city councillors of Antwerp to an emergency meeting. Parma had been for nearly three months before Maestricht and unless generous relief could be sent immediately the garrison must surrender. This meant troops, munitions, guns, transport: it could not be done without money. Almost the whole day William argued the vital necessity of a loan, to be met by querulous reproaches for the bad condition of the army, and the absurd suggestion that it would be better to send the volunteer town guard. No one knew the mettle of such volunteers better than William; they could manage very well to barricade a handful of frightened courtiers and unarmed priests in the cathedral; but relieve Maestricht in the teeth of Parma . . . ? He did not say so in words. Covering his face with his hands, he sank wearily into his chair, unable to argue further. 'Do as you will', he said, 'but do not blame me when Maestricht falls.'[2] Ten days later Maestricht fell.

They blamed him then not only for Maestricht, but for all else, for what he had done and not done, for what he was and for what he was not. At least he had no illusions, closing his eyes and ears to nothing that was said of him: by the Calvinists that he took bribes from the Catholics, by the Catholics that he took them from the Calvinists; that he wasted public funds on his family, that he was sacrificing all the Netherlands to the sole interests of Holland, that he intended to set himself up as absolute ruler. . . .

He had learnt in his maturity to observe the swift changes of popular favour dispassionately and without resentment and could write of them with cynical calm. Yet, he kept his faith, for he still believed that out of so many contradictory factions he could make a united nation.

VIII

Gradually the storm died down. Parma came no farther; as after Gembloux, William managed yet again to stabilize the front and hold him off

[1] La Noue, 89.   [2] Blaes, IV, 184.

from Brabant and Flanders. With the finances in chaos, with the army mutinous, with the southern nobility intriguing simultaneously with Parma and clamouring for offices from the Estates, he could hardly have done more. Meanwhile his strategy in the Estates General was masterly; here, week by week, he regained the ground he had lost.

So persuasively had Parma made use of propaganda that, earlier in the year, the Spaniards had declared the Prince of Orange beaten at his own game. Using a lie covered over by a superficial appearance of truth, Parma persistently asserted that the King would have given his people peace had not the Prince of Orange alone prevented it. There was certainly some truth in this, for William had discounted the Perpetual Edict and persuaded the Estates to break with Don John. He had done this because, quite rightly, he had not trusted Philip's offers, knowing by experience that they were, in his mother's simple words, 'Satan in a coat of sheepskin'. But how prove that? He could only appeal to the people to trust his judgment, rather than Philip's promises, and when defeat undermined their confidence in him, the foundations of his position were gone. How rebuild them again?

He did it, during the summer, by the exercise of absolute forbearance, refusing to exculpate himself, never in the most painful circumstances laying himself open to yet more bitter attack by too personal a defence; so all the summer he faced mutinous murmurs in the camp and embittered speeches in the Estates and the city councils of Antwerp and Brussels with a studied silence, a tacit appeal to his accusers to judge for themselves. The climax came at a meeting of the Estates General on July 28th, 1579, when an anonymous letter crammed with damaging accusations was handed in under the guise of a petition. Already William's restraint had had its effect, for the delegate who was reading it out stopped suddenly, embarrassed by its contents, and some at least of his fellows applauded his decision. But William, stretching out his hand for the document, restored silence, and with businesslike clarity completed the reading himself. When he had finished he rose to speak. Simply, he summarized what he had read. Was this, he asked, their opinion of him? If so, then he would resign and withdraw. If not, then his life and services were at their command, but he must have leave sometimes to speak his mind to them, and sometimes to be listened to. He was ready to abide by their decision, to go or stay.

It was a test case, a moment on which he had frankly staked his entire hope of holding the South. He would know now whether their blame and criticism reflected their real distrust of him (in which case he was already useless to them) or merely their general fears and their own guilt and failings. 'With one sole voice', as the report of that session tells us, the delegates implored him to stay. The members from Catholic Brabant and Calvinist Holland, from Dutch-speaking Utrecht and French-speaking Tournai, protested alike their need and their devotion. This after the preaching in the pulpits and the hissing in the streets, the black looks and the whispered words, the open criticism and the private slander which he had borne since Maestricht fell ... It meant something, this eleventh-hour vote of confidence, something more than the proof that he was still the only man in whom anything approaching universal trust could be placed. It meant that, for all the bitterness and the factions, the reunion of the Netherlands might yet be possible, and that he might achieve it.

CHAPTER VIII

'UNITED WE STAND'

1579—1581

I

THE test vote had been taken for a definite purpose. The first of those defenders whose help William had counted on for the Netherlands, the Archduke Matthias, while he absurdly continued to use the empty title of Governor-General, had become politically useless; he trailed pathetically after the Prince of Orange, hiding in his shadow from the hostility of the people.

There remained only Anjou, the titular 'Defender of the Liberties of the Netherlands', Anjou whose importance had greatly increased since he had been put forward as the prospective bridegroom for Elizabeth of England. The direct help of Elizabeth had failed to come, but should she marry Anjou she could hardly refuse him oblique support in the Netherlands which, combined with what he would bring from France, might be decisive in the war. Anjou therefore must be substituted for Matthias. Every consideration of strategy and policy pointed to it: France as an ally would cover the flank of the Netherlands and cut off Parma; France and England and the Dutch would hold the Narrow Seas; money and men had already come from Anjou, and more would follow. No ally could have been more satisfactory, had but Anjou been other than he was. The Calvinists recoiled at the thought of an alliance with a son of Catherine de Medici who had perpetrated the horror of St. Bartholomew, and the Flemish-speaking provinces resisted the introduction of a French ruler; but these objections might well have faded had Anjou himself been anything but a caricature of a Valois and a Frenchman. Nothing that anyone had seen of him and nothing that anyone could say of him was likely to reconcile the Estates to his coming. Yet come he must, for without his help the inexhaustible forces of Spain would gradually, inevitably, beat down the fighting Netherlands. William put the case for Anjou on the only grounds he could, on those of pure necessity, and sought to carry the Anjou alliance on the shoulders of his own popularity.

That was why he had engineered that vote of confidence in July, so that in August, province by province, the Anjou alliance might be gingerly put forward.

Sainte Aldegonde first pressed the claims of the unseemly champion at Utrecht, saying as little as he could of Anjou, but crisply outlining the quandary in which the Netherlands now stood. They had all seen Imperial mediation fail; the congress gathered at Cologne under the aegis of the Emperor Rudolf to bring peace to the Netherlands had proved only that Philip would not offer terms which his people could accept. With Parma so strong in the field, though he had but four provinces, the ultimate victory of Spain seemed, if distant, yet sure, and the need to offer tolerable terms had vanished. Soon the congress was to disintegrate. Meanwhile at Utrecht Sainte Aldegonde declared the desperate need of foreign help; if they did not take Anjou on their own terms, the Estates would be forced to have Philip on his. Could they hesitate at the choice? They did hesitate, of course, out of inexperience and optimism and dislike of Anjou, arguing that they could manage well enough for themselves; had they not done so already? But it was for William and Sainte Aldegonde to make them see that such valiant revolt and desperate defence are of little avail when the opponents are ill-matched, that time was on Philip's side, not theirs, and that in the long run a small people unaided are at the mercy of a greater. They might have added that no amount of courage will help, if it is always last-minute courage, if money is rarely voted and never in large enough quantities, and forethought usually lacking.

While Sainte Aldegonde pursued his unpopular task at Utrecht, at Ghent Hembyze had acted. He had been gathering his forces ever since William had left the pacified city in the previous January. In the spring, with an outburst of image-breaking, he had again established his ascendancy. Now in August 1579 the projected alliance with Anjou gave him his cue for vengeance against the Prince of Orange. He issued a crudely phrased pamphlet unmasking the Prince as an impious traitor both to his religion and his country, bent on handing over the Netherlands to a French Catholic potentate. But the fickle mob of Ghent were sick of Hembyze and his posturings; there was strife and division in the town and William was once again called in. As his popular strength had waned for the first half of the year, now it was as steadily rising, and when he reached Ghent it was Hembyze who had to go, fleeing before his approach and taking the preacher Dathenus with him. The majority of the city councillors then cheerfully voted his final deposition from their body and for the first time in two years it seemed that Ghent would settle down to peace, order and moderation. It was the measure of William's popularity that he repeated the same success at Bruges three weeks later.

The whole of Flanders had now been brought to order, and since at about this time the annual happy event took place, William and Charlotte offered their infant daughter – the fourth girl – to the newly pacified province for a godchild. She became Flandrina.

II

The autumn of 1579 thus found William in a position strong enough to speak more sternly to the Estates and the cities. No easy and lackadaisical winter lay before them: Parma was consolidating his position fast and making ready – so it was thought – for an important spring offensive. Now was the time to reorganize and strengthen the resistance. Except when he was in the camp or inspecting and advising on the fortifications, William was present at every meeting of the Estates and his hours from dawn to evening were filled with private interviews, committees, negotiations; even walking from the assembly back to his own quarters there would be Norris of the English brigade, or one of Anjou's diplomats, or some provincial magnate deep in talk with him all the way. Perhaps it was not always necessary; he protested once in the Estates that too many people seemed to regard him as the only *deus ex machina* in every minor crisis.

It was uphill work restoring order, not only in practice but even in theory, to the muddled finances of the South. When William saw the Antwerp council about further subsidies for the coming year, they blandly met his proposition for a general levy with the suggestion of a heavy tax payable by Catholics only. Hours of argument barely convinced them that it was not merely wrong but impolitic to penalize their fellow citizens, more especially in a war fought for toleration.

On November 22nd, 1579, he opened the winter session of the Estates General and as soon as the preliminary formalities were settled laid before them an important remonstrance, drawing a grim picture of Parma's plans for the spring, and indicating the need for a thorough revision of their finances and their methods. This was no moment for quarrels and delays, since war demanded a certain sacrifice of their individuality in the interests of the country as a whole: the idea of union ran through this remonstrance like a recurrent theme. At the end William thought it wise to answer yet again Parma's personal attacks on his motives. The picture of himself as an ambitious man standing alone against the peace offers of King Philip might be untrue, but it was insidious. At Lille, not long before, the mob had trailed a puppet shamefully through the gutters shouting 'Hé, bougre de Prince';[1] such demonstrations, though in the sphere of Parma's influence,

[1] Blaes, IV, 319.

might prove infectious if not anticipated. Once again, therefore, William emphasized his personal disinterestedness, and put up his offices as Stadholder and lieutenant-general for the confirmation or annulment of the Estates. Once again and with the usual enthusiasm they confirmed his power; but they failed to take up his financial suggestions with the same immediacy or heat.

So the winter wore on, the short, raw days spent one after another in session with the delegates. On Sundays only, for sheer exhaustion, William had made it his rule not to attend, spending the day quietly at his devotions with his family. But by December even his Sundays could not be kept free, and on Christmas Eve itself, almost to the dawning of Christmas Day, he was with the delegates. At length on January 9th, 1580, they broke up with something — but too little — decided. To speed them on their way to their own provinces he drew up a further and more exhaustive remonstrance, which he spoke before them at their last meeting, and later, for full effect, had printed at Antwerp for general circulation. Thus he made the Antwerp press serve a double purpose, for the remonstrance was in part a demonstration and, as it were, a submission of his policy to the public, in part propaganda for the united Netherlands.

Once again he emphasized the need for some general unity, some emergency body to control and regulate the subsidies offered by each province. The problem, as he clearly stated it, was to circumvent the delays and disputes between the delegates and the local Estates who had chosen them, without curtailing the ultimate power of the citizens of individual provinces. It was a matter, largely, of administration. Too often, in these times of haste and need, did the Estates General hold up its decisions because the delegates dared not act without reference to their provincial assemblies. 'We cannot act without our masters,' they would say, and each time they said it the army in the field would have to wait another fortnight, another month, for urgent supplies. William put forward the idea of some kind of control committee with emergency powers to meet the exigencies of the war. In the past the leading nobles and the Knights of the Golden Fleece had to some extent filled this part; with their international connections, administrative experience and local prestige, they had been in a position to take important and immediate decisions where necessary. But the last ten years had altered all that. The Chapter of the Golden Fleece had lost all political significance; the patriot nobles were dead or dispossessed — there remained of all those great ones only himself, Sainte Aldegonde and Culembourg, the rest having now, almost without exception, gone over to Parma. This left the burghers and the lesser men in control of the Estates, a group more representative of the country's needs and interests, but still unused to the power which circumstance had given them, seeking always to diffuse and transfer the ultimate responsibility. There is something to be said for the easy assurance of those who have been born to rule; in a time of emergency a certain fearlessness, a certain indifference to criticism is essential. Strongly as William believed in representative government, religiously as he laid his every action open to the Estates and the cities, behind all he did was an absolute self-confidence, the natural gift of the man who, from childhood, has expected to take weighty and responsible decisions on his own authority.

III

Leaving the remonstrance to make its impression, William made a two months' tour of the North. On the way, for the first time in thirteen years, he visited his old home at Breda. Here for a little he had settled Charlotte and the children; but the rare leisure on which he had counted to revisit his house and lands had not come. Breda was never again to be his home. He stayed for two or three nights on this hurried journey in January 1580 with the Archduke Matthias as his guest, and the little town crackled and shone with fireworks for his coming, fireworks in the old tradition of his great entertainments there so long ago. So the night sky behind the great gothic church had been lit up when the Prince of Orange had been a boy of sixteen, and Philip of Spain his royal guest.

The North received him well. The majestic city of Amsterdam had thrown open its gates, its councillors having recognized at last which way the wind was blowing, and joined themselves to the rest of Holland. At the little old-fashioned Hague, once the medieval capital, now as George Gascoigne called it, 'the pleasantest village (as I think) that is in Europe', the flags were out and the cannon booming. At Delft he had indeed come home. Typically he slipped back at once, though only on so short a visit, into the fashion of the North. In the South, at Antwerp, he had lived for two years with a grandeur suited to his high offices and the southern conception of a nobleman's place; his clothes simple but rich, his household impressive, his table amply served. Crossing the frontier of Holland he was 'Vader Willem' once more, unpretentious and comfortable in his old clothes; it was in this very February of 1580 that Fulk Greville coming to Delft found him seated among the burghers, or as he put it, 'fellow-like encompassed with them'. 'His uppermost garment', the elegant Englishman observed, 'was a gown, yet such as — I dare confidently affirm — a mean-born student in our Inns of

Court would not have been well-pleased to walk the streets in. Unbuttoned his doublet was, and of like precious matter and form to the other. His waist-coat – which showed itself under it – not unlike the best sort of those woollen knit ones, which our ordinary watermen row us in.' Interesting, but more interesting still when we recollect that had Fulk Greville found him a month earlier or a month later in Antwerp, his doublet would not have been shabby nor his knitted underwear showing. This was the style of Delft, as natural to him there as the Dutch language.

His brother John, Stadholder of Gelderland, had been with him during this tour of the North, assisting him in his interviews with the city councils and delegates. The eight weeks in the North had been no holiday; many outstanding quarrels and arguments had to be resolved and in Gelderland the excessive zeal of the Calvinists, over-encouraged by John, had to be damped down. The question of Anjou needed tactful and persistent canvass-ing. Writing to their mother, John gave news of his brother as always too busy to write himself – 'His Excellency thinks often of your ladyship', he wrote, 'and sends his love to my own dear wife and the children and all his friends, but all day without respite he is weighed down and driven hither and thither by his duties so that he cannot write.' Even John with his own high standards of work was exhausted by William's mode of life, this squeezing into eight weeks of the work of as many months. 'His Excellency is, God be praised, in good health', he continued, 'but so burdened and plagued by weighty business as is hardly to be believed. Indeed he is much to be pitied and, to judge by any ordinary measure, he could not withstand the strain, but God is with him, through Whom he is able to endure so much exertion and such continual unrest . . . he hardly has time to eat or drink, seldom gets his dinner before two or even three in the afternoon and cannot sit down to table more often than once a day.'[1] But with all his labours William could not calm the religious animosities of the North, and when in the spring of this year, a foolish irresponsible, the Count of Renneberg, attempted to sell Friesland to the Spaniards, the failure of his coup precipitated outbursts of bitterness against the Catholics amounting almost to civil war.

Charlotte met him at Zierickzee on his way back to the South. They came back to an atmosphere less hostile than that of the previous summer, yet tense with a kind of hysteria. The great spring offensive of Parma had come to very little, for supplies from Spain were once more lacking. But William – unlucky as always in the misfortunes of his best men – had lost La Noue, the finest of all his soldiers, taken prisoner this spring. Persistent anxiety, doubts and rumours hung over Brussels and Antwerp, and the pro-

[1] Jacobs, 486.

longed argument over the Anjou alliance stretched nerves to the breaking point. Nobody wanted him, yet still William persisted, for the deadlock with Parma would not last for ever and some foreign help they must have.

Another more questionable benefit attended the Anjou alliance, for the fickle nobility of the South, who had chiefly gone over to Parma because they were jealous of the Prince of Orange, now began to think that to serve under a royal Governor of the ancient Valois dynasty might be more bearable and more profitable than serving under Parma and the always unappreciative Philip. They were swarming all over Brussels and Antwerp again, intriguing for power and place, and once again William was dining with Aerschot and supping with Hèze and even playing tennis with Aerschot's son the Prince de Chimay. Politics with these people, as with the envoys from Anjou, could only be conducted in a round of drinks and parties. There were weddings and masked balls; the steward of his household got married and William gave away the bride, elegant in her white damask. There were games and horse-shows, and Charlotte set her heart on a stout little Danish pony, a toy among ponies, just the size for her brother's little son, and just the present she had been looking for.

It was difficult to keep the balance even between necessity and extravagance, difficult to keep down the expenses of a big household. It was above all difficult to strike the balance between the austere views of the outspoken Calvinist minority and the natural expectations of the people; when William's household was swept with an epidemic of influenza, there were some in Antwerp who said it was a judgment, but there would have been more to complain if meanness and cheeseparing had been the rule and there had been no shows to stare at. William had a large family, all of whom must now have suitable attendants and clothes and pocket-money to keep up their position. Maurice and his inseparable lifelong friend, his cousin William Louis, must inevitably have good clothes and good horses and a liberal supply of silver for the kind of tips which would be expected of them. Then there was Justin of Nassau, on whose illegitimate birth the Calvinists might frown, but whom it was not in William's nature to treat other than as his son. Justin, a rather bovine young man of one and twenty, had been in his father's household through thick and thin, ever since he was six years old, and although his father never put him forward beyond his abilities – which were small – paternal affection once at least prompted him into an error of social judgment. He suggested a marriage for Justin with the daughter of the Sea Beggar Admiral Dirk Sonoy; Sonoy, in politics the most loyal of William's friends, came of a proud if not a very important family: they did not marry bastards.

William's daughters were less expensive and he had less time for them than, as a father, he might have wished. Marie, 'Mademoiselle d'Orange', at twenty-eight was still unmarried; both leisure to conduct negotiations, and the necessary marriage portion had been continually sacrificed to the immediate needs of the Netherlands. Marie, her father's daughter, was content they should be. Her younger sister 'Mademoiselle Anna', a bouncing blonde of seventeen, had already planned to marry her cousin William Louis who was extremely willing, which certainly saved her father the trouble of looking for a husband for her. Even so the girls had to have a reasonable wardrobe between them, and suitable attendants; it could not be done for nothing. Charlotte's conventual training seems to have come out in a predilection for plain black velvet, but the household accounts mention a head tailor and two assistants for 'Madame': black velvet with a difference, then.

The stupendous munificence of the old days could never come back, but even a modified noble household was expensive and lay open to ceaseless exploitation. When William at length, in some anxiety, laid down new regulations, their phrasing revealed clearly enough the casual pillage to which a great man was persistently subjected: his servants, William commanded, were not to have their friends in to feasts in kitchen or pantry or cellar – or indeed anywhere; they were not to help themselves from the dishes being carried in or out from his own table, nor to dispense drinks from the sideboard to their acquaintances in the ante-room. A certain severity ran through these regulations, the outcome of too many misdemeanours, though here and there a word or a line throws a warm light on the great household; the pages come in for special consideration, they are to have proper leisure for their lessons and their sports, and abundance of good and nourishing food suitable to growing boys, while on the long summer evenings extra beer and bread is to be placed in the pantry for any who feel the need of a second supper. The distribution of cutlery, silver, linen, sugar and spices is the sphere of 'Madame', under whose gentle sway came the entire female household, from Marie de Sainte Aldegonde, the chief lady-in-waiting, to the menial cleaners 'Cyprienne de la chambre' and 'Anneken la povre fille', the least of the laundry maids.[1]

Whatever the Antwerp mob thought of the household and its gaieties, the burghers were growing restive. They were not reconciled to the Anjou alliance by the expenditure which they saw lavished on the French envoys, nor did they approve of the entertainments exchanged between their Prince of Orange and such turncoats as Aerschot. But the quality of their criticism had changed in the last year: they criticized the policy but not the man, or

[1] Arend van Dorp, I, pp. 296, 304 seq.

at least if they criticized him it was with a proprietary affection. They felt, when they saw him smiling and laughing with Aerschot or listening gravely to one of Anjou's people, that he was being imposed on. Like Juliana, they mistrusted his confiding nature, thinking him as little capable of evading the wiles of 'the lubricious and fraudulent French'[1] as she had thought him of seeing through Don John. Thus when a fanatical fellow rushed upon him, coming out of dinner with a French envoy, and loudly hailed him as a traitor for selling the Netherlands to France, the general feeling in Antwerp was one of indignation against the rogue, and when William refused to take any vindictive action they were impressed by his generosity.

IV

This was in June 1580, and before the month was over Philip of Spain had perpetrated an action which redoubled William's popularity and strengthened his hand throughout the Netherlands. Ever since the beginning of the revolt, Philip had regarded assassination as a legitimate secret instrument of policy and more than once plots had been brought to light; but not until this summer of 1580 did he throw off the outward decencies and give to murder his open approval. He was right in thinking that without the Prince of Orange the revolt would be crippled, and Granvelle, grown ever more malevolent as he brooded on his wrongs, had written urging him to put a price on William's head; even if no assassin could be found bold enough to venture for the reward, he suggested that William, a notorious coward, might always die of fright! Granvelle put a strange interpretation on William's celebrated mildness.

The first step was to proclaim the Prince of Orange an outlaw, to release his subordinates from their duty and to make it a crime to obey him. The value of such a proscription was not politically speaking very great while William was successful, but it would be an excuse for wholesale desertion if his fortunes changed. Meanwhile it was a necessary preliminary to Philip's open proclamation declaring William, so-called Prince of Orange, 'the chief disturber of the whole state of Christendom', his subjects absolved of their allegiance, and everyone 'authorized to do him injury or take him from this world as a public enemy'. The reward — twenty-five thousand écus, a patent of nobility and free pardon for all past offences — was in proportion to the risks the murderer would take: he would scarcely himself live to claim it, for the man who killed the Prince of Orange had little chance of escaping the Netherlands mob.

[1] Archives, VII, 229.

Yet a fanatic or a wastrel might brave the danger, and Charlotte's ordeal was beginning; presents of food, homely sausages sent by admirers in the North, fruit and the like, she scanned with anxious eyes. William had a schoolboy appetite for his favourite dishes which some traitor might turn to account — poisoning an eel-pie would be a good way. Charlotte could not guess whence or how the murderer might strike. She could not know that, in his shop near the Antwerp quays, Gaspar Añastro, a Portuguese merchant, sat in consultation with one of his clerks, Juan Jauréguy, and a priest, reckoning that twenty-five thousand écus was a handsome sum, even divided by three, and that to rid the world of the heretic traitor would be a noble deed. She could not know — and indeed might have feared little had she known — that a cabinet-maker's apprentice, called Balthasar Gérard, at Dôle, had dramatically driven a dagger up to the hilt into a slat of wood crying that thus he would strike the Prince of Orange. An older man, among the onlookers, reproved the foolish boast; it was not for the likes of Balthasar Gérard, said he, to murder great princes.[1]

Parma did not like it. He saw, as Philip did not see, that to offer a price for the Prince of Orange was to victimize him personally in a manner which could not but bring his own people in close alliance round him, while his position with the Estates and with foreign diplomats was far too strong to be shaken by a writ of outlawry which must remain a dead letter. Sooner or later some murderous fanatic, tempted by the glory rather than the gain, would win that fearful prize; but was it worth the opprobrium to the Spanish cause?

v

Illumined by the lurid and dangerous light of Philip's threat, William had become infinitely more dear to the Netherlands. They saw now the very proof of his importance to them, sharply lit up by the Spanish menace. Borne forward by this fresh wave of devotion, William carried the Anjou alliance to its unwelcome conclusion. He had a double problem, first to persuade the Estates and the city councils to accept Anjou, secondly to content Anjou himself with the semblance, not the actuality, of power. The second task was likely to prove as difficult as the first, for Anjou was no fool and he was ambitious. Fortunately he was also lazy.

Reiterant persuasion throughout July 1580 brought the Great Council of Antwerp to agree. There were long arguments and long pauses while

[1] Gachard, VI, 164.

William walked in the adjoining gallery and waited to hear what the burghers had to say. The people in the streets noticed his face as he left the town hall evening after evening, and guessed by his grave, dejected or confident air how the unpopular alliance progressed. Anjou was certainly a distasteful mouthful for the Netherlands to swallow; none of the stories current about him did him any good with the people, and the army resented the idea of this unsoldierly 'protector'. But what had to be had to be and, one by one, the provinces bowed to the inevitable. Gelderland, Utrecht and Brabant were the last to hold out. They did not want Anjou for protector of the Netherlands, they said simply: they wanted the Prince of Orange. But no, he argued, endlessly patient and explanatory; it would not do. He was their servant always, but he could not be the figurehead they needed to give them consequence and standing against the King of Spain. So they, too, yielded.

In August at length the alliance was drafted; Sainte Aldegonde sailed from Flushing on the 24th (unhappy omen — Saint Bartholomew), to lay the offers of the Netherlands ten days later before the dapper Anjou at Tours. William had chosen wisely in sending Sainte Aldegonde, whose impressive gravity and incisive wit were likely to intimidate the 'lubricious and fraudulent' advisers of Anjou, and whose knowledge, skill and resource could be relied upon should differences arise. Differences arose almost at once. Anjou, who was perfectly capable of understanding a political document, pounced immediately on all the safeguards against his absolute power with which William and the Estates had so carefully fortified the proposals. For instance, why was he offered only the titles 'prince et seigneur'? Why not 'souverain'? Sainte Aldegonde had the answer pat: the word 'souverain' had no Dutch equivalent. Anjou, who had no means of checking this statement, let it pass, but proved more argumentative on the clauses which forbade him to employ any but native ministers, and gave to the Estates the final selection of his councillors. Anjou was indignant, Sainte Aldegonde explanatory but immovable: this had always been the custom of the Netherlands, from which only the King of Spain had departed. Anjou, announcing that he would see about altering that later, gave in for the time being. The culminating insult to his pride came when he learnt that he must take a separate oath to the constitution in each province. Seventeen humiliating promises to respect the so-called privileges of the boorish Netherlanders? It was too much. Again, Sainte Aldegonde wore him down. Anjou was sick of France, where opportunities were too limited for his ambition; he wanted a new field and, while he hoped to marry the Queen of England, the Netherlands were the safer, nearer offer. Since he had no respect for promises, it did not matter very much what terms he accepted. The important thing was to secure the Netherlands.

Cunning as Anjou thought himself, he made no allowance for the cunning of others. Had he done so, he would not have made it so contemptuously clear to Sainte Aldegonde that he yielded only to gain his immediate ends. But then, neither Sainte Aldegonde nor William had ever doubted that they would have to keep him under the closest watch. What mattered to them was the subsidy of two million four hundred thousand florins a year which he undertook to pay and the troops he could raise in France for the defence of the Netherlands.

VI

The draft-treaty signed at Tours, on September 18th, 1580, Sainte Aldegonde rejoined his master in the North. William wintered that year between Dordrecht and Delft, gladdening Holland once more with his presence, while, tactfully, Charlotte kept her annual lying-in at Dordrecht where the fifth of her little girls was born in October. Brabantina this time — as a compliment to Brabant for having at length agreed to the Anjou alliance. William himself was constantly on the move, for he had only a few months, before Anjou came, to settle outstanding troubles in the North and prepare the unenthusiastic country for its new protector. John, whose tenure of the Stadholderate of Gelderland had so fatally increased the zeal of the Calvinists, had at length decided to retire to Germany. One could not speak of anything so violent as a quarrel between the brothers, but by this time they disagreed radically not only on religious policy but over Anjou in particular. They parted nevertheless on friendly terms, John leaving his eldest son to complete his education in his uncle's army, and to continue his authorized flirtation with Mademoiselle Anna.

John had family reasons, too, for leaving the Netherlands. His wife had died and he wanted to find another as soon as might be. But it was the death of the matriarch Juliana which made his return to Dillenburg essential. At more than seventy she had been still so energetic that William and Charlotte had suggested that she should come on a visit to them. Letters were infrequent for William had no time, and even Charlotte, taken up with her young family, her husband's health and the great household at Antwerp, could not write often. But they managed a joint letter now and again: 'We are as deep in war', William had written to Juliana in the summer of 1580, 'as ever we were; to-day we win, to-morrow we lose,' he said, hoping by this commentary on the see-saw of loss and gain to reassure the old lady, should she hear depressing rumours. Charlotte, adding her postscript, said that little Louise Juliana was getting very big for her age, was talking German as well as French, sent her duty to grandmamma, and had recently asserted that she was sure she would be grandmamma's favourite because she had grandmamma's name.[1] We do not know whether the old lady ever read these letters, which are dated from Antwerp only ten days before she died at Dillenburg. Her death was a sad but not a tragic bereavement. She had lived her life fully and died content, leaving her surviving children and her one hundread and sixty-eight grandchildren to grieve for her without remorse. But since she was no longer at Dillenburg, John had his excuse to return, and took it.

Thus, without his brother, William visited the cities and provinces of the North and summoned the Estates General from Antwerp to Delft. The winter had set in very cold, the Prinsenhof was draughty and William as usual paid no great attention to his health. When Charlotte joined him from Dordrecht she found him feverish and coughing, insisted at once on his going to bed and fed him on spoonfuls of syrup which she made herself of rose-hips and honey. Determined to get up and preside over the Estates, he was a petulant patient, and at first would not have a doctor. When Forest was at length called in, and prescribed rhubarb, he would not take it. Instead Charlotte rubbed his chest with camomile and almond oil and swathed his throat in wool, until he grew more amenable. On the following day, after much persuasion, the protagonist of the Protestant Cause and the hero of the Netherlands was induced to take his medicine, though only after it had been made up into comparatively tasteless pills. How serious his illness was it is hard to say, but serious enough for Charlotte to feel deep gratitude to the invaluable Forest, and to give him later 'with her customary sweetness' a pair of golden goblets in memory of the occasion. Forest, who had been deeply impressed by the spectacle of a real princess acting as a sick-nurse and had added her honey and rose-hip recipe to his own pharmacopoeia, looked upon his two cups for ever afterwards as 'a perpetual memorial of her and of her goodness'.[2]

Between them they soon had their patient well again and on December 13th, 1580, he opened the Estates at Delft. Ever since Sainte Aldegonde's return he had been at work with William's notes and advice on an important document which was now placed before the Estates for their approval. Philip's accusations against the Prince of Orange embodied in the writ of proscription published in June could go no longer unanswered. Now in

[1] *Archives*, vii. 366-9.   [2] *Bijdragen*, iii, iii, 24-5.

December the answer was ready, which, under the name of the *Apology*, was to be read in every language of western Europe during the ensuing months

VII

This was the document which William laid before the Estates, asking their authority to publish it, in vindication of their honour and his before all the world. Appealing for their support, he uttered for the first time openly his renunciation of Philip's overlordship. 'Je vous reconnais seuls en ce monde pour mes supérieurs.'

The *Apology* was an attempt at the same time to make clear a position far clearer to posterity than it was to contemporaries, to justify William's opposition to the King and the revolt of the Netherlands, and to vindicate the invidious, dangerous and disapproved part of rebel into which circumstances had thrust him. In order to understand the *Apology* it is necessary to remember that moral and practical justification *alone* were insufficient in the sixteenth century. It was essential also to be right with the law.

Respect for authority was the keystone of political theory, and respect for authority meant respect for the sovereign, divinely appointed, or the feudal overlord, sanctified by tradition. William knew the importance of this respect: he had asserted a theoretical loyalty to Philip through so many years of rebellion, because it alone made him an acceptable ally for other kings and princes. 'Point une revolte', he had written to Catherine de Medici; 'not a revolt but a resolution taken by the whole State of the Netherlands for the preservation of their lives and privileges.'[1] No ruling prince could wholly approve him as a rebel, and, while they might occasionally help him, they would have no compunction, if it suited them better, in treating him as an unprivileged, unprotected outcaste, to be betrayed and deserted. The man who threw off the bonds of allegiance could expect — *even from seeming friends* — no better treatment, since the sanctions he had himself flouted could no longer protect him, and there were no others. Proscription, the ultimate punishment of traitors, was always, as it were, inherent in the situation.

The *Apology* was to alter all that by turning the accusation against Philip himself, by proving that Philip the sovereign, not William the vassal, had first failed in his duty. It falls into line in the history of political thought as the first practical expression of the new political theory, advanced by the Calvinist philosophers. Where the sovereign fails in his duty, said

[1] Gachard.

they, the people are not only justified, but morally bound, to dethrone him. Among the Frenchmen at William's Court at this time was Duplessis Mornay, himself generally believed to be the author of a recent book, the *Vindiciae contra Tyrannos*, which gave its first clear statement to this theory. His personal influence on the *Apology* is implicit.

In a covering letter addressed to the Estates and printed with the *Apology*, William declared that he could have no greater badge of honour than that of being proscribed by their enemies. In the opening paragraphs he compared the antiquity and high services of his family favourably with those of the Habsburgs, and described the valour and loyalty which had characterized the house of Nassau in the service of their rightful overlords. Having thus built up his own position in a way which seems strange to us, but was important in his own time, he turned to demolish Philip's. The preliminaries were personal, as Philip's had been in that 'mass of injuries', the ban; there William had been held up to obloquy as the bigamous husband of a nun and the probable murderer of his wife. Turning the tables on the King, William in answer accused him of the murder of his eldest son and his third wife and of incest in marrying his niece. This personal onslaught, shocking but not unfamiliar to the modern mind, did not aim to enlist a public eager for savoury details; it was rather directed to politicians and educated men as a proof that Philip was no fit vessel for the divinity which God invests in kings. Only for this reason did William sanction the propagation of those scandals which, in the long years of his reign, had collected about the secretive King of Spain. He may have had his mad and violent son, Don Carlos, strangled (the evidence is to this day baffling); he had certainly married his niece, though with the necessary and usual dispensation; as certainly as he had not murdered his much-loved third wife. It has so long been the fashion to think a man's private life of no public concern that it is easy to forget how large these things appeared to an age which, though often coarser than our own, regarded divine sanctions as all-important. The state of Philip's, or of William's, soul had direct bearing on his authority under God.

Next William discussed the principles of his policy, and the reasons he had had for acting as he did. He revealed the indiscretion of the late King of France in the woods at Chantilly in 1559, and the sentiments of pity and obligation which had inspired him to adopt the cause of the Netherlands. He had put the arguments together as best he could, trusting to memory, for his papers of that period were all destroyed and so much had happened since that the overtired human brain blurred and confused events once separate. As an historical account of policy the *Apology* is unreliable, but as a psychological document it is valuable, for it shows what events and what scenes stood out in William's mind, what others had become merged or confused. No particular purpose is served by its errors and indeed it would have been more extraordinary if, instead of an impression, William had been able to give a clear and accurate account of all his past, if he had remembered word for word fourteen years later exactly what Egmont had said to him, and when and where.

Oddly enough when he came to the revolt he emphasized first his own personal wrongs – the seizure of his lands, the abduction of his son – in order to show that he had fought only for what was his own. This again was sound feudal theory, and he made little at first of his political belief in the rights of the Netherlands. Yet for the better information of European sovereigns he added that the so-called revolt of the Netherlands was no casual disorder of the mob, but a reasoned movement sanctioned by the wisest and the best in the land. He spoke at length and eloquently of the rights of the Estates, the sole true repository of authority in the Netherlands, under whom and for whom he had acted. Finally he rebutted Philip's accusation of personal ambition with an impassioned appeal to the Estates whose servant, and the peoples', he held himself to be: 'Let us with one heart and good will go together and let us together embrace the defence of this good people . . . and if you will yet continue towards me the favour which heretofore you have borne me, then, whatsoever things may be resolved upon by you for the good and preservation of yourselves, your wives, your children, whatsoever things are sacred and holy, these by your aid and God's grace, I will maintain.' The pedestrian English 'I will maintain' does not give the effective meaning of the ancient French 'Je maintiendray'. It is more than to maintain, it is to uphold, for the word carries in it the sense of mutual obligation, of the oath given by the laying of the overlord's hand on that of the vassal, and of the vassal's within that of his protector. This was the proclamation of William's plighted word to his people: he was sworn, hand-fasted, to the Netherlands. Indeed – to the Netherlands; for up to this time the device had been, like all ancient feudal devices, not general but particular to the family of its bearer. The words on his coat of arms were 'Je Maintiendray Nassau'. To omit his family and thereby to endow the narrow phrase with wide significance was a touch of genius.

VIII

The ban and the *Apology* were to introduce a new phase in the drama of the Netherlands. Philip's proscription and William's reply put an end to the absurd fiction of the 'loyalty' of the revolted provinces. Step by step, through the breaking of negotiations with Don John, through the respective alliances with the Archduke Matthias and the Duke of Anjou, the ground had been prepared for a declaration of independence. It followed naturally from the *Apology*.

William, the most discreet of politicians, both to his contemporaries and to posterity, rarely explained the theory behind his policy, and Sainte Aldegonde, who of all men knew his heart, left no memoirs. The best the modern historian can do is to read back from his acts to the policy behind them. But his acts were often and inevitably opportunist, aimed at securing some immediate and perhaps momentary vantage point; to make out the guiding policy underlying acts of daily expediency is the work of deduction and conjecture. How soon had William planned this final act of revolt? Earlier, it may be, than we have any evidence for stating. Perhaps about the time of the siege of Leyden, when he first refused the offered terms? But he had held his hand all these years, to strengthen the moral position of the revolted Netherlands, and to ensure the participation of the greater number of the provinces. Looking back over the nine years since his first successful return, the broad line of his policy begins to emerge through the complexity of his actions: he had played for time, for prestige, and for unity.

How far had he succeeded? Not altogether, yet beyond all expectation. The more dangerous of the Calvinist extremists had withdrawn, the religious peace was working, more or less, in the South. Parma held the Walloon provinces, but only the Walloon provinces, and the outlying Luxembourg. Thirteen of the seventeen had agreed to accept Anjou; thirteen of the seventeen had set up that central executive council to deal with war and finance which William had proposed. In this winter of 1580-81, after three years of struggle and storm and disappointment in the South, he might look back on an achievement surely beyond his hopes. He had saved not only the Flemish-speaking Netherlands, but saved them entire, with all their conflicting rights and internal quarrels, and brave, dangerous, unguarded independence. On Christmas Day, at least, this year, he made merry with his family, and Marie de Sainte Aldegonde, the daughter of his chief minister and principal lady to his wife, choosing an informal moment, brought out her album for the Prince and Princess of Orange to write in. 'Je maintiendray' wrote William with a flourish across the page. Below Charlotte added in her pretty French flowing hand a Spanish phrase: 'Un sola aurora ha de vencer mi noche.' 'One dawn alone can break through my darkness.' Spanish was no language of Charlotte's and one suspects some pretty tag of her husband's once or twice used tenderly, and so remembered by her. 'Un sola aurora . . .' their dawn had indeed come.

While the *Apology*, in edition after edition, poured off the printing presses of Delft and Leyden, in four different languages, and was shipped to booksellers over all western Europe, the Estates General of the United Netherlands had assembled at Amsterdam in May 1581, to draft their declaration of independence. It took them longer than they expected, and, as the summer heat drew vapours out of the canals and the arguments showed no signs of being quickly settled, they moved to the pretty, cool, aristocratic country town, scarcely more than a village, which in days gone by had been the ancient capital of Holland, and whose name, 's Gravenhage, or the Count's Hedge, still recalled those feudal times: it was the first odd chance which was to restore to the Hague its old glory. Here on July 24th the Estates General prefaced their final break with their overlord the King of Spain by proclaiming William, Prince of Orange, head of the government until such time as the new sovereign should be found. Here on the following day they celebrated his new elevation at a formal banquet. We do not know very much about this banquet, not even whether Charlotte was present, or whether, as seems more likely, it was confined to men only. Nor apparently did William bring his son, the boy Maurice, now nearly fourteen, for this was no occasion on which to emphasize his dynasty; he had again refused the sovereignty. They celebrated that night in the Hague the birth of a nation, not the triumph of a man, or, if the triumph of a man, then only because to so many of the delegates there assembled the Prince of Orange had become the nation personified.

We know what he looked like in this year, 1581, for the occasion was important enough for delegates to want his picture to hang in their town halls, and by far the greater number of the portraits in the public galleries and municipal buildings of the Netherlands to-day derive from that which Adriaen Key of Antwerp painted at this time. The Prince of Orange had changed almost out of recognition in the thirty years since Antonio Moro drew him. The lean outline of the face has thickened, and wrinkles have gathered about the mouth and eyes, the high forehead is deeply lined, and the auburn hair, once so thick, has thinned and receded. To hide this defect, he wore in the fashion of the older men of his time a black velvet skull cap. The face is that of a man with twenty more years to his life than William's bare forty-eight, and the responsibilities he had borne so long and so much alone are written in every line of it; but the eyes are still large, observant and bright, and the expression of the mouth more humane and more humorous than the close, judicial young man's mouth of thirty years before. Looking at Adriaen Key's portrait, it is easy to understand why the ordinary people called him 'Father' openly, and came to him with their troubles.

On the following day, July 26th, 1581, the Abjuration was solemnly ratified by the Estates General; the provinces of Holland, Zealand and Utrecht, of Gelderland, Friesland, Groningen and Overissel, of Malines, Flanders and Brabant, solemnly foreswore their allegiance to Philip of Spain, a king who had forfeited all sovereign rights by breaking his oath to his people, abandoning his obligations and conspiring against the common weal of the Netherlands. In the opening phrases rings out the new political theory of the time, the very arguments of the *Vindiciae contra Tyrannos* published only eighteen months before. Both the Prince of Orange and Sainte Aldegonde had talked much with its author and his words and theories had filtered through their minds into action. The Abjuration marks a period in the relation of princes and subjects, marks the first practical expression of the theory which was in some lands at least to prevent the solid entrenchment of Divine Right.

Not that this aspect of the document was of any great significance to William. For him the Abjuration was the climax of his long struggle for reunion. The first step towards the restored Netherlands had been taken nearly five years before at the Pacification of Ghent; now, after delay and struggle and disappointment, in the teeth of faction and misunderstanding, he had imposed his wiser will on the straining, quarrelsome provinces and brought them one great step further towards independence and unity. As he himself had written in his *Apology*: 'Maintain your union: Keep your union, not in words, not by writing only, but in effect also, so that you may execute that which your sheaf of arrows, tied with one band only, doth mean.' . . . *L'union fait la force.*

CHAPTER IX

'DIVIDED WE FALL'

1581–1584

I

'A PRINCE is constituted by God to be ruler of a people, to defend them from oppression and violence, as the shepherd his sheep; and whereas God did not create the people slaves to their prince, to obey his commands, whether right or wrong, but rather the prince for the sake of the subjects, to love and support them as a father his children, or a shepherd his flock . . . and when he does not behave thus but . . . oppresses them, seeking opportunities to infringe their ancient customs, exacting from them slavish compliance, then he is no longer a prince but a tyrant, and they may not only disallow his authority, but legally proceed to the choice of another prince for their defence.' So the Act of Abjuration. Philip of Spain, hereditary ruler of the Netherlands, was deposed; the choice of a new ruler followed logically. '*Legally* proceed to the choice of another prince . . .' – that was the essential to the sixteenth-century mind; we are not yet in a period where the 'rights of man' flourish, as it were, *in vacuo*, and the State has to be evolved in accordance with them. We are still barely beyond the rigid framework of medieval theory, in a world where order is essential, in a world, moreover, where personal sovereignty is gaining ground, not losing it. The Act of Abjuration proclaimed no objection to monarchy in principle; it proclaimed simply the right to alter an allegiance.

Seen in its widest implications the Act of Abjuration was an important milestone on the road of European liberty; but seen in its narrowest aspect it was but the legal preliminary to the acceptance of Francis of Anjou as the new master of the Netherlands. As such it was an ingenious piece of state-craft. For one thing it got rid of the superfluous Matthias without the need for any further action. He had been – technically – Governor-General under Philip II, so that with Philip's deposition his office came to an end automatically. Matthias, knowing what was coming, had gracefully resigned in June. By October he was back in Austria, his Netherlands escapade at an end.

In the meantime the Prince of Orange was lieutenant for the sovereign-elect, for that ruler whom no one except himself wanted. In nine years he had rescued and held together the greater part of the Netherlands, given them the framework of unity and the moral strength to claim their independence. Now in the three years which remained to him he was to wreck that very unity for which he had striven — and still strove — by forcing on the unwilling provinces the distasteful protectorship of Anjou. Yet it is impossible to regard his action as a political misjudgment. There are occasions — all too many — in politics where the only choice is a choice of evils. Of the dangers and evils inherent in the situation of 1581 the Prince of Orange undoubtedly chose the lesser.

The Netherlands still stood, a resisting fortress backed against the sea, which through the negligence, not the weakness, of Spain the Dutch still controlled. Hesitation, half-hearted mistrust of his lieutenants, inadequate forethought — all these things had hampered Philip's battles; but strength for strength, if Philip would but throw in what he had, the Netherlands were far outmatched. At their back lay England, part-mistress of the Narrow Seas, a valuable ally, a dangerous enemy. On their flank lay France, and the survival of the Netherlands hung now, as the success of the revolt had hung once, on the quiescence of France. That France and Spain, rival claimants for the dominance of western Europe, could not be friends for long was plain political sense, but they would not need to be friends for long to annihilate the Netherlands. A year might have done it. Thus to have England and France quiescent was essential even to the most precarious survival; to have them friendly the first step towards the real defeat of Spain; to have them hostile plain ruin.

Anjou was the pivot of the situation. His elevation into 'prince et seigneur' was the price of French collaboration, and since his courtship of the English Queen had been enthusiastically received by Elizabeth, it was the price of English friendship too. To reject him would bring with it the displeasure of Elizabeth and the hostility of the French, would destroy the fruits of William's years of diplomacy, and deliberately give allies to Spain. Even as late as this, it must be remembered that there were Spanish sympathizers in England, and something more than Spanish sympathizers in France; the Guise family were little less than a Spanish faction, while the King wavered, uncertain how far to back his brother.

Anjou, therefore, was the only solution of the external problem; in him alone lay the chance of military survival. But the internal traditions and prejudices of the Netherlands dragged against the alliance, for these two essential friends, France and England, had never before been essential friends, and historic memory of commercial and national rivalry told against present needs.

But in a small country, among an impressionable people, much may be done by personality. Had Francis of Anjou had the qualities of a statesman, or even a leader in war, the dangerous situation might still have been saved, but luck in this matter was against William and his people. Francis of Anjou was at once politically essential and personally impossible. He lacked neither ability nor character, had nimble wits and a ready tongue, self-confidence, gaiety, even a kind of charm. But he had grown up in a society at once dangerous, stormy and vicious, learning nothing of politics save the dubious expedients which characterized the rule of his mother, Catherine de Medici. At twenty-eight he was a cunning, ambitious egocentric, overplaying even this part, since at the Court from which he came it had never been necessary to conceal characteristics which were common to everyone. Moreover, with a strangely heartless stage-management even of his attachments he had made a habit of playing his minions against those of the King his brother. When the favourites of Henri III cultivated the aesthetic pose, those of Anjou became tough. Their rivalry had become so much a part of life at the French Court that Anjou himself was probably unaware of the bad effect which his male harem would have in the Netherlands. Not that this would have made him alter his conduct, for if he had one virtue it was a total indifference to other people's opinions.

Few as were the illusions William had as to the personal impression which Anjou was likely to make, he knew his presence to be essential. While the Duke loitered in England making grotesque love to Elizabeth, the provinces might sicken of the alliance, strain and break away, arguing truly enough that their Protector showed little enthusiasm for his part. And the military situation was extremely menacing: Breda itself had been seized in a sudden night attack, all Tournai had been overrun, and with infinite difficulty did William manage to drag out of the Estates sufficient funds to keep the army paid. Rather than vote supplies from their own pockets, the deputies of Brabant had voted for the sale of Church lands throughout the province, a decision which, whatever the Calvinist fervour of the moment, was bound to cause very serious trouble among a population of whom the majority were Catholic.

In December 1581 William once more issued one of his public exhortations to the Estates General now again in session at Antwerp. They had been promised that Anjou should help them, and waiting for Anjou they were sulkily disinclined to help themselves. Yet if allies were essential, an absolute trust in them to the neglect of all personal effort was mere irresponsibility. Moreover, William sensed the beginning of a new danger; the members of the Estates were murmuring slightly – as they had done twenty-five years before when subsidies were needed for Philip's French war – that they did not see why they should wage Anjou's battles. This was to misrepresent the whole matter: whatever Anjou's personal ambition, the war *in* the Netherlands was essentially the war *of* the Netherlands. 'There is no war in this country', William wrote, 'but your own war; you deliberate now only of what is your own.' The Abjuration had made them in fact responsible only to themselves; but *responsible* was the operative word.[1]

Meanwhile repeated letters went to Anjou in England imploring him to come. Still he delayed, hoping to win Elizabeth against the evident will of her people, until at length Sainte Aldegonde was dispatched to fetch him away. In token of his personal devotion to the Duke, William included his son Justin in the deputation to take his place, if Anjou agreed, as a gentleman of his household. The offer was accepted, could indeed hardly have been refused, and the dutiful young man became one of Anjou's gilded retinue. What Justin, with his Flemish bourgeois origin stamped on every feature of his round and placid face, thought of his fellow servants history does not relate — probably nothing very much, for he was to go through his long and virtuous life with the vaguely puzzled and genial expression of one who is always a little out of his depth. He had been born out of it.

Not until February 1582 did Elizabeth at last say farewell to 'her little Frog', promising to be his wife as soon as he had established himself in the Netherlands, and sending with him to William and the Estates fervid letters of recommendation by the hand of the magnificent Leicester.

II

If the first part of William's task — that of persuading the Estates to take Anjou — had been difficult, the second — that of persuading them to like him — was impossible. Elizabeth had been right to call the little creature her Frog; he would have made a passable frog. His extraordinary physical appearance was set off with suggestive and dazzling clothes, with pomade, powder, paint, with lacquered cheeks and silken, fantastic, wig. Not that this would have mattered had he been trustworthy, or failing that, stupid. He was neither. Respecting nothing and no one in the Netherlands, he had planned for himself an unrestricted sovereignty, and as he sized up, one by one, the grave statesmen who greeted him on his landing at Flushing, these ponderous Netherlanders, this elderly Prince of Orange, he thought himself a match for them all. But he erred; for William, keeping his own counsel, as he had done long ago when Anjou's father had been indiscreet, was well aware that frogs were slippery.

[1] Gachard, IV, 367-8.

Anjou's reception in Antwerp bore the outward sign of friendship. There were the usual speeches and tableaux, triumphal arches and salutes, but no great spontaneous enthusiasm, and in certain details the mistrust of his new subjects was already clear: he had to take the oath to respect the charters of Antwerp — with great pomp and reverence it is true — but outside the city walls. Proceeding at length into the town Anjou was formally installed as Duke of Brabant in the cathedral. Three weeks later he took his formal oath before the Estates General.

With every mark of personal friendship and formal reverence William strove to throw the cloak of his own popularity over Anjou, being with him constantly, watching him at tennis, dining at his table, bringing Anjou back to dine at his. All his efforts served but to increase the mistrust of the mob. The great southern nobles who, discontented at their prospects with Parma, had come back to Antwerp to scout out the lie of this new situation, were few of them friends to William, and the people of Antwerp felt only anxiety and distress when they saw their Prince of Orange strolling from the dining-hall to the *jeu de paume* among a group of time-serving younger nobles each one of whom — so the mob thought — would be more than willing to stab him in the back.

Nevertheless William believed that he could, gradually, make Anjou, if not popular, at least acceptable. His household, first, must be rearranged with great care, putting Flemish gentlemen in most of the higher posts. He himself was to be Anjou's Grand Chamberlain, his son Maurice his Master of the Horse as soon as he should be old enough. The bastard Justin was of course prominently displayed among the gentlemen-in-attendance. None of this helped much and perhaps the only real assistance which William got in this difficult situation was from his wife. Charlotte's exceptional sweetness and charm had made her a popular figure in Antwerp where no one thought of her as particularly 'French'. But French she was, incontrovertibly, and moreover 'ma cousine' to Anjou. He had in his suite her only brother, that brother for whose advantage she had been forced to renounce her dowry and take the veil, but the past was forgotten, and Charlotte's longing for reconciliation with her family was now to be fulfilled. The welcome which she gave to her brother extended to embrace all of Anjou's suite; she was, as people indulgently said, like a mother to them all.[1]

It needed more than William's tact and Charlotte's kindness to do a miracle for Anjou. He remained his own worst enemy, seeing no reason to modify his conduct to suit Flemish manners. The minions swaggered about Antwerp, disgusting staid burghers by their extravagance and the mob by

[1] C.S.P.F. 1582, 8.

their French airs of superiority, while in Anjou's private apartments they wrangled and fought and insulted their master in a manner grotesquely unsuitable to the gravity and splendour of his new position. William, urging on the Duke the necessity of a more formal atmosphere, met with nothing but rudeness. When the irrepressible St. Luc, ex-favourite of Henri III, now favourite-in-chief of Anjou, slapped a rival's face, William broke in with uncontrollable exasperation. Ill-manners like this, he protested, could not be permitted in any decently conducted Court, Anjou must punish the offender whatever his rank or privileges: why, if such a thing had happened when he was a young man at the Court of the Emperor Charles — 'Marry', broke in St. Luc, before William had finished or Anjou could answer, 'you're not one to talk to me of your Emperor Charles. If he were here now your head would be off your shoulders.' With which undoubtedly just surmise, the favourite flung out of the room, leaving William speechless and the rest of the company giggling.[1]

Yet with all his drawbacks Anjou was bringing genuine help. The King of France, unwilling to quarrel outright with the King of Spain, feigned a lack of interest, but nevertheless recruits were already collecting for the Netherlands, and Charlotte's brother was to go back to France to assemble and command them. In the field it looked, for the first time in three years, as though the Estates would be able to counter-attack when Parma opened his spring offensive. Altogether William seemed confident, cheerful, and master of the situation.

III

Sunday, March 18th, 1582, was the Duke's birthday and expensive festivities were planned, with riding at the ring and charging the quintain, concluding by an evening collation with eighteen meat courses at Anjou's residence. It was the coming event of the spring season. Two or three days before, a Portuguese merchant named Añastro applied for a pass to go into the Walloon provinces on business; it was routine work for William to sign it. Impossible to keep a check of every foreign merchant in the hive of Antwerp, impossible to follow every traveller on the roads. Añastro rode with all the speed he could to Parma at Tournai. There, gaining an audience, he joyously boasted that he had set up a clerk in his warehouse, Juan Jauréguy, complete with pistol, ammunition, a new suit of clothes and full instructions, to shoot the Prince of Orange as he came out of dinner on Sunday, March

[1] Busbecq, III, 314.

18th. Congratulating himself loudly on his courage, he reminded Parma of the twenty-five thousand écus for the murder of the Prince of Orange. Parma answered with distaste that the murder had not yet happened, and in his opinion Juan Jauréguy was the one who had the courage. Meanwhile Añastro could await events in his camp.

On Sunday, March 18th, the Prince of Orange went over to Anjou's lodging to congratulate him on his birthday, then returned to his own house for dinner. Jauréguy had confessed at daybreak and been given the last sacrament; wearing his new French suit and a heavy cloak he made his way to the Prince's lodging, a silent, docile, lethargic youth of twenty, with nothing much to say for himself. If no one had told him that it would be a fine thing to destroy the Prince of Orange, he would never have thought of it for himself. But Añastro had explained it all to him and he knew it was his duty to obey his master. Had he taken in any of Añastro's finer flights of fancy? Had he understood the improbable story that no harm would come to him, for, although he would be arrested, the life of William's own son, prisoner in Spain, would be held in pawn against his own? It seems probable that Añastro had used his fertile imagination and persuasive powers super-fluously, for Jauréguy, if slow in the uptake, always did as he was told, and he was about to murder the Prince of Orange with — it may be — only a fraction more emotion than he would have felt at making him out an invoice. The pistol, however, was a new instrument to his ink-stained knuckles; just to make sure, he had put a great deal more gunpowder into the charge than he had been told, ramming in the bullet with heavy, careful, inexpert fingers. Undismayed and unquestioning, therefore, did the little clerk make his way to the place where he was to earn that afternoon his undeserved immortality.

William was at dinner with a few guests and the men of his household only; the talk had been of tapestry apparently, because, when they came out of the dining-hall, he led his guests across the big ante-room, crowded with sightseeing loiterers, to examine a set recently made; young Count Maurice walked behind his father, his half-brother Justin near him, and somewhere close at hand was Sainte Aldegonde. Armed with halberds and swords, William's bodyguard brought up the rear, but according to his custom, he was not directly protected, preferring to be free for the approach of petitioners and friends. Juan Jauréguy therefore pushed through the crowd without hindrance, until he came up with his quarry, carefully levelled the unfamiliar firearm and carefully released the trigger.

William's first thought, so he afterwards said, was that the roof had col-lapsed; a strong smell of singed hair and the astonishing realization that his ruff was on fire seemed irrelevant, and he was still beating out the flame when the sour taste of blood filling his mouth forced his mind to make the necessary connection and he understood that he had been shot.

Jauréguy gaped, his fingers limp and bloody. Rammed solid with charge and shot, the pistol had blown to pieces, shattering his hand. But the on-lookers had been quicker than William to realize what had happened. Swords and halberds flashed into action and the murderer went down under the feet of the guards, while William, half-inarticulate, the blood now choking him, called out to them in vain to stop their ghastly work. Blinded, stunned, he did not doubt the murderer's success: 'I forgive him my death,' he gasped. By this time, two of his servants were helping him out of the room; stumbling, still conscious, he walked between them.

Once he was gone, tumult broke out over Jauréguy's corpse. Was this Anjou's work? From his clothes this murderer was a Frenchman. Keeping his presence of mind in spite of his powerful emotions, Sainte Aldegonde sharply ordered search to be made of the murderer's body, in the hope of finding evidence to show who set him on. Jauréguy's pockets contained some cheap metal crosses, such as the poor devout buy at places of pilgrimage, a prayer written on a torn shred of paper, two little pieces of beaver skin (Añastro dealt in furs) and a green wax candle-end. This pitiful haul was brought over to young Maurice, who, in the general hubbub, had escaped notice; stricken and frightened, he clutched the insignificant treasures and began to cry, until one of his father's attendants, more intelligent and calmer than the others, led him out of the room, showed him where he could safely stow his finds, dried his tears and urged him to go back to help Sainte Aldegonde. By the time Maurice came back, a more exhaustive search of Jauréguy's body had yielded two letters both incontrovertibly written in Spanish, thus enabling Sainte Aldegonde justly to give out what he would have given out in any case — that the Spaniards, not Anjou, had set the murderer on. The body meanwhile was exposed in the chief square of Antwerp, until it should be identified, and the city guard doubled to prevent disorder.

With the news of the murder brought to Anjou came also a request to him and his suite to stay within doors; they knew the temper of the people and needed no second warning. Anjou may have been genuinely upset, for William's death at this moment would be fatal to his hopes; he beat his head three times against the wall and broke into loud tears. Or was it merely annoyance at the loss of his birthday party?

As soon as she heard what had happened Charlotte fainted dead away, while Catherine of Schwartzburg and the two elder princesses broke into loud weeping. It was some time indeed before the ladies of the household had recovered their self-control enough to enter the sick-room. Charlotte indeed came round, at the ministrations of her women, only to faint again, three times. When she was at length mistress of herself she proved, as once before, a patient and skilful nurse, nor was Catherine — trained long since by Juliana — less efficient than her sister-in-law. The hysterical scenes which greeted the first news of the attack must therefore be taken all the more as proof of the nervous pressure under which William's family had lived ever since his life had been held up for sale.

While cries and agitation filled the women's quarters, the surgeons were consulting round William's bed. By an extraordinary chance the bullet which had passed from right to left at an upward angle through the cheeks and palate had struck no vital organ and broken no bone. So close had the pistol been fired that the wounded right cheek was spattered with gun-powder and fragments of the paper used to ram in the charge, while the flame of the explosion had burnt away all the hair on that side of the face and cauterized the outer surface of the wound. But the heavy and extended contusion of the flesh made it extremely difficult to investigate the injury inside the mouth. There was more than a chance that the maxillary artery had been grazed, and though the bleeding had now almost stopped, some of the surgeons feared to probe the wound exhaustively for fear of inadvertently breaking it open. There were too many of them, perhaps. Cynics said that if the Prince of Orange had been a private soldier, bandaged up in a hurry on the field of battle, he would have healed in forty-eight hours. But the surgeons were to prove right about the artery, though uncertain in their treatment. For the present they reported with sober optimism, forbade the patient to speak, and ordered rest and quiet as far as possible.

Rest and quiet, of all things, William could not have. As soon as the streets were safe enough Anjou came round to see him, and continued his visits daily, making a special point of being present whenever the wound was dressed, a courteous attention which can hardly have been appreciated by the harassed doctors. But even in the first painful hours William had had to think of policy and the people; all over Antwerp they clamoured that he was dead, and nothing would satisfy them but one of the officers of their local volunteers must be admitted to see him. Propped on his pillows William received the delegate and even managed to give him a spoken message, bidding the people trust in Anjou, before his doctors intervened to stop him talking.

There was nothing more to do but wait and hope, while beyond the whispering ante-rooms the tense groups in the Antwerp streets, the congre-gations praying 'in the churches of both languages', over all the Netherlands, all Europe waited for news from that darkened room where the Prince of Orange, grotesque in bloodstained bandages, conducted the urgent affairs of his people by talking on his fingers and scribbling notes to Sainte Aldegonde. On the frontier of Luxembourg, half-way from his native Dôle to Antwerp, Balthasar Gérard, who had also set out to kill the Prince of Orange, had heard with bitter disappointment that he had been forestalled; learning that his quarry yet lived, with grim joy he resumed his quest. Granvelle praised Heaven for the Prince's death, and, when the rumour was contradicted, joined with his other enemies in wishful thinking. Shot through the jaw and cheek? He could not live. Granvelle pursued his unpleasing speculations: what would become of 'the little nun and her bastards'? he unkindly asked, and went on to wish that Sainte Aldegonde, who so loved his master, would elect to be buried with him 'like an Indian's wife' — a sidelong insinuation of a particularly offensive kind.[1] Crabbed with age and spite, he remembered the attractive young nobleman, so beloved of the ladies: 'he has a fine face now for his little nun to kiss', he gloated, pleased that death should treat him so ungraciously.

Jauréguy had struck on March 18th, 1582. Seven days later it seemed that William was out of danger: he was eating solid foods, talking, and attending to the urgent business of the State. Parma was threatening the passage of the Meuse at Bommel and Venloo, and hasty reinforcements had to be sent, as well as orders for an assault on Alost. While William read and signed letters and transacted his affairs, the Estates sat in judgment on two of Jauréguy's accomplices, the priest who had given him the sacrament on the morning of the murder, and one of Añastro's servants who had known the details of the plot. Knowing only too well what measures the outraged deputies might take, William sent a personal message by Sainte Aldegonde requesting the gentlemen of the Estates to spare the conspirators any 'great torment', and to content themselves, if they found them guilty, with a speedy death. Reluctantly, the gentlemen of the Estates gave up their plan for dragging by wild horses.

Fortunately for them, the two poor devils had gone to their last account before March 31st, when the wound, apparently healed, broke open again. William had spent a long afternoon talking to Anjou; after he had left, at half-past eight in the evening, the haemorrhage began and went on until midnight, when one of the surgeons at last found its vent, and closed it by applying a small pellet of lead held in place by the pressure of a finger inside the patient's mouth. By that time he had lost four pounds of blood. At five on the following morning, either somebody's finger slipped, or the grazed vein broke in

[1] Granvelle, IX, 168.

another place; the second haemorrhage lasted for three hours and by the time the bleeding slackened William had lost another pound of blood and his case seemed desperate. Striving in vain to stop the flow, the surgeons argued and probed while the room filled with anxious servants, soldiers and onlookers whom no one somehow managed to keep out. Fresh from street or stable, the men's boots stank, and some, who had hurried from their meal to see how the Prince did, were eating spring onions and spitting out the stalks. In this hurly-burly the physicians applied their agonizing cauteries to their fast-sinking patient. A Doctor Schoutemans of Antwerp at length stemmed the blood with a mixture of vitriol and red copper. But they were still nervous lest the cautery should not work for long enough, and took it in turns to apply a finger to the place, for seventeen days without intermission.[1]

Not that, at first, anyone imagined that there was the slightest hope. The doctors gave him a week at the most, and on the third day it did not even seem worth while to prolong life by avoiding effort. William, with a hand scarcely able to lift the pen, had scrawled four lines to Anjou commending the people to him, and four to the Estates bidding them trust in Anjou. Sainte Aldegonde, who carried the letter, delivered it silent and in tears. That night he asked to see all his family, 'to say good-night'. They stood round the huge bed, Charlotte the beloved wife, her young children, Catherine his sister, Marie, Maurice and Anna. He could only say indistinctly that they were in God's hands, 'Es ist mit mir getan — All is over with me'. The scene comes to us from the homely pen of Marie, writing to her uncle, John of Nassau.[2] Whether in the last weariness he spoke German, the language of his childhood, or whether she merely translated the French, which was his habitual speech, for her correspondent's benefit, we cannot know.

Contrary to every expectation William lived. On April 19th the surgeons felt they could safely leave off holding the vein and no longer did they tremble with anxiety every time their patient coughed. He was warned to be careful about talking, but he could eat solid food again after nearly three weeks of water gruel. On Sunday, April 22nd, five weeks after Jauréguy's attack, he got up for the first time and appeared for a brief moment at the window: some of the crowd saw him; others, who had not, became so wild with excitement at the rumour that they forced an entrance to his house and insisted on looking into his room. He was asleep by then, and they began to clamour that he was dead and they deceived; there was nothing for it but to waken him so that he might make a sign to them. Six days later he was

[1] Gachard, VI, 87-8; *Bijdragen*, III, iii, 26; C.S.P.F., 1584, 635, 646.
[2] *Archives*, VII, 87-9.

walking up and down his room practising his strength; Venloo and Bommel had been saved and Alost taken, all as the outcome of his last orders from his sick-bed. These were joyous omens for his recovery, but he could not rejoice, for Charlotte, worn out with five weeks of ceaseless watching, was desperately ill. Six pregnancies in seven years, months of anxiety and the crisis of the last weeks had been too much for a constitution never strong. Her husband had fought for life when all had given him over, but Charlotte's resistance had gone in the struggle for him. It was said that she had contracted a chill at the thanksgiving service for his recovery. By April 28th the illness was diagnosed as 'double pleurisy'; she had a high fever, her surgeons let blood recklessly to reduce it, and in the small hours of May 6th she died. Only eleven days after she had knelt in the great church of Our Lady to give thanks for her husband's life, she was herself laid to rest in its dispassionate shade.

Some thought that William himself must fall under this final affliction. His grief had little outward expression but 'the separation of lovers secretly gnaws at the heart', wrote the English agent, and his sympathetic fears were shared by many. Deeply indeed had Charlotte been loved, and those who came from all over the provinces with expressions of official sympathy often broke down in William's presence so that he was left to find words of faith and philosophy to comfort his comforters. His only solace lay in the pursuit of that task for which Charlotte had saved his life in sacrificing hers. Alone but for the faithful and undemonstrative Sainte Aldegonde, he shouldered once more his gigantic load.

I V

All this while at Rome and Madrid they were still impatiently waiting for him to die. 'This pestilent Orange will never be done with his dying', complained Granvelle, who for a time firmly believed that he was indeed dead and his supporters merely concealing the fact. When at length reports of his recovery could no longer be disbelieved, his enemies still cheated themselves with the vain hope that he had recovered his health but not his reason, and Granvelle's last consolation when this, too, proved false was that God had a yet more fearful end in store.[1]

When, towards the end of May 1582, William was once more fully at the service of the State, he found that the situation, eased by the taking of Alost, had again worsened. Anjou's reinforcements were not as large as had been hoped, nor, unfortunately, as efficient. The brunt of the defence

[1] Granvelle, IX, 150, 156, 237, 258-9.

still fell on the Estates' own army, while Parma, who had received fresh troops from Spain, now had sixty thousand men in the field, more than half as many again as William could muster. Determined with these superior forces to win himself at last an outlet to the sea, Parma pushed forward, taking Oudenarde in July, and clearly aiming to cut off Dunkirk, or even, should his strength prove great enough, to carry Antwerp by assault on the landward side.

Anjou's French officers co-operated very ill with William's staff, so that the counter-attack for which all had hoped proved impossible. Once again, for the third summer in succession, William shortened the line and stood on the defensive. When Anjou first came, some cynic had foretold — 'he promises marvels, but he will have to do something quickly or the people will tire of his ugly face'.[1] Sure enough, this third summer of retrenchment and retreat was a bitter disappointment to those who had only accepted Anjou as Protector for the sake of the help he could give. The South was more disillusioned than the North, both because they had expected more and because their country was more critically endangered. Moreover, neither Anjou's presence nor William's personal efforts had in the slightest degree eased the religious situation: the Calvinist minority throughout Brabant and Flanders continued to attack and offend the Catholic majority. With all his efforts William could only guarantee one single church in Antwerp for Catholic worship. Bitter discontent increased daily, and those Catholics who had hoped for alleviation from Anjou turned now more and more towards Parma. While the Catholics tacitly dropped away, the Calvinists continued restive and critical.

William's personal danger had released once again a flood of popular devotion, but during the summer his persistent advocacy of Anjou turned the flood to an ebb-tide. It was at this time that William, reorganizing his personal finances with the help of his old friend Arend van Dorp, drastically cut down the expenses of his household in order to take over half the monthly pay of the army, together with all such extra charges as guns, ammunition, postal services, pigeons, espionage and scouting. That autumn of 1582, therefore, the Estates had only to find the balance, which probably they would do: but they took their time. Daily the delegates came and went, hurrying to their native provinces to report progress, hurrying back to Antwerp with fresh instructions. It happened that meetings were held up because some important delegation had slipped home for orders; by the time they got back, some other group had gone away. The Estates General were behaving very much as they usually did, like a pack of unruly sheep eluding

[1] Granvelle, IX, 216.

the vigilance of their dog; William's idea of a central executive committee seemed quite forgotten. Anjou, who had never experienced anything like it, took the whole thing for a deliberate insult to himself.

Furious, he came storming round to William's house early one November morning. He found him in bed, where since his illness he had made a habit of transacting much of the day's business before getting up at about noon. William managed to calm the angry young man by explaining the situation and pointing out that what he complained of was mere disorder, not calculated ill will; to satisfy him he sent Sainte Aldegonde down with a special message imploring the Estates in their own interests to reach a quick decision. Anjou retired, apparently satisfied. But by this time the real hostility between them was thinly concealed by good manners. Anjou was plotting something and William knew it, though narrowly as he watched, he underestimated Anjou's infamy.

For he planned nothing less than to overthrow both the Estates and the Prince of Orange, and make himself by one *coup d'état* the unquestioned master of the Netherlands. He had, or imagined he had, suborned the commanders in the more important garrisons, Termonde, Bruges, Alost and Nieuport: his plan was to rush Antwerp, thus giving the signal for a general rising of his adherents. Some rumours of his plan got out, as rumours will; his conduct became a little odd, yet not inexplicable.

William, who guessed the purport, but not the date or the scope of the conspiracy, grew ever more guarded in his handling of the Duke; yet some of his most intelligent friends, Duplessis Mornay for instance, were still urging him to trust Anjou more fully, when Anjou treacherously struck. He filled the suburbs of Antwerp with his troops, on the plea that Antwerp stood in need of defence, but the citizens had cautiously refused to let them come within the walls, and had rejected the apparently harmless suggestion that the gates should be left open after dark to allow food carts to pass in and out. On the night of Sunday, January 16th, 1583, the Antwerp authorities, instituting one of their quarterly checks on foreigners lodging in the town, were dismayed to find no less than three thousand French 'visitors'; unable to think of any better or more immediate way of checking disorder, they commanded lighted candles to be put in all windows giving on the streets, thus to ensure enough illumination to discourage secretive violence. The night did indeed pass without disturbance, but on the following morning Anjou came prancing in to William, as usual transacting business in bed, with an apparently innocent request for his presence at a review of the troops in the suburb that afternoon. Misdoubting his intentions, William excused himself and the Duke took his leave, still in high good-humour. He had satisfied his conscience by trying to get the Prince of Orange out of the town and into safety; if he would not take a hint, his blood would be on his own head.

Anjou next heard mass, dined extremely early, and, when most of the townsfolk were sitting down to their midday meal, rode out towards the suburbs, accompanied only by a few friends and the Flemish officer in charge of the Antwerp garrison, laughing and joking as he went. As the city gates were opened for them, two of his followers levelled their pistols and shot the sentries dead.

'Ha, Monseigneur!' exclaimed the astonished Flemish officer at Anjou's side, 'what are you doing?'

'I am going to make myself master of the town, with the help of my own men,' declared Anjou, and pointed to the French troops drawn up just outside the gates. He had time to say no more, for as the sentries fell, the French charged the undefended gates, and with shouts of 'Ville gagnée! Vive la messe!' poured into the town, Anjou himself prudently cheering them on from a point well outside the gates.

Contrary to his calculation the Catholic population did not rise, for 'Vive la messe!' meant less to them than 'Ville gagnée'. Antwerp taken by the French? Not if they knew it. Leaping from their dinner-tables, snatching up their arms, the burghers ran into the street. In a matter of minutes the volunteers of the town guard were at their posts, the chains, kept against the Spanish danger, went up across the streets, and every window and housetop had become a sniper's post. Half-way up the great main street from the city gate to the central square the mad onrush was halted and held, while more French soldiers trying to scale the ramparts were hurled backward into the moat. Checked in the main street, driven back by a hail of shot and stones and slates — from the pavements, from the rooftops — the foremost troops fell back, only to be caught in the narrow gate by the inward surge of their own reinforcements. By this time they were in panic; fighting to get in or fighting to get out, they cut each other down, and meanwhile the city cannon from their dominating batteries ploughed furrows of destruction through them.

At about this juncture William rode up and immediately stopped the cannonade, 'as he is of a very gentle nature', commented a spectator, frankly disappointed. The remaining French ran for safety; even so the toll of life had been heavy, two thousand or more. Some had been killed at the barricades, but more in the press at the narrow gate, and many, jumping or falling from the walls, had been drowned in the moat. One Antwerp fisherman found sixteen hundred écus in the pockets of a drowned man and afterwards the banks were black with optimists dragging up the corpses. Along the main street, where the fighting had been hottest, among the corpses of the soldiers lay 'two hundred gentlemen or what you will dressed in velvet and rich brocade'. The velvet and rich brocade were not left long on those undefended bodies, and soon the arrogant younger sons of the French nobility, the painted darlings of Anjou's retinue, lay bereft and naked to the winter sky.[1]

Anjou slept that night outside the city walls at Berchem — if he did sleep. But he claimed a spotless conscience, writing the same evening to William, to declare 'the just reasons I have had to take offence'.[2]

V

This time William could do nothing to save Anjou's face or to gloss over what had happened. He told him as much: words could hardly be found for the moral depravity of the action; for its political folly — a thing which even Anjou could understand — William could, however, find words enough. 'The people are now so incensed against you', he wrote, 'that they openly say they would rather die at the hands of their enemies than be in hazard every day to such dangers as these.'[3] In the circumstances it was utterly impossible for Anjou to re-enter Antwerp, where such of his suite as had not taken part in the attack remained imprisoned in their various lodgings under guard against the indignant mob. There was even an attempt to stop food supplies to the French camp, which William with difficulty circumvented.

Anjou had done all he could to forfeit the title of Protector, and when William gathered his principal advisers to discuss the situation all agreed that Anjou must go. William did not think so; neither his perfidy nor his ambition could alter the incontrovertible fact that he was indispensable. Once again he put the case to the Estates General. They had — as he clearly saw — three alternatives: to make peace with Spain, to make war on their own resources, to continue the alliance with Anjou. The first was plain surrender, the second inevitable defeat; if Anjou left he would take his troops with him, denuding a great stretch of their country to Parma's advance, alienating both his brother of France and the Queen of England from their cause, cutting off two powers whose friendship was essential, jeopardizing the trading connections which were life-blood to the Netherlands, and perhaps even driving the French crown into a Spanish alliance. Arguing in

---

[1] *Analectes*, v, vii, 506-11.   [2] Garchard, v, 78-9.   [3] *Archives*, VIII, 144.

Anjou's cause, yet without attempting the hopeless task of excusing his wickedness, William eloquently cited the classic cases of rulers, otherwise great and wise, who had perpetrated treacherous crimes – the great Theodosius, for instance, and the massacre at Thessalonica. But William knew more even than he could say to the Estates General; he knew, for instance, that Anjou was determined to have the Netherlands, with or without the Estates to help him, that he was ready to abandon his pretensions to Elizabeth of England and marry his own niece, the King of Spain's daughter, if she could have the Netherlands for dowry. Essential therefore to keep him an ally and under control, rather than to have him join his troops to Parma and come as a conqueror.

It was an appalling choice, yet William, as a statesman, could see no way out but to keep a hold on Anjou. For the first time in his life Sainte Aldegonde disagreed, radically and irreconcilably, threatening, if William persisted, to resign his offices and retire from public life. William persisted and Sainte Aldegonde kept his word; for the first time in fourteen years the Prince of Orange faced the darkening future absolutely alone. His popular favour, too, had ebbed with Anjou's treachery, and the people who a year before had prayed and watched for him were again openly hostile, declaring that he was in league with the Duke. Was not his bastard employed in Anjou's household? Some even claimed to have seen Justin shooting down the burghers of Antwerp on the French side of the barricades. Still William would not yield, not realizing perhaps that by forcing Anjou on the recalcitrant South, smarting from his betrayal, he was pressing them too far. Or if realizing it, unable even so to act otherwise. He did not underestimate the peril to which his policy was exposing the precarious unity of the provinces, for the North, more remote from Anjou's prejudicial presence, more entirely confident in all that their Prince of Orange did, was more willing to renew the French alliance; so that this matter of Anjou deepened the fissure between North and South, threw the latter back into the arms of Parma and left the former to become a separate nation.[1]

If indeed, as seems possible, the question of Anjou caused the final breach between North and South, if until that time William might have saved the united Netherlands for which he had fought, if indeed he sacrificed his Union on the altar of this alliance, then it was one of the bitterest ironies of all history, for it was a sacrifice utterly and entirely in vain.

Posterity, seeing the mistakes made by statesmen, is often blind to their reasons, for posterity has the advantage of knowing more than those on whom it delights to sit in judgment. The passage of time restores proportion

[1] See *Bijdragen*, III, ii, 306 *seq.*; IV, iv, 1 *seq.*

to events magnified or distorted in the eyes of contemporaries. It is very easy for us to forget how real in the spring of 1583 was the danger of Anjou's hostility: for we know that Anjou had barely a year to live. It was the one thing that William could not know.

Duplessis Mornay had left the Netherlands shortly after the Duke of Anjou came, rejoining his own master, Henry of Navarre, the Huguenot leader; at the news of Anjou's treachery he wrote at once praising God that so evident a proof had now been given of the worthlessness of this ally and imploring William to abandon the miserable Valois dynasty and make an alliance instead with the French Huguenots as he had done of old, during his exile. Strongly as this policy might have appealed to William, he could not adopt it, for it did nothing to settle the problem of rendering Anjou innocuous. Indeed to throw over the Duke for the Huguenot King of Navarre would have been simply to strengthen the Catholic and Guise party in France by forcing Anjou into their arms, with sinister consequences for the Netherlands. The Huguenot party was not at present a strong enough ally to make such a risk worth the taking.

There was, however, much to be said for gaining their alliance without losing that of Anjou, so as to have something at least to fall back on in case the renewal of the treaty with Anjou proved after all impossible. A private understanding with the Huguenots might reconcile the Calvinist populace to the French connection and emphasize the existence of some more respectable element in French society as a counterpoise to the disreputable Anjou. For this reason in the early spring of 1583 the Prince of Orange opened double negotiations with two leading Huguenot families, for the marriage of his eldest daughter, and for his own. But whether 'Mademoiselle d'Orange' was bashful, or her dowry too small to please the bridegroom's family, her part of the negotiations was soon discontinued.

William himself had offered the sober and unromantic part of his fourth wife to a sober and unromantic widow. Louise de Coligny was the daughter of that old friend of his exile, the great Admiral Coligny. If he had ever set eyes on her — which is highly improbable — it must have been during his French campaign of 1568 when Louise would have been a girl of fourteen. Presumably he knew her only by report, as a woman of character and discretion whose life had been scarred by fearful tragedy. Married at seventeen to the Seigneur de Teligny — a person of whom history has nothing but golden opinions — Louise had accompanied her father and husband to Paris in August 1572, a bride of only a few months. The same night had made her orphan and widow. When her father had been dragged out to death, her husband, preferring to meet his end voluntarily and at his own time, had gone out in the streets to confront the murderers; twice he stopped a group of them, offering himself to their swords, and twice they recognized him for a man whom no one had heart or conscience hard enough to strike. The third time he met strangers who did not know whom they were killing and did their work. So at eighteen Louise put on the black which, but for a short interval, she was to wear all her life. Now at twenty-nine she was to put it off — briefly — for the Prince of Orange.

By an odd chance Louise was to be the ancestress of the dynasty, the mother of that son who alone himself had a son. Cousin-marriages between Charlotte's descendants and hers ultimately brought forth the House of Orange we know. For that reason, politically and historically, Louise de Coligny is important, and it is seemly that she should lie in the same grave with her husband at Delft. But she can hardly have been very important in William's personal life. Mutual respect there was certainly, a similarity of tastes and interests, tranquil contentment. The reasons for this new marriage, so soon after the death of the much-loved Charlotte, are easy enough to imagine, if difficult to establish. There was a family of very young children, all girls — always a bewildering problem for a widower. Possibly there was feeling between Catherine of Schwartzburg, a lady of strong character, and the gentle Marie; Marie had the prior right to look after her father's household, Catherine very possibly made the bolder claim. Just before Charlotte's death William had been struggling to retrench and reduce his expenses to those of a private gentleman once more. It is an obvious supposition that, between the divided control of two ladies, this retrenchment went very ill. A sensible wife would solve the difficulty. And finally William at fifty was — but for the lines on his face — young for his age even by modern standards; by sixteenth-century standards, very young. Since he did not care to face the prospect of a long and lonely middle-age, it was reasonable enough to take a new wife as soon as possible, and complete the family for his young children before they grew conscious of the gap.

In all its personal aspects the marriage was successful. Louise, a conscientious, upright and affectionate woman, with a good business head, took firm if rather austere charge of the household, and her heart went out at once to the five little girls, 'mon petit peuple', as she called them. Politically it was a failure. William met his bride at Flushing, and conducted her to Antwerp where they were married very quietly in the castle chapel on April 12th, 1583; the mob, making no distinction whatever between the depraved Anjou and the virtuous Madame de Teligny, broke into offensive cries; Huguenot or Catholic, Valois or Coligny, they were all 'French' to them.

No joyous cheering, no demonstrations of goodwill came to sweeten the first months of this marriage. All William's efforts to regain the confidence of the people broke down on his persistent advocacy of Anjou's alliance. Gangs of citizens assembled threateningly outside the castle, so that the women of his household were virtually prisoners and even he dared not always trust himself in the streets. Once at least, when he had spent the afternoon in the town hall pressing the Antwerp councillors for food supplies for the army, the mob outside grew so menacing that he had to spend the night in the building and return next morning to the castle under guard.

Meanwhile Anjou had been relegated to Dunkirk out of harm's way, where he kicked his heels in boredom until July, and then took ship for France, jocosely telling the officer whom he left in charge, that if he surrendered, 'his neck would learn the weight of his backside'. Undeterred by this threat, the governor yielded Dunkirk on July 16th, 1583. Parma now had his outlet to the sea and was ready to cut off Antwerp.

The situation was appalling, all the more so that William himself had altogether lost control of the South. The fall of Dunkirk shattered whatever fragment of respect for Anjou he had managed to build up again. His own credit went with it. He saw only one way to tide over the disaster: if Sainte Aldegonde — known to oppose Anjou — would come back to Antwerp and take over its defence, then he himself and his family could withdraw to the North, once again consolidate his position there, and be ready to return to the South when his credit should be a little redeemed.

Sainte Aldegonde did not need to be asked twice; little as he had approved William's policy, recrimination was not in his nature. He came with all the speed he could. Meanwhile secretly and with the mob mistrustfully spying on all his movements, William and his family made ready to go, and on July 22nd, under cover of darkness, embarked with his wife and children for Middelburg. When the news trickled out the furious people stormed the castle and would not be quiet until they had entered and seen for themselves the empty rooms. Then they cried out, unreasonably, that they had been deserted.

VI

Was it desertion? Was it a surrender of his policy? Did this secret and hurried removal from Antwerp signalize an admission of defeat, a retirement from the South to the faithful stronghold in the North? William had but eleven months to live, and his death removed from the Netherlands the only man strong and patient enough to reunite North and South. Had he lived, he would not have abandoned his ideal of the United Netherlands; nothing in the last months of his life suggests it. Rather, it would seem, he had gone at the urgent request of the four northern provinces, to strengthen and encourage them, but to persuade them above all into joint action with the South. It was essential to him to hold both North and South, essential therefore, after two years' absence, to revisit his devoted North. But during that visit he died, so that this going from Antwerp was final not by intention, but by chance alone.

Anjou's withdrawal, had it not been for the disastrous loss of Dunkirk, might have eased William's task of persuading the provinces to renew the treaty. Anjou as an absentee was far less prejudicial to his own cause than as a present source of irritation, and his French troops, however half-hearted, were still better than nothing, for they constituted a sizable quarter of the entire army at the disposal of the Estates and were sorely needed. Thus William's first task, when he met the delegates of Holland, Zealand, Friesland and Utrecht at Middelburg in August, was to repeat all the arguments in favour of the French alliance and once again to exploit his own personality as a cover for Anjou. They met him, as once before, with the request that he, and he alone, would accept the office of Governor of all the Netherlands. Again and for the same reasons he refused.

William's strongest argument had always been the lack of an alternate protector; now suddenly the extremists in the South, led as usual by Ghent, had found another champion. Even their experience of John Casimir had not taught them wisdom. Gebhard Truchsess, the unprepossessing scion of a north German Catholic house and Archbishop of Cologne, a diocese conveniently abutting on the Netherlands, had fallen in love with a lady to whose bed there was no way save through a well-lighted church. Following a precedent by this time well-established, Truchsess gave up his religion, but not his bishopric, married his lady and announced the secularization of Cologne. The Emperor instantly sent troops against him, thus turning him at once into a Protestant crusader. It needed no more for the Southern Calvinists to shout for Truchsess instead of Anjou, while the obstreperous Hembyze, suddenly reappearing at Ghent, suggested the amalgamation of Cologne with the Netherlands as a single Protestant power.

Man for man, there was little to choose between Anjou and Truchsess. Both were egotistical, irresponsible intriguers; but Anjou had France behind him and no other war on his hands, while Truchsess had no one behind him and the potential strength of all Catholic Germany against him. Anjou was of the same blood as the old Valois rulers of the Netherlands; Truchsess was not. Politically, he was not the champion for whom William was looking. Ghent, however, wholly wrapped up in its own affairs, remained deaf to his arguments. Circumstances fortunately prevented the armed descent of Truchsess on the Netherlands. He had depended on the help of John Casimir, but at this critical moment John Casimir's elder brother the Elector Palatine died, and the flighty crusader flung down his sword and scurried to Heidelberg to demand his share in the regency of the young heir.

All that winter the military situation grew steadily worse: Antwerp blockaded, Brussels threatened, treachery and intrigue undermining all the South, where William's return to the North, and his calling of the Estates General thither, were blackly interpreted as evidence of his neglect of the common weal, his preference for Holland and his personal ambition. Nor were affairs in the North altogether smooth; personal and politicial anxieties came together, for his eldest sister's husband, Count van den Berg, always a dubious supporter, was found in this winter of 1583-84 to be in correspondence with Parma for the handing over of the whole province of Gelderland. Discovered, he was lodged securely in prison, where his faithful and tearful wife insisted on joining him. Parma, meanwhile, had offered to treat separately with Anjou and it became evident even to the Estates that the protector of the Netherlands could only be prevented from betraying them entirely into Spanish hands if they made him a better offer themselves. In such inauspicious circumstances was the alliance renewed at Termonde in March 1584. William had won his point, at a price he would not live to pay.

The Estates General, shifting before the threat from Parma, had moved from Middelburg to Dordrecht, and from Dordrecht to the Hague. A few miles off at Delft the new Princess of Orange kept her homely little Court at the Prinsenhof, the old unpretentious red-brick house which had once been a nunnery. Small, inconvenient and draughty, it yet had its own peculiar charm, with its sunny refectory, its cool wide corridors and walled fruit garden. Here Louise reigned over her simple Court for the few months of her brief marriage; here 'Mademoiselle Anna' carried on her blissful flirtation with her cousin Louis, approved of by her own father, disapproved of — from a distance — by his. Here came Maurice on brief visits from his studies at Leyden, astonishingly mature at sixteen, harsher, more inhibited than his father, brilliantly gifted: 'of great towardness, good presence, and courage, flaxen-haired, endued with a singular wit', as an English agent described him.[1] On him as the successor to his policy William was forced to rely, for now long intervals went by with no news from his eldest son, sixteen years a prisoner in Spain. All attempts for his release had failed. Politically he was dead; and indeed what relation now can William's recollections of the child he had left at Louvain have had to the man past thirty immured in Spain?

[1] C.S.P.F., 1583-84, 631.

Louise had been pregnant before she left Antwerp and the jolting of the springless Dutch cart which carried her from Middelburg to Delft had all but robbed her of her burden, but not quite. Late in January 1584, William had news at the Hague where he was with the Estates General that her time had come, and rode the few miles distance to Delft to reach the Prinsenhof, while his wife was in labour. Outside the crowds gathered, excited, praying that their Prince's return to live among them should be greeted by the best of all omens. 'Is it a Count of Holland?' they asked.[1] And on January 29th Louise was delivered of a son.

Rejoicings swept the North, for the child's birth seemed to bring hope and reassurance. William himself, having to choose a device for the occasion, selected the Latin words, *Saevis tranquillus in undis*, Calm amid the raging of the tempest. Reflecting at the time his own persistent confidence and hope, the device proved wonderfully apt as the years went by to the life and work of this, his youngest child, Frederick Henry, whose name was to stand for the Golden Age of Dutch history and under whose benevolent hand, while all Europe was torn with conflict, the Dutch people achieved their glorious apogee. Called after Europe's two leading Protestant Kings, Frederick of Denmark and Henry of Navarre, the child was christened on June 12th at Delft, with a great gathering of delegates from over all the Netherlands, his half-brother Maurice standing proxy for the kingly godparents.

William used the joyful occasion for more serious matters: to discuss the military situation with those from the South. He sat long with Sainte Alde-gonde considering how Antwerp was to be saved, cut off from all but the sea. Debating the strategic situation, they pored over maps: William was for cutting the dyke in the rear of Antwerp, so as to widen the sea-access and keep open the communications with the North, but the plan was not likely to be well received, for these were no longer the heroic days of Leyden, and the disillusioned South, bemused with its internal, petty jealousies and sectional interests, was drifting fast towards separation and peace. To prevent this fatal drift towards Parma William had planned before the summer was over to be in Antwerp again. He had been cheered and hissed so often in Antwerp that he did not seriously doubt his ability to redeem himself once again, and so also to redeem the policy for which he stood. Feeling that the permanent interests of the Netherlands lay in union, he was convinced that, fundamentally, the Estates would see it too. Parting from Sainte Aldegonde, he promised to be with him before the autumn. They never met again.

It cannot have been many days after the christening of his youngest son that startling news reached Delft. The Duke of Anjou had died of typhoid

[1] Granvelle, XI, 467-8.

fever at St. Omer. Was it good news or bad? For the first few weeks it would be hard to tell, for while his death removed the danger of his enmity it also loosed the bonds which bound the essential allies, France and England, to the cause of the Netherlands.

William, accepting the news with a decent show of regret, wrote suitable letters to the King of France and the Queen-mother. He was not a man who immediately expressed his political decisions on paper and we do not know with any certainty what project he had in mind to re-establish the shattered unity of the provinces under some new head. But certainly in June 1584 it was not too late — had he but lived — to close the fissure which Anjou had made. The situation had altered, opening new possibilities. In the Prinsenhof at Delft, confident and resourceful, William faced a future from which at least one problem had been removed.

CHAPTER X

MURDER AT DELFT

1584

I

In spite of the twenty-five thousand écus on his head, William would not alter his habit of receiving petitioners and keeping his doors open to all. He could perhaps hardly have altered his custom so late in life and after it had become so well established, but in any case he was a fatalist. If his religion was undogmatic it had become in these last years a profound and important reality in his life, and he accepted the Calvinist doctrine of predestination with logic and consistency enough to believe that taking precautions against an inevitable end was waste of time.

Since Juan Jauréguy, several men had tried in vain for the reward, none of them coming within firing distance before they were discovered. But Balthasar Gérard continued in his quest; he had no money and his plans were vague; for nearly a year he hung about in Luxembourg, acting as secretary to a distant cousin, remotely connected with Parma's army, until one day he noticed some blank passes on an officer's desk and pocketed a handful. Then he fled. By the spring of 1584 he had reached Tournai, where he was refused an audience by Parma, and had to explain to an intermediary that he wanted to murder the Prince of Orange. While his offer was being reported he suddenly took fright, remembering the blank passes he had stolen, and fearing that Parma might be angry. So he slipped away, penniless.

By May he had reached Delft, where he found the Prince of Orange more approachable than the Duke of Parma. Giving his name as Guyon, he asserted that his father had been martyred for the Protestant cause at Dôle, and that he himself only wished to serve the greatest of all the Protestant leaders, adding that he had in his possession some blank passes signed by one of Parma's officers. William, who could imagine no use for the passes, was unwilling, with his customary gentleness, to discourage a young man come so far to serve him; but, thinking that Anjou might have more use for him, dispatched him with a courier just going to France with letters for the Duke. Gérard stuck to his plan. He had no dagger, no pistol, not so much as a penknife of his own, otherwise the Prince of Orange would have been killed in May. As it was, he had travelled almost to the French border when he heard the report that Anjou had died, and volunteered to carry the news to Delft, not the preliminary news, which outdistanced him by some way, but the more detailed report which followed later.

At Delft, William occupied the long summer days with affairs of state. He worked in the mornings usually in his bedroom, his custom since Jauréguy's attack, receiving petitioners or messengers before he got up. Gérard was thus shown into the bedroom to contemplate with disappointment a conveniently defenceless victim, when he himself was unarmed. For the next few days he hung about the Prinsenhof, ostentatiously talking religion with anyone who would listen, and disarming the suspicions of the porter by borrowing his Bible. William at length sent someone to know why he had not gone back, as arranged, to the French commander to offer his services. Gérard answered simply that he had not a penny in the world and his shoes were worn out. Fatally, William sent him twelve crowns, and that afternoon, explaining that the roads were very unsafe, he bought from one of William's own lifeguard a serviceable pair of pistols.

Tuesday, July 10th, 1584, was an ordinary enough day, with the usual programme of official business. William gave the burgomaster of Leeuwarden an audience all the morning and, when their conversation was interrupted by the trumpet sounding the dinner-hour, asked him to stay and eat with his family. The burgomaster was the only guest, the others present besides William and Louise being only the Countess of Schwartzburg, Mademoiselle d'Orange and Mademoiselle Anna. Just as the party was entering the dining-room, Gérard, pushing forward, evidently very nervous, asked — in 'a hollow and unsettled voice' — for a passport for his journey. Louise distrusted his manner and his face, but William, smiling at her imaginings, promised the passport and gave his wife his arm in to dinner. Outside Gérard investigated the means of quick escape, noted the doors and passages, examined the stables and outbuildings, measured the garden wall with his eye, then strolled back to the corridor between the dining-room and the stairs, joined a growing crowd of petitioners, and waited.

At table they discussed politics until the servants brought round the finger-bowls, when some officers came in to talk business: after dinner was the hour for military affairs. All three who spoke to William during his last ten minutes were foreigners: first a Welsh officer, next an Italian whose business would have taken longer, and who was asked upstairs to discuss it further. Then, at the door as they went out, the veteran Captain Roger Williams. He had dropped on one knee and William, pausing a moment, laid his hand lightly on the bowed head: the last, typical gesture. At that moment Gérard fired.

The double charge of the heavy pistol tore diagonally from left to right through his lungs and stomach, and embedded itself in the whitened wall beyond, spattering plaster and blood. William staggered forward and with colossal self-mastery did not fall. 'Mon Dieu', he cried, 'ayez pitié de moi, je suis grièvement blessé,' and then, with fearful certainty, knowing that no second miracle would work for him, 'Mon Dieu, ayez pitié de mon âme; mon Dieu, ayez pitié' – his voice had weakened to a gasping breath – 'de ce pauvre peuple.' Supported in the arms of his equerry he had sunk down until he was resting on the low steps of the staircase. Louise and her stepdaughters stood transfixed, but someone had run for Peter Forest. Only the Countess of Schwartzburg, watching the grey face of her brother, knew that Peter Forest could do nothing now. Kneeling at the foot of the staircase, she took his hand in hers and, speaking low and clear, for the distance was already great through which her words must reach to him, said 'Do you die reconciled with your Saviour, Jesus Christ?' Who can tell what far memories that familiar voice called back to the fast darkening brain, what pictures flickered for the last time on the retina of consciousness – the thronged courtyards and the happy schoolroom of Dillenburg, the strait precepts of his earliest teachers? He opened his eyes for the last time on the blurred and crowded faces, and his lips moved. 'Yes,' he said. He did not speak again. He was unconscious before they had carried him back into the dining-hall among the empty chairs and tables, and dead before Forest came.

11

The Prince of Orange had not lived to forgive his murderer, who was seized within a few minutes of the attack, as he tried to vault the garden wall. Search of his person revealed nothing save a little pair of water-wings, deflated, with which – since he could not swim – he had planned to cross the canal. He confessed immediately and with pride in the porter's lodge, and passed his last days on earth with the ecstatic constancy of a martyr, exulting in his deed. This was his only reward, although the blood-money was punctually paid to his family out of revenues which the King of Spain confiscated for the purpose from the imprisoned eldest son of his victim. Gérard's execution was conducted in public at length and with gusto, a woman spectator who began to whimper at the sight being all but lynched by the people. He prayed in a low and constant voice throughout: when a hammer used with too much violence by the executioner, split from the haft, causing one of the assistants to jump, the victim was seen to smile with remote satisfaction. So died the cabinet-maker's apprentice, Balthasar Gérard, who had been told that it was not for such as he to kill a great prince, and who had proved otherwise.[1]

III

'When I recollect that we are now all orphans and do not know whither or where to turn, my heart is so full of sorrow that I hardly know what I do,'[2] wrote Marie, the eldest of the children. 'Sorrow has given me no rest,' cried Louise de Coligny, 'nor leisure to think of any other thing.'[3] Characteristically, William had disregarded the possibility of his death, kept open house and received petitioners as if no assassin's pistol had ever been hidden under Jauréguy's cloak, as if no such thing were likely to happen again. In other ways he had shown a casual face to the danger of death; he left no adequate will and in ready money for his family and household not more than a hundred guilders.[4] 'My lord always thought', wrote Marie, 'that there was no great hurry.'[5] So death had caught up with him, in the fifty-second year of his age, unprepared, leaving his wife, his children, his people to the mercy of God.

His loss left the Netherlands, North and South, stunned, unbelieving. Even in the ranks of the Spanish army they refused to rejoice. 'Great is thy loss, and greater will be thy misery, O Flanders, for want of thy prince, who did guide thee, and governed thy people, with wisdom, love, policy, and continual care for thy quietness; he was thy comfort and the stay of thy state in all extremities. The widow, the sucking babe, and the fatherless child, shall have cause to bewail his death,'[6] lamented a Dutch writer, but that was later, for at first there were no words. The silence of sorrow fell on the city of Delft, while Louise lay prostrated in a room draped even to the windows in black, and the townsfolk gathered in stricken groups, and the children cried in the streets.

He lay in state for a long time while his people took silent farewell of the Father they would never know again. Some had wanted to take his likeness as he lay there, but this was forbidden lest his enemies should find means to mock the dead by unseemly cartoons. Yet one man defied the prohibition and later painted from surreptitious drawings the last portrait of the great Stadholder. For now at last, the endless hurry over — the travelling and the meetings, the days in public council and the nights in private debate, the snatched and hasty meals — the frantic tempo of his life slowed to its final standstill, and there was time to fix those quiet features for the last time;

[1] Gachard, III, 192-3.   [2] *Archives*, VIII, 451.   [3] *Archives*, VIII, 457.
[4] C.S.P.F., 1583-84, 631.   [5] *Archives*, VIII, 452.   [6] Somers Tracts, I, 407.

time and to spare to portray the body which Peter Forest had laid out and embalmed, to draw the beloved face which death had emptied of all content. The eyes closed, the strong vitality gone, the mouth relaxed, the obstinate chin sagging on the breast, nothing of expression was left in that most expressive of faces but unspeakable exhaustion. Never did man more weary go to eternal rest.

He was buried with ceremonies too tragic to be splendid on August 3rd, in the great cool church, called the New Church, at Delft, and even the minister who preached the last sermon over his coffin had seen and understood the dead man's face. His text was from Revelation: 'And I heard a voice from Heaven saying unto me, Blessed are the dead which die in the Lord from henceforth: Yea, saith the Spirit, that they may rest from their labours: and their works do follow them.'

Later the Estates ordered to be set up over his grave a baroque tomb of black and white marble, with his image in bronze, as he had been in the days when he first came back to the Netherlands, a lithe figure, seated, in armour with the famous white pug dog on guard at his feet. The long inscription, engraved at their orders, opens nobly: 'To the Glory of God and to the ever-lasting memory of William of Nassau Father of the Fatherland who valued the fortunes of the Netherlands above his own.'

Father of the Fatherland . . . he had lived and died as Stadholder, as the highest official in the republican provinces, but still as an official under the elected government of the Estates. His authority ended with his life; but his two younger sons were to serve the Provinces with equal devotion, Maurice as the brilliant dictatorial soldier who consolidated what his father had begun, Frederick Henry as the generous ruler of Holland's Golden Age. The eldest son alone achieved nothing, frustrated by that fate which kept him a prisoner in Spain until after his fiftieth year. When he came back to the Netherlands it was only to die a free, but a broken, man.

The work to which he had devoted his life, and for which he had died, was never to be accomplished. The Netherlands, as he had known them, were never to be one nation. The struggle for their liberation had trans-muted the past and destroyed the possibility of its revival. What he had done was to create a new State, the United Provinces of the coming century, the 'Holland' of the future. Even though it fell short of what he had wanted, his achievement was very great. For it was a hard and desperate task, to restore the self-respect and freedom of a people borne down by apparently inescapable doom, to fight a great power with such small instruments, and to fight it for five years without hope and alone. It was a strange, almost a unique, thing to be the idol of a nation and to remain uncorrupted, to be oneself the guardian of the people's rights sometimes against the emotional impulse of the people themselves. In times of emergency and war, in political crisis and national danger it is often expedient to sacrifice the forms — even the spirit — of popular government. Was not this one of the chief reasons why popular governments withered in so many lands during this stormy century? There lies his greatest claim to recognition: he sought not to impose his own will on the embryo nation, but to let the nation create and form itself. He belonged in spirit to an earlier, a more generous and more cultured age than this of narrowness and authority, and thin, sectarian hatred. But he belonged also to a later age; his deep and genuine interest in the people he ruled, his faith in their development, his toleration, his convinced belief in government by consent — all these reach out from the mediaeval world towards a wider time. Few statesmen in any period, none in his own, cared so deeply for the ordinary comfort and the trivial happiness of the thousands of individuals who are 'the people'. He neither idealized nor overestimated them and he knew that they were often wrong, for what political education had they yet had? But he believed in them, not merely as a theoretical concept, but as individuals, as men. Therein lay the secret of the profound and enduring love between him and them. Wise, wary, slow to judge and slow to act, patient, stubborn and undiscouraged, no other man could have sustained so difficult a cause for so long, could have opposed, with so little sacrifice of public right, the concentrated power of a government which disregarded it. He respected in all men what he wished to have respected in himself, the right to an opinion.

There have been politicians more successful, or more subtle; there have been none more tenacious or more tolerant. 'The wisest, gentlest and bravest man who ever led a nation',[1] he is one of that small band of statesmen whose service to humanity is greater than their service to their time or their people. In spite of the differences of speech or political theory, the conventions and complexities which make one age incomprehensible to another, some men have a quality of greatness which gives their lives universal significance. Such men, in whatever walk of life, in whatever chapter of fame, mystic or saint, scientist or doctor, poet or philosopher, and even — but how rarely — soldier or statesman, exist to shame the cynic, and to renew the faith of humanity in itself.

Of this number was William of Nassau, Prince of Orange, called the Silent.

[1] G. M. Trevelyan, *Introduction to Fruin, Siege and Relief of Leyden.*

INDEX